Genre and the New Rhetoric

Genre and the New Rhetoric

Edited by

Aviva Freedman and Peter Medway

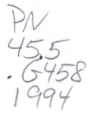

Taylor & Francis

Taylor & Francis Group

LONDON AND NEW YORK

First published 1994
By Taylor & Francis
11 New Fetter Lane, London, EC4P 4EE

A Catalogue Record for this book is available from the British Library

ISBN 0-7484-0256 X (cloth)
ISBN 0 7484 0257 8 (pbk)

**Library of Congress Cataloging-in-Publication Data are available on
request**

Typeset by Euroset, 2 Dover Close, Alresford, Hampshire SO24 9PG

Transferred to Digital Printing 2003

Printed and bound by Antony Rowe Ltd, Eastbourne

Contents

Series Editor's Preface

I am not sure whether editors are supposed to enter into critical debates between contributors or between books in the series. The conventional rules of the genre are to be bland, complementary and encouraging – which is why many of us never read series editor's introductions, much less cite them as having anything to say.

No tricks here, but I will try to shift the genre of the introduction a bit sideways. Because Aviva Freedman and Peter Medway's *Genre and the New Rhetoric* directly takes up issues raised by another recent book in this series, Bill Cope and Mary Kalantzis's *The Powers of Literacy* (1993), and because my own work on literacy and pedagogy is cited here as a link in the argument, my aim here is to use the introduction to critically reassess issues and questions that the two books raise – issues that have been the topic of ongoing conversations with Freedman and Medway, Cope and Kalantzis over the past year.

Now in its eleventh volume, this series has featured cross-disciplinary work that looks at language and literacy in institutional contexts, including schools, universities, the mass media, new technological infrastructures, workplaces and scientific disciplines. The books have critiqued dominant approaches that treat literacy/illiteracy as an individual mental attribute or deficiency, a virtue or pathology. They have presented alternative analyses that have drawn from critical social theory, feminist theory, social history, linguistics, and cultural studies. The principal theme running across the series has been the connection between literacy and power. It has, hopefully, provided a forum for debate over how literacy enables and precludes particular kinds of political enfranchisement, social life and cultural identity, for debate over who gets included and who gets left out. But the key question about what kinds of practical, pedagogical intervention might alter the literacy/power relationship in schools and universities, workplaces and public life remains up for grabs.

Genre and the New Rhetoric mixes groundbreaking articles in the field, by Miller, Freadman, Freedman and others, with new and recent pieces. The result is an excellent primer on current American and Canadian debates over genre and pedagogy that pushes beyond formalist and individualist approaches to writing. It begins from a social and cultural approach to literacy, in this case drawing strongly from rhetoric, speech act theory and the philosophy of language, pragmatism and symbolic interactionism. At the same time, much of the work here is strongly influenced by humanist approaches to writing, and by applied American work in the field of College Composition. That work on writing has been pushed along by practical issues of how to teach writing in universities and colleges that have progressively opened their doors to cultural minorities, working class and other 'non-traditional' students. These, of course, are not new issues, nor are they restricted to US and Canadian institutions. The 'crisis' of writing in tertiary studies and attempts to 'fix' the problem of composition standards via the imposition of formalist approaches have long histories (Heath, 1989). It is in this North American context that the current demand for instructional approaches has encouraged a more systematic analysis of text types and the social practices of writing.

A good place to begin is to ask why 'genre' has become of such pedagogical importance for educators at all levels. Part of the explanation lies with the overt mixing, blurring and shifting of cultural forms that characterizes late-capitalist cultures and economies. It is increasingly hard to tell the difference between grunge and folk, between funk and rap. The airwaves are filled with hybrid cultural forms: from infotainment to docudramas, from 'hard copy' to the written soundbites of *USA Today*, from Aboriginal Reggae to Californian ice hockey. As the contributors to this volume point out, the shifting and mixing of genres is not new, and would not have surprised rhetoricians from Aristotle on. However, the processes of textual hybridization are accelerated under fast capitalism and a globalized economy.

Global corporate culture establishes a product-driven 'culture of the new', where nuance, pastiche, slight changes in product design or textual inflection are part and parcel of the construction of new audiences and markets. Sony, Fox, Nike and Coke have become participants in an advertising-driven avant-gardism that is based on the near continual experimentation with new text forms and audiences. At the same time as products and texts cross national boundaries, we are living in an era of unprecedented global migration: with multilingual, multicultural and multi-code lifeworlds in our communities, schools and workplaces.

At this historical moment, I suspect that 'genre' gives us a vocabulary for talking about, for making sense of, for giving order to this explosion of forms – what Catherine Schryer here calls a 'stabilized-for-now' view of the world. Perhaps the danger lies in going too far towards analysing and reproducing genres, in effect, freeze drying them in a way that would obscure the dynamic cultural, economic and political forces vying for airpsace and airtime, image and voice. To describe these forces and to make decisions about how to intervene in institutional sites like workplaces and schools, there is a need to develop a politics of representation, a task taken up by recent work in cultural studies.

Genre and the New Rhetoric pivots around a series of key issues: about worthwhile analytic frames and degrees of precision for analyses of written texts; about the adequacy with which such frames and models explain the dynamic relationships between texts and social contexts; and about whether 'explicit' or 'implicit' pedagogies are appropriate for teaching writing.

I agree with Freedman and Medway's introductory observation that work both in the North American 'new rhetoric' and the Australian 'genre pedagogy' raises but does not resolve these contentious issues of public culture, difference and social power. The Australian systemic linguistics work begins with the axiom that genres are 'functional' social processes. Similarly, the rhetorical traditions here presented by Carolyn Miller, Anne Freadman, Charles Bazerman and Richard Coe argue that texts are dynamic cultural forms, subject to heteroglossia and play in local, contested ways. So far so good. But what occurs in many of the contributions to *Genre and the New Rhetoric* and *The Powers of Literacy* is a tendency to 'write over' culture as given, as conflict-free, to assume that 'speech communities', 'contexts of situation', 'socio-rhetorical networks' or particular clinical, laboratory and workplace sites are benign, consensual social bodies, where (mostly monocultural and patriarchal) discourse norms, 'common goals', 'motive strategies' and 'private intentions' occur naturally and unproblematically. The danger here is that failure to acknowledge the material sources of 'difference' and power, marginality and exclusion naturalizes these as 'context' variables outside of the scope of genre and rhetorical studies – as something that just 'naturally' occurs in institutional life and societies (Fairclough, 1989). Where this is the case, what appears to be a social and cultural explanation of texts risks becoming the same old psychological romanticism: a world where texts work in 'mysterious' and 'unpredictable' ways, a world where which genres count, where and in whose interests can be traced back to 'private intentions' and 'individual motives'.

All of the chapters in both books acknowledge some kind of dialectical reflexivity between text and context, between genre and culture, between writing and subjectivity. Schryer explicitly takes up this point, when she describes genres as 'stabilized-for-now or stabilized-enough site[s] for social and ideological action'. She, and later Russell Hunt as well, quite profitably draws from Bakhtin to acknowledge that scientific articles or medical records are 'sites for struggle' where battles over values and power are played out. A.C. Van Norstrand also recognizes that political parties and 'informal alliances' that generate 'systemic abrasion' are at play in the communities he studied. But no normative grounds are proposed for judging or analysing 'ruling communicative purpose'. For me, the issues that he concludes with – the generalizability of his model of analysis to other texts – are far less important than the need for some system of analysis that enables normative judgement of genres and texts, that foregrounds whose interests they serve, how they construct and position their writers and readers, and who has access to them.

The very fact that the practices and texts of Defense Department procurement can be taken as 'just another' textual 'place' underlines the danger of a rhetoric and genre analysis detached from questions of knowledge and human interests, cut off from questions of discourse and power. Many of these applications of genre as 'typified rhetorical actions based in recurrent situations' and as 'goal-oriented cultural processes' alike, manage to avoid a harder-edged political analysis of the institutions they are describing. Which genres have power, where, when and to whom has to do with sociologically material and symbolic resources. In this way, what Coe calls 'the social availability and efficacy of particular forms' is crucial.

Here Freadman's 'Anyone for Tennis?' and Miller's 'Rhetorical Community' recognize the need to theorize the social beyond broad brush-stroke references to the importance of 'context of situation'. Freadman's work on genres as ceremonial language games with unstated rules and tricks sets the ground for a fuller, cultural studies analysis, an analysis rich with pedagogical implications. Yet Aviva Fredman's

' "Do As I Say" ', the collection's strongest and most important pedagogical statement, tends to rely on psychological models of learning (e.g., Krashen, Ellis) rather than on cultural analyis. My point here is that if genre is in the first instance a social and cultural phenomenon, then claims about its teaching have to be based on culturally-located models of teaching and learning and on discourse analyses of talk around the social practices of writing. Freedman takes this challenge up in her advocacy of 'scaffolding', which has strong cross-overs with the 'authoring cycle' work of Martin, Rothery, Christie and colleagues, the social literacy model of Kalantzis and Cope, and the rhetorically-based process writing models of Coe and others.

The move towards a culturally-based pedagogy is crucial, as Cope and Kalantzis insist. For all claims about how one can and should learn are by definition culturally contingent; that is, cross-cultural work on literacy has shown us that response to institutional literacy training depends on how one learned to learn, 'ways of taking' in communities (Heath, 1982) – not on any absolute claims about the efficacy of rote or progressive, explicit or implicit, transmission or negotiated teaching. If the ways that we use the social technology of literacy are indeed the products of history and culture – not nature or biology – than the whole pursuit of the 'right' method for teaching writing and reading is spurious. The task in workplaces and schools, universities and colleges, then, becomes how to shape pedagogies that use and build upon peoples' discursive, local resources and that generate significant, innovative and critical cultural action.

Many of the chapters focus on textual description, ranging from the rhetorical descriptions of Zimmerman, Paré and Smart, to Giltrow's cognitivist description. The legal, workplace and institutional texts described in these chapters indeed operate as speech acts of power: sanctioning, authorizing, positioning, controlling, with very real material consequences for human subjects in courts of law, corporations, clinics, workplaces. What is needed, then, is a new rhetoric tied to an analysis of power, or, to extend Miller's model of pragmatics, a communicative ethics that provides some means for classifying types of knowledge, action and their political consequences. Such a rhetoric also would need to take up the connections between writing practice and face-to-face talk around texts, between text, talk and other forms of semiosis in everyday literacy events.

The contribution of *Genre and the New Rhetoric* is its continual emphasis on the social fluidity and institutional location of genre, which has been lost in the rush towards formulaic teaching. But in my opinion, the debate over genre needs to move beyond issues of technicality of text description and correctness of teaching method.

'How to teach' a genre is culturally contingent and 'whether to teach' a genre is sociologically contingent. The next move would have to be towards a rhetoric that takes up issues of textual access and power, and engages with matters of pedagogical variance and difference across cultures. Without such an analysis, genre risks becoming simply a new 'unit' of psychological skill, individual competence or cultural virtue. And, in the midst of all our talk of play, difference and game, rhetoricians and linguists could wind up wiring the circuit of post-industrial social reproduction as uncritically as educational psychologists oiled the machinery of industrial capitalism.

Allan Luke
Townsville, Queensland
June, 1994

References

COPE, B. and KALANTZIS, M. (eds) (1993) *The Powers of Literacy*, London: Falmer Press.

FAIRCLOUGH, N. (1989) *Language and Power*, London: Longman.

HEATH, S.B. (1982) 'What no bedtime story means: narrative skills at home and school,' *Language in Society*, **11**, 49–76.

HEATH, S.B. (1989) 'Talking the Text in Teaching Composition,' in DECASTELL, S., LUKE, A. and LUKE, C. (Eds) *Language, Authority and Criticism*, London: Falmer Press.

Preface

Most of the essays in this collection were first presented as papers at a colloquium, entitled 'Rethinking Genre', held at Carleton University, Ottawa April 1992.* That colloquium provided a forum in which a range of intellectual perspectives was brought to bear on the evolving notion of *genre*, and one in which participants from different disciplines and different national traditions struggled with, challenged, qualified, and extended each others' ideas. Those whose papers were first presented at that conference found their thinking and their writing considerably enriched by that forthright, vigorous, and generous exchange of ideas (as did the editors of this volume). And so, our first debt of gratitude is to the participants in that colloquium: Richard Andrews, Charles Bazerman, Carol Berkenkotter, Don Bialostosky, Richard Coe, Pat Currie, Patrick Dias, John Dixon, Janet Giltrow, Elizabeth Hoger, Tom Huckin, Russell Hunt, Carolyn Miller, Leslie Olsen, Sigmund Ongstad, Anthony Paré, Cathy Pettinari, Cathy Schryer, Graham Smart, John Swales, A.D. Van Nostrand and Eugenia Zimmerman.

The discourse at that conference was filled with explicit references to, and implicit assumption of, ideas developed in two key articles: Carolyn Miller's 'Genre as Social Action' and Anne Freadman's 'Anyone for Tennis?' We are grateful to have been accorded the right to republish these pieces in part, as an introduction to the body of the collection.

We are grateful as well to the Social Sciences and Humanities Research Council of Canada, whose generous support made this conference possible, as well as to the Carleton University Office of Research and Graduate Studies which provided seed money for the enterprise. Thanks are also owed to the sponsor of the conference, the Carleton University Centre for Rhetorical Studies, and to its Director, Professor Albert Halsall, always an inexhaustible fund of advice, encouragement, and good humour.

For aid in the publication of this collection, we thank both the Social Sciences and Humanities Research Council of Canada and the Carleton University Dean of Arts.

Aviva Freedman
Peter Medway

*The colloquium also gave rise to a second and different collection of essays: *Learning and Teaching Genre*, ed. A. Freedman and P. Medway (Portsmouth, NH: Heinemann, 1994).

Acknowledgements

The editors are grateful to the Speech Communication Association for permission to print a revised version of Carolyn R. Miller's 'Genre as Social Action' which appeared in *Quarterly Journal of Speech*, 70, 1984; to the National Council of Teachers of English for permission to print a chapter substantially based on Aviva Freedman's 'Show and Tell? The Role of Explicit Teaching in the Learning of New Genres' and 'Situating Genre: A Rejoinder' which appeared in *Research in the Teaching of English*, **27**(3), 1933; and to Ian Reid, Director of the Centre for Studies in Literary Education, Deakin University, Australia, for permission to print a condensed version of Anne Freadman's 'Anyone for Tennis?' which appeared in *The Place of Genre in Learning: Current Debates*, edited by Ian Reid (1987).

Part I
Introduction

Chapter 1

Locating Genre Studies: Antecedents and Prospects

Aviva Freedman and Peter Medway

The essays in this collection represent a newly emerging field of scholarship in North America: genre studies. For those familiar either with traditional conceptions of genre or with the recent work on genre associated with the Sydney School in Australia, the approach to genre in this volume will require explanation on our part and rethinking on yours. The introduction that follows is intended to offer some of the necessary orienting explanation. We believe the rethinking entailed well worth the effort for teachers, researchers, and students of language in general; current reconceptualizations of genre can enlarge our understanding of how it is and why it is that we produce the kinds of discourse that we do – in our classrooms, in our boardrooms and workshops, and across the range of situations in which the diversity of culture realizes itself within a society.

Traditional definitions of genre focused on textual regularities. In traditional literary studies the genres – sonnet, tragedy, ode, etc. – were defined by conventions of form and content. Descriptions of non-literary genres drew attention to textual features such as the inverted pyramid of a news story, the 'purpose, methods, procedure, observations, conclusions' organization of the lab report, the bottom-lining and you-attitude[1] of a business letter. Current genre studies (which incidentally tend to concentrate on non-literary texts) probe further; without abandoning earlier conceptions of genres as 'types' or 'kinds' of discourse, characterized by similarities in content and form, recent analyses focus on tying these linguistic and substantive similarities to regularities in human spheres of activity. In other words, the new term 'genre' has been able to connect a recognition of regularities in discourse types with a broader social and cultural understanding of language in use.

This theoretical rethinking has led to or been accompanied by a growing body of empirical studies of school and workplace writing. Since Odell and Goswami's pioneering 1985 collection, *Writing in Nonacademic Settings*, researchers have used 'ethnographic' research methods drawn from anthropology to study such instances as the writing of professional biologists (Myers 1990); the documents produced by tax accountants (Devitt 1991); the production of the experimental article (Bazerman 1988; Swales 1990); the discourse produced at a central bank (Smart 1992, 1993); the recording and reporting of social workers (Paré 1991); the evolution of the memo and the business report (Yates 1989); the role of text in private enterprise (Doheny-Farina 1991); and writing for the disciplines at university (Herrington 1985; McCarthy 1987; Freedman 1990; Berkenkotter *et al.* 1991).

All these studies unpack the complex social, cultural, institutional and disciplinary factors at play in the production of specific kinds of writing. For example, Yates (1989) has shown how changes in management philosophy as well as the introduction of new technologies elicited new business genres: the memo and the business report. At the same time, other researchers have pointed to the social consequences of textual creation: how discourse communities use mastery of writing to enrol and initiate new members, as well as to exclude others; and how texts themselves reshape the social and even material environments in which they are produced. For this reason, Bazerman and Paradis call their 1991 collection of essays, *Textual Dynamics of the Professions*, pointing to the complex interplay between texts and their social contexts.

This work is as relevant to teachers as to researchers with a theoretical interest in the social nature of written discourse. For teachers, too, there is a powerful heuristic advantage to establishing the primacy of rhetorical or socio-cultural purpose, 'rhetorical' here being used in the classical sense referring to speech or writing used to achieve some purpose within a social situation. It forces us all to reanalyse and rethink the social, cultural, political purposes of previously taken-for-granted genres, and leads to an archeological unearthing of tacit assumptions, goals and purposes as well as the revealing of unseen players and the unmasking of others.

Genre studies thus opens new perspectives on language use. As a result, we can begin to see how much more is at play in the production and reception of specific genres than we had suspected – the nature of the multiple invisible participants involved in the production of even such familiar school genres as fill-in-the-blank response sheets, multiple-choice exams, or personal reflective journals. Perhaps most significantly, as Miller points out (1984; reprinted in this volume as Chapter 2), understanding genre as social action enables us to understand what is being learned when we (or our students) learn new genres: 'we learn – what ends we may have... We learn to understand better the situations in which we find ourselves... For the student, genres serve as keys to understanding how to participate in the actions of a community.'

For teachers, consequently, a failure to understand genre as social action 'turns what should be a practical art of achieving social ends into a productive art of making texts that fit certain formal requirements'. This is the main importance of the reconceived genre studies for teachers. Put positively rather than negatively, they enlarge our sense as teachers of the ends *we* may have, and allow us to see our work in the teaching of writing as contributing to an emancipatory *social* agenda.

Overview of the Introduction

We have organized this introduction in three sections. We hope that the first, 'The Discursive Context', will be helpful primarily for those less familiar with genre studies in general and the North American tradition in particular. In this section, we set out some of the theoretic notions that have been appropriated by genre studies, especially those concepts and approaches whose understanding is assumed rather than explicated in the essays that follow.

In the second section, 'The Next Stage', we assess the state of the art of genre studies in North America, presenting some of the political implications of the 'paradigm' that has evolved, and pointing as well to its blind spots and to the possibilities for new directions in a second stage of genre studies. The directions taken so far reflect the specific intellectual and also social origins of the field and are not the only ones conceivable. Besides offering our thoughts on ways forward we discuss how the North American genre studies differ from the work of the Australian Sydney School which represents one existing alternative approach.

In the third section we present an overview of the essays in this collection.

The Discursive Context

Here we lay out some of the central concepts and theoretic approaches that underlie current North American thinking about genre. First we briefly describe four twentieth-century perspectives on human knowing and language use that have been drawn on in genre studies: the 'rhetorical turn' in disciplinary studies; social constructionism; rhetorical versions of rationality in the field of argumentation; and speech act theory. Next we discuss the work of two scholars who have in different ways shaped current thinking about genre by describing and theorizing patterns of regularities in discourse from a social perspective: Mikhail Bakhtin and John Swales. Finally we discuss recent research studies investigating academic and non-academic discourse which use the socio-rhetorical perspective of current genre studies.

The 'Rhetorical Turn'

Beginning in the mid-century with the brilliant and prescient work of Kenneth Burke, rhetoric has increasingly taken centre stage amongst ways of understanding human behaviour. If twentieth-century humanists and social scientists have tended to define and differentiate human beings by their ability to use language, more recently it is the rhetorical dimensions of that capacity that have captured our attention.

Thus, while along with Langer and Cassirer, Burke insists on the primacy of our symbol-making capacity, he alone stresses the degree to which symbol-making is inextricably bound up with persuasion. Even before Kuhn, he pointed to 'language's symbolic action' as 'exercised about the necessary *suasive* nature of even the most unemotional scientific nomenclatures' (1950: 45). However, it required the authority of Kuhn, with his status as a scientist and philosopher of science, to allow for the widespread acknowledgement of the degree to which theories even in the pure sciences are established rhetorically and communally. Sociologists of science have developed these insights and have painstakingly explicated the ways in which scientists construct the knowledge of their fields in response to rhetorical constraints (examples include

Latour and Woolgar 1979; Mulkay 1979; Knorr-Cetina 1981). The recent spate of works on the rhetoric of the social and pure sciences elaborate on these insights (see for example, McCloskey 1985; Gross 1990; Simon 1990).

The teaching of composition, too, was affected by this rhetorical turn. From our current vantage point in time, the possibility of a disjuncture between rhetoric and composition seems absurd especially since composition undoubtedly derived from the ancient study of rhetoric. By the mid-twentieth century, however, at least in North America, the teaching of composition had degenerated into an impoverished discipline that bore little trace of its origin. As described by Young (1976), composition instruction involved little more than attention to editing and rules of usage.

By the 1970s composition scholars, alert to the new developments in rhetoric, began to reinfuse the field of composition with classical concepts such as 'invention', 'audience', 'occasion', and '*kairos*', and these notions began to extend and shape thinking, research and teaching. Particularly attractive was the ability of these concepts to provide a systematic basis for a *process* pedagogy which could help students with the decisions and strategies necessary in the course of writing, rather than simply commenting, as current-traditional practice did, on faults in the written product, with appeal to a few very general maxims. As a result, students were encouraged to think as much about the demands of the *occasion* of their writing as about the textual characteristics of some general, unspecified or universal 'good writing'.

It is not surprising that such rhetorical notions soon informed considerations of 'genre' as well, especially from the perspective of its composition. At the same time, the larger recognition of the rhetorical dimensions of knowledge-making and the primacy of the rhetorical impulse in human communication (and all linguistic and semiotic processes) have profoundly shaped current thinking about the nature and role of genres.

Social Constructionism

By the 1980s, a different but related set of notions began to take hold in the field of composition studies; imported primarily from philosophy (psychology and sociology have their own versions), social constructionism has begun to shape research, thinking and pedagogy. The figures most commonly associated with social constructionism in composition studies are the philosopher Richard Rorty and his follower in composition studies, Kenneth Bruffee.

At the beginning of his essay, 'Solidarity or Objectivity', Rorty (1991) sketches two principal ways by which humans 'try to give sense to their lives'. One is to 'describe oneself as standing in immediate relation to a nonhuman reality' – whether this be through religion or science or traditional philosophy. The second is 'by telling the story of [one's] contribution to a community' (p. 21). Rorty argues that attempts of the first kind require a belief in some external set of universals on the basis of which we can spin our theories; these 'foundational' beliefs, however, have themselves been shown to be unverifiable. Therefore we would do best to turn instead to the second way of making sense of our lives, by focusing on communal constructions of meaning and *pragmatic* evaluations of the good and the true: 'truth is . . . what is good for *us* to believe' (p. 22). In this view, knowledge is something that is socially constructed in response to communal needs, goals and contexts. The social constructionist alternative to foundationalist assumptions is that

> there is only agreement, a consensus arrived at for the time being by communities of knowledgeable peers. Concepts, ideas, theories, the world, reality, and facts are all language constructs generated by knowledge communities and used by them to maintain community coherence. (Bruffee 1986: 777)

Further, as cultural anthropology has shown, it is not just knowledge that is so shaped. To quote Clifford Geertz (1983) in *Local Knowledge*, 'cognition, emotion, motivation, perception, imagination, memory . . . whatever' are 'directly social affairs' (p. 153). These emphases on the community and the socio-cultural, the acknowledgement and indeed celebration of the shaping power of the social, provide some of the groundwork on which social and contextual redefinitions of genre are based. The difference that philosophical social constructionism can make to views of writing is potentially radical; the composing of texts traditionally regarded as containers of knowledge comes to be seen, far more dynamically, as part of the social process by which that knowledge, 'the world, reality, and facts' are made. It is in the writing of students, as well as scientists and managers, that Bruffee's 'language constructs' come into being in the first place and receive regular reactivation thereafter.

Rhetorical Versions of Rationality

Equally important, but somewhat different in emphasis, is the work of the philosopher, Stephen Toulmin. Beginning with *The Uses of Argument*, Toulmin (1958) has reconceived the notion of 'argument' and has rejected the conventional notion of 'rationality' as an abstract analytic category, applicable across all disciplines and forums. Instead, he has developed a notion of 'the reasonable', in which what counts as appropriate and convincing varies according to historical, disciplinary and/or social context. Toulmin and his colleagues, Rieke and Janik (1979), have developed a descriptive framework for specifying the potential elements in any argument, and have described the instantiation of these elements in ways that differ according to the forum: claims (theses), grounds (evidence), warrants (approved ways of connecting claims to evidence), for example, differ in fundamental ways according to the context and the players. As in current genre studies, Toulmin places great emphasis on context: 'every text has to be understood in relation to a situation' (interviewed in Olson 1993: 290). Further, behind the notion of situation and especially recurrent situation is the Wittgensteinian concept of 'life-forms', something that is echoed in current genre theory (see especially the two chapters by Miller in this volume).

For teachers, Toulmin's work points to the degree to which specific subjects or courses of study differ in their modes of reasoning. Even the composition class privileges specific warrants, claims and grounds, which differ from those preferred in other disciplines. The different genres of school writing thus entail and elicit specialized and rhetorical versions of rationality.

Speech Act Theory

A different intellectual tradition feeding into current thinking about genre also derives from philosophy: speech act theory. With the title of his book, *How to Do Things With Words*, the philosopher John Austin (1962) indicated the underlying premise of this work: words do more than make statements about the nature of the world. For example, the sentence, 'the window is open', is typically more than a factual statement about a physical phenomenon. Such a statement may also be a demand that the window be closed; a complaint about lack of cooperation in the household; an explanation of why the puppy has disappeared; a request for a translation into French – depending on the context, the speaker, and the social roles and relative power of the speaker and addressee(s).

There are two points to note here. First, language – and especially utterances – are ways of acting in the world. Second, for the utterance to be comprehended as an action, researchers must take the context into account and understand it in the way that it is understood by the participants. Context, and the participants' understanding of it, define the meaning (or at least its range of possible meanings).

As Bazerman elaborates in Chapter 5, a focus on speech acts alone is too narrow to account for the complexity and richness of what is entailed in the social action undertaken in many texts (as the analyses in this collection reveal). Nevertheless, the central recognition underlying speech act theory – that discourse is usefully understood as action – has been immensely generative, not least in genre studies.

Bakhtin

The work of Mikhail Bakhtin, especially his essay 'The Problem of Speech Genres' (1986) and his essays in *The Dialogic Imagination* (1981), has been very influential in North American genre studies. For Baktin as a linguist, the fundamental unit of analysis is the 'utterance' rather than the word or the sentence. The utterance itself is socially defined, in terms of its relationship to other speakers' (preceding and succeeding) utterances; an oral utterance is one conversational turn.

'All our utterances', writes Bakhtin in 'The Problem of Speech Genres' (1986), 'have definite and relatively stable *typical* forms of construction'; that is, 'we speak only in definite speech genres' (p. 78). These primary speech genres 'correspond to typical situations of speech communication' (p. 87) such as greetings, military commands, requests for information, marriage proposals, and their regularities derive from the situations that evoke them. From these primary speech genres, the more complex 'secondary' genres of writing are derived.

Other concepts seized on from Bakhtin's work include his emphasis on 'dialogism', and on the 'addressivity' of discourse in anticipating a reader/hearer's response and in responding to the larger textual conversations already in progress. Hunt's pedagogy, as described in Chapter 13, is founded on just such an understanding of language use. In their chapters, Miller and Schryer draw on the Bakhtinian insight that genres are sites of the centrifugal and centripetal forces at work in discourse.

Particularly significant for North American genre studies has been Bakhtin's insistence that, while both primary and secondary genres involve regularities and typification, generic forms 'are much more flexible, plastic, and free' (1986: 79) than grammatical or other linguistic patterns. Furthermore, creativity is possible and visible everywhere, although Bakhtin insists that 'genres must be fully mastered to be used creatively' (1986: 80).

Swales

The applied linguist John Swales is a more recent participant in the ongoing conversation about genre. His monograph, *Genre Analysis* (1990), includes detailed discussion of influences from applied and socio-linguistics, as well as closely argued redefinitions of 'genre', using terminology (as well as attendant assumptions about the role and use of language) more familiar to applied linguistics: a genre is defined primarily by its common *communicative* purposes; these purposes, and the *role* of the genre within its *environment* give rise to specific textual features.

More relevant to the essays that follow is the fact that Swales locates genres within *discourse communities*, which are defined as 'socio-rhetorical networks that form in order to work towards sets of common goals' (p. 8). Swales's notion of discourse communities is distinct from social constructionist notions of community. Neither 'assimilation of world-view' nor 'a threshold level of personal involvement' are criterial (p. 31); in fact, involvement in such communities and use of relevant discourse conventions may be entirely instrumental.

The term 'community' has lately become a contested notion on philosophic and political grounds[2] (see Kent 1991; Fairclough 1992). Questions have been raised about the circularity of the relationship between genres and discourse communities: which comes first? In this collection both Miller and Van Nostrand qualify and/or redefine the notion of community entailed by genre analyses in substantive ways – such that, minimally, audience and community are differentiated, while contestation, competition and struggle are acknowledged as significant.

The Next Stage

Our discussion of the discursive context was framed rather as if ideas developed and exerted influence without human intervention. In fact, of course, while people

7

have indeed been influenced they have also, consciously and unconsciously, made choices. It would be naive in the extreme to suppose that positions were adopted purely from perceptions of the inherent validity of the ideas, and not in ways that to some degree reflected social and material interests. Taking full account of these factors would have resulted in a very different history.

While constructing such an account was not the task we set ourselves, we respect and regard as necessary the attempts of others to find sources of intellectual developments in the economic, social and political sphere, and we can speculate in a preliminary way about how genre studies might appear when viewed as a manifestation of broader tendencies that extend far beyond the academy. We might note, for a start, striking common themes running across many 'reconceptualizations' in contemporary thought, of which the 'reconceptualization' of genre is one: for example, the limitations of reason, logic and system; the disintegration of Enlightenment and Modernist certainties as guides to truth and to behaviour; the replacement of transcendent endorsements by the local norms of professional communities. Science advances not by the inexorable logic of successive revelations of nature but by the persuasion of influential groups; arguments are only locally valid; there are no truths, only assertions with a backing that is not universal but communal. Correspondingly, genre researchers evaluate professional texts by purely local criteria – what 'works' in the context – without reference to more general values. Reviewing this collection of North American intellectual trends, we might point to the pervasive, though unspoken, parallel (perhaps, even, endorsing metaphor) of the market, where what is right is what sells and what sells depends on the current consumer values of the particular socio-economic niche.

Alternatively, at a more particular level, a different story might be offered by way of hypothesis concerning the relationship of composition teachers to the resources of rhetorical, social constructionist, speech act and Bakhtinian theory.[3] Since the 1970s this group has been seeking a body of legitimating theory as a basis of academic respectability and parity of status with the more traditional branches of English. The teaching of writing needed to be enhanced from a somewhat menial craftlike occupation (assigned where possible to graduate students) to a professional discipline with research traditions, professional associations and the rest. Rhetoric in particular offered the possibility of more systematic and theoretically based instruction and research, and seemed a promising basis for a distinctive epistemic community. (It should be added, of course, that, as noted above, recourse to rhetorical theory was *also* pedagogically effective.) Genre studies now promise a further status-enhancing stiffening of the subdiscipline's intellectual backbone.

North American and Sydney School Conceptions of 'Genre'

Whatever the particular social formations and interests that lie behind the emergence of North American genre studies, their origins have imparted to them a particular ideological profile. It contrasts strikingly with that of the parallel genre project that has developed from quite different sources in Australia. Sometimes referred to as the 'Sydney School' after its main institutional base in the University of Sydney's Department of Linguistics, formerly headed by M.A.K. Halliday, the Australian genre movement is an educational application of the systemic functional linguistics of Halliday and his followers (for instances of such work, see the collections of essays edited by Reid 1987, and Cope and Kalantzis 1993). The two developments – North American genre studies and the Sydney School project – seem to have evolved largely independently of each other.

To be sure, there is considerable and important overlap. Common to both traditions is the explicit recognition of the primacy of the social in understanding genres and of the role of context. Applications in research and pedagogy, however, have differed in ways that reveal implicit differences in theorizing. For example, there is far greater emphasis by the Sydney School scholars on explicating textual features, using Hallidayan schemes of linguistic analysis, while North American work has focused on unpacking complex relations between text and context.

The most striking difference, however, is both the prescriptivism and the implicit static vision of genre (unless genres are static, why should they be, and how can they be, taught?) expressed in the Sydney School project (although, significantly, not in the Hallidayan linguistic theory from which this work originally derived). In contrast, North American theorizing has emphasized the dynamic quality of genres, and application in research has followed suit. In her 1984 essay (reprinted with revisions in Chapter 2 of this volume), Miller argued that genres evolve, develop and decay. A corresponding focus of research has been to trace the evolution of specific genres in response to socio-cultural phenomena in their contexts. Yates (1989) has traced the origin and development of the memo in response to changes in the management philosophy, organization and material conditions of business; Bazerman (1988) has described the evolution of the research article in response to changes in scientific knowledge. In this collection, both Zimmerman and Giltrow point to the historical evolution – over relatively long and short time-frames, respectively – of specific genres.

Viewed from another perspective, the meaning of 'genre' is quite distinct in the two traditions. Schryer (Chapter 6, this volume) speaks for many North American theorists when she argues that genres represent 'stabilized-for-now' or 'stabilized-enough sites of social and ideological action'. The conception of genre thus is far more provisional and fragile, and far more sensitive to contestation and struggle (see Miller, this volume) as well as to the tension between Bakhtin's centrifugal and centripetal forces (see both Miller and Schryer, this volume).

Related to the notion of fragility is the greater recognition – and again celebration – of the possibility of 'play' within genres, to use Freadman's term. While Freadman's piece (which is included here as Chapter 3, with revisions) has not been part of the North American canon, the degree to which its insights have been seized on when it has become known (and the degree to which it is cited in the more recent literature) reveal how closely her analysis fits with North American concepts. The notion of 'play' incorporates, among other senses, a recognition of the range, scope and potential freedom possible within genres – not to speak of the power of the individual to choose from among options within specific genres. Bakhtin too talks of the plasticity and freedom of genres (as opposed to the rules of syntax, for example), and significantly, it is Bakhtin, rather than Voloshinov, whose voice is heard most frequently in North American discussions of genre.[4]

Central also to North American notions of genre is the concept of *inter*play and *inter*action. If genres respond to contexts, they also shape such contexts (as Devitt 1993 and Freedman 1933a, 1993b argue). Similarly, if genres show us what motives we may have (as Miller argues), Bazerman's studies of figures such as Newton and Edison reveal the ways in which genres can be reshaped by those who use them – in major ways, by exceptionally powerful or forceful individuals, and in small ways presumably, by the incremental adaptations of routine users.[5] Significantly, the social theorist of choice among North American scholars is Giddens rather than Foucault or, even Bourdieu (in this collection, see the relevant discussion in chapters by Bazerman and by Miller). Giddens, it should be noted, as quoted in Miller, mediates 'the postmodern dilemma of whether the human subject can be the subject of conscious control or must be decentered into oblivion'.[6]

The teaching implications and applications in North American genre studies, as compared with those of the Sydney School, are affected by these fundamentally different conceptions of genre. First, direct translations into teaching are almost entirely absent, and indeed the very possibility of such translation is questioned directly in Freedman's chapter in this collection. In addition to drawing on language acquisition research and theory, as well as research from the field of situated cognition, Freedman points to the very reconceptualization of genre as current in North American studies to ground her argument. If genres are understood as typified responses to social contexts, and if such contexts are inevitably fluid and dynamic, what sense can it make to explicate features of historical genres (and all genres are historical) as a way of teaching or learning? (In any case, she argues, students are remarkably adept at responding linguistically to just such shifting contexts, and the intrusion of rules and formulas is often enough to put them off balance.) A complementary view is offered by Hunt (Chapter 13, this volume), who shows how in fact new genres can be taught or rather elicited: by focusing on the primacy of context and reshaping that context, through shifts in the curriculum, in the power organization of the classroom, in student–teacher and student–student relations, and in the role of technology. New genres emerged, in his study, as a result of a radically different pedagogic intent and context, carefully staged by the teacher.

There is one further set of differences between the stances of North American scholars and Sydney School genre educationists. The latter conceive of themselves and their project as effecting social change.[7] This liberationist stance has been absent from North American genre studies, as currently constituted (though not from composition studies more generally). Nor has the vocabulary of 'power' and 'domination' been in evidence. Systems of belief, ideologies, and values are indeed probed (see as examples Schryer, and Giltrow, this volume), but are treated as relatively self-contained rather than as integrally related to economic and political formations.

Towards More Critical Genre Studies

The main reservation to be entered about North American students of genre, as suggested by the comparisons with Sydney School scholars, is that they have tended to be descriptive, with the accompanying tendency to an uncritical acceptance of the status quo. As Herndl (1993) noted recently, partly because of its reliance on the research methods and cultural pluralism of anthropology, research into scientific and professional writing (the core of genre-based research) 'lends itself to a mode of reporting that reproduces the dominant discourse of its research site and spends relatively little energy analysing the modes and possibilities for dissent, resistance, and revision' (p. 349).

In the essays collected here, for example, researchers have set themselves the task of describing such genres as those of government and social work, without yet extending their inquiry to encompass the political issues entailed. In general, there has not been much critical analysis of questions such as the following. How do some genres come to be valorized? In whose interest is such valorization? What kinds of social organization are put in place or kept in place by such valorization? Who is excluded? What representations of the world are entailed? The absence of such questions is the ideological limitation we see as most needing to be addressed in the next stage of genre studies.

The questions hitherto addressed have been ones, as it were, internal to the specialist field of composition studies: how are texts brought about and how do they function within social contexts? The answers have been in terms of situational elements and the situatedness of the participants. The approach is to plot the dynamics: 'This party had these interests that affected his/her reading in this way', and 'This aspect of the context was weighing on the writer as a factor to be addressed'. Such an 'internal' mapping of the dynamics of a rhetorical situation can be neutral in terms of politics and ethics. In contrast, the inquiry now needed, and referred to by Coe (Chapter 11, this volume) as neglected, is one 'that should take us from consideration of strategies to consideration of the ends those strategies serve – and hence from rhetoric to ethics' – and, we might add, to politics. After all, in a society marked by many harmful inequalities and inhumane relations, any important form of social action (which our contributors agree genre to be) may as reasonably be expected to serve injustice and exploitation as justice and equality.

The questions that need to be brought into genre inquiry are those that inform other contemporary critical studies, such as feminist and post-colonial cultural studies and critical socio-linguistics, questions about, for instance, the gender and racial ideologies underpinning writing practices, the ways that texts 'position' writer, reader and those represented, and the construction of the Other through writing. They are pregnant with possible conflict not just about theory but about practices affecting real interests such as the flow of power, status and resources. What, for instance, about the *exclusiveness* of academic genres? What about the arguably *gendered* nature of scientific discourse? What about the status of genres of indigenous science among such groups as aboriginal Americans and Australians?

There are several possible reasons why the ethical and political implications of genres have received little comment. First, texts such as routine workplace reports which had previously appeared mechanical and impoverished in their stereotypical dryness have now become so fascinating when viewed in the new rhetorical perspective that the predominant attitudes informing genre analyses have been wonder and delight. Second, the sensitive, complex and deeply implicated way in which workplace texts are found to be responsive to multiplicities of contextual factors has tempted us into ecological analogies and a disposition to display the same respect for the intricacy and functionality of a social system as we have learned to show for a biological one. The 'intricate, richly interwoven complexity of the processes at play' (Freedman, Chapter 12, this volume), brought out by Marilyn Cooper (1989) in the metaphor of a web, has been extensively documented by, amongst others, the researchers we cited at the opening of this introduction. For something so intriguingly balanced, so finely evolved, criticism or distaste, we might feel, are hardly appropriate responses.

The feeling is, of course, misplaced. To see human relations as ecology or system involves suppressing the consciousness that it is people, experiencing beings like ourselves, and not abstract systemic elements that are the constituents of these networks. It is, moreover, entirely possible to give full acknowledgement to the achieved complexity and delicacy of an institution's working while offering a radical critique of its purposes and effects.

That said, it is still understandable if an ethical or political critique is not what first suggests itself to the scholar examining the mundane procedures of the firm down the road or the average government department. Of course, we are aware that the internal memo reflects the unequal power relations of the organization, but those inequalities are not news. They are, after all, in the nature of firms and government departments, institutions that are central to our society. No 'cruel or outlandish' exploitation or unusual oppression normally confronts us, beyond what we are accustomed to and what seems part and parcel of administrative structures in general. So what more can we do than map the generic workings? Thus we might reason.

Thus we might reason wrongly, however, because the effect will be simply to 'naturaliz[e] the discourse practices of the professional middle classes' (Trimbur 1993: 390). Genre studies are a particularly promising instrument for illuminating the social process in its detailed operation, and afford an opportunity we should not refuse of examining what it means to be part of an institutional process. For despite the superficial familiarity of the institutions in which workplace genres are to be found, the experience of those who write, read and act on the documents is not something we know much about in ethical and political terms.

So we need to ask specifically, what does participation in a genre do to, and for, an individual or group? What opportunities do the relationships reflected in and structured by a genre afford for humane creative action or, alternatively, for the domination of others? To what extent and how does the set of genres in an institution facilitate or impede that consideration of ends of which Coe speaks?

There are a number of ways, we might hypothesize, in which genres can have ethical and political implications. A useful initial distinction might be between 'internal' and 'external' effects, those on the genre's participants and those on others who are not the writers and readers of the documents. The insiders are affected through what is required of or permitted to them as readers or writers, the outsiders through being represented – or significantly not represented – in the texts. The two dynamics interact, since what is required of or permitted to writers may be particular sorts of representation of parties outside the generic network; constructing these representations may be experienced as morally distasteful or desirable.

A young professional we observed, skilled in the production of the sort of rhetorically complex documents we have recently learned to respect, shocked us with the testimony that writing them was largely an experience of frustration and stultification. Extended involvement in the genre left him with an overwhelming urge to engage in very different sorts of writing away from the office that offered scope for thinking, reflecting, imagining, discovering and creating, capabilities he felt were endangered by his weekday labours at the workplace genres. Writing is labour, potentially as alienating as other sorts – or worse, since it implicates more of the self.

If the genre was in this instance oppressive, it was so as work which denied the writer the chance of expression, or of activating more than a specialized part of himself. Writers can also, as we indicated above, find oppressive those representational requirements which would seem to bear most heavily on the individuals written *about*. McCarthy (1991), for instance, investigates the effects of a highly prescriptive genre of reporting used by a psychiatrist in work with children. The procedure, known as DSM-III, ensures coverage of a range of topics considered significant and enables the parent interview to be completed more quickly than a more open-ended procedure would permit. There is some indication, though, that in the case reported the resulting efficiency was not necessarily to the patient's benefit, and, in addition, caused professional frustration for the psychiatrist. She missed the insights which may sometimes be gained by rather looser interviews: 'I just can't let the parent go off on tangents. Which is too bad, because sometimes by following the parent's lead you get the richest material.'[8]

Clearly, the way in which people are represented within the genres of controlling agencies can have far-reaching implications for their well-being. For files kept on the population a Foucauldian analysis in terms of surveillance and discipline, the formation of disciplined bodies through inscription, seems irresistible. Likewise, where those who will be affected by a course of action are not represented in the documents which prepare the action, or are represented in less than their full humanity, as were the Vietnamese and Cambodian people in the Pentagon Papers, the writing practice can be complicit with and enable real violence: 'These men who were determining the course of millions of lives did so largely through the instrument of writing' (Ohmann 1976: 192, in an essay also referred to by Coe, Chapter 11, this volume).

Less obvious, however, but also worth studying is the possibility that generic activations which harm the people written about (we are speaking of more serious instances than the US psychiatry case – though, with Herndl, we are uncertain from McCarthy's account how serious that is) may also do violence to the writers. We as yet lack documented evidence of this, but imagine an agency employee required to report in a bureaucratically callous manner on a group of which she is a member.

(The extreme case would be the presumably tormented and reluctant writers of many Stasi reports.) Green and Lee (1994) relate an educational instance that they see in a similar light: a student with a deeply felt anti-racist awareness would in their view have been compelled by the standard school geography genre in which she was writing, had she chosen to accept its authority, to represent a traditional forest people as simply cipher-like functionaries of a particular cultivation system, in a way that would have unacceptably reduced their humanity.

There is, however, another possible interpretation of that episode. The fact that the student gained a high mark despite departing from the expected treatment of the topic suggests that the genre may have allowed alternative instantiations. We need, therefore, to know the range of tolerance of different genres. After all, many institutions (school subjects being an example; see Goodson 1984) operate only as coalitions of partly overlapping interests, more or less loosely held together by common concerns and conventions. Genres that are capacious and flexible may be just what some organizations need to create the sense that the different parties are involved in more or less the same enterprise. We can speculate further: not only are genres not bound to be oppressive to writers, they may even, beyond allowing them to write what conscience or desire dictates, actively make possible the realization of their political aspirations. A genre may, for instance, sanction the advocacy by a subordinate in an organization of the cause of a suffering group to which she feels commitment.

Presumably it is the genres that are hospitable to a measure of difference that are most likely to adapt to changes in the context within which they operate. There are some genres which, in terms of the way an organization needs to evolve for its own good, are clearly dysfunctional (cf. Schwom 1993, on the loan analysis report in certain banks and medical reports produced by physicians for attorneys). Frustrating to many of those who have to use them, and especially to younger employees who have visions of change, such genres seem to serve only the maintenance in power of some existing '-ocracy', and function primarily as a means of resisting change. Because of their association with precedent and proper procedure, and their solid existence as social fact, genres may be ideal symbolically charged landmarks over which to mount a not-an-inch-further last-ditch defence of the status quo, under the banner of 'This is how it is done'.

Outsiders, too, can be repelled with generic defences from positions of privilege. Here the decisive factor may be the difficulty and inaccessibility of some genres, and particularly the arcane tacit rules and background knowledge which inform some of them. Sociologists, but not yet students of genre, have considered academic discourse in this light (consider, for instance, Bourdieu's 1971 account of the bizarre discourse practices of the élite French academy). Genre theorists, like the social constructionists Trimbur refers to, 'in general...show much less interest than Ohmann in the circulation of knowledge and how it creates differential access to the means of producing, distributing, exchanging, and consuming knowledge' (Trimbur 1993: 390).

As Herndl acknowledges, this critique of current genre studies is not a devaluation of what has been accomplished but a claim that such work has further yet to go.

In fact there are suggestions in the research reported in this volume that a more reflexive and critical turn is in the making. Schryer, for example, raises critical questions about the genres she describes, and probes at underlying ideologies, as does Giltrow in her analysis of the background knowledge of newspaper descriptions of violence. Certaintly, the social theory of Giddens, now much referred to in genre studies, encourages such a reflexive turn.[9]

In mapping the agenda for the next phase of genre studies in the light of all the above considerations, it appears we need to commit ourselves to critical examination of at least the following specific issues: what we might call 'the labour process of genre'; the nature of the sanctioned representations, and their implications for people's lives and experience, moral and material; the degree of accessibility of a genre to potential users, as common resource or as means of exclusion; and genre maintenance as power maintenance.

More generally, we need to take from the Australian genre researchers their commitment to the explicit acknowledgement of the political dimension of genre. The Sydney School position will not, however, serve as it stands, for, ironically, it too is subject to the criticism that it accepts existing genres uncritically as they are, placing them at the foundation of a prescriptivist pedagogy which locates possibilities for enfranchisement simply in extending *access* to the genres and not in subverting the power of existing genres and/or legitimizing new ones. As Luke (1994) points out, many Australian teachers and Sydney School educationists see scientific genres as transparent, or only secondarily as ideological in function. We therefore need to see genres as inescapably implicated in political and economic processes, but at the same time as shifting, revisable, local, dynamic and subject to critical action.

Overview of Essays in This Collection

The essays in this collection themselves attest to recognition in North American genre studies of the 'play' possible within genre. As a reader, you will encounter many different voices (even within the same essay), and a range of instantiations of the genre 'collected essays within the discipline of genre studies, circa 1990'. Many of them were first presented in earlier versions at a colloquium held at Carleton University, Ottawa, in April 1992.

The collection is divided roughly into three: Genre Theory; Research into Public and Professional Genres; Applications in Education. In the end, though, some of the theoretic pieces entail reports of research, all of the reports on research feed back into theory, and the section on education includes both discussions of research and theoretic qualification. So much for neat categorizations.

The section on theory begins with two classic pieces, much cited and powerful influences within the textual context of genre studies: the seminal piece by Carolyn Miller, 'Genre as Social Action', and the essay by Anne Freadman, 'Anyone for Tennis?' which has had a more underground circulation. Although located in different disciplinary traditions, each essay foregrounds the rhetorical and socio-cultural dimensions of genre, as well as the centrality of 'action' and 'play' (as opposed to traditional definitions which focused on static textual regularities).

The other two chapters extend and enrich these seminal redefinitions. In 'Rhetorical Community: The Cultural Basis of Genre', Miller considers, probes, and extends the implications of her original argument from the perspective of cultural criticism. In the course of doing so, she fundamentally redefines 'community' as a 'discursive projection' or a 'rhetorical construct'; the discourse community implicit in genre theory becomes a 'virtual community', a point at which Bakhtin's centrifugal and centripetal forces meet. Charles Bazerman's essay, 'Systems of Genre and the Enactment of Social Intentions', bridges the 'theory' and 'research' sections. He focuses on the example of the legal patent in order to examine 'how people create individual instances of meaning and value within structured discursive fields...through the performance of genres'. He describes the evolution of the patent genre historically, defines its action contextually, and locates it within a complex web of interrelated genres.

The section 'Research into Public and Professional Genres' is composed of chapters by Schryer, Zimmerman, Van Nostrand, Paré and Smart, and Giltrow. Cathy Schryer's essay, 'The Lab vs. the Clinic: Sites of Competing Genres', examines two competing scientific traditions and their recurrent ways of representing their problem-solving and knowledge construction. In her essay, 'On Definition and Rhetorical Genre', Eugenia Zimmerman shows the effect of historical context on genre by examining the classical rhetorical genres and their modern-day counterparts. A. D. Van Nostrand focuses on a specific set of genres within a government agency in his chapter, 'A Genre Map of R & D Knowledge Production in the US Department of Defense'. The genres produced are analysed as cultural artefacts on the one hand, and as forces 'that power the system' on the other. In their chapter, 'Observing Genres in Action: Towards a Research Methodology', Paré and Smart compare genres produced in two bureaucratic organizations (a social welfare agency and a government financial institution) to make the following theoretic point: genres can be defined not only by their distinctive actions, but also according to the specialized and distinctive composing processes and reading practices entailed. In the final piece in this section, 'Genre and the Pragmatic Concept of Background Knowledge', Janet Giltrow expands our understanding of the operations of genre by pointing to the distinctiveness of not just what is said, but rather what can remain unsaid. Each chapter in this section thus shows the power of current redefinitions of genre for illuminating the operation of specific genres; at the same time, each adds texture and nuance to the theoretic reconceptualizations at play.

The final section focuses on 'Applications in Education'. In ' "An Arousing and Fulfilment of Desires": The Rhetoric of Genre in the Process Era – and Beyond', Richard Coe looks at the role that pre-existing genres play in the creation of new texts. Drawing on the work of Kenneth Burke, he points to the generative power of form and to the potential role of teaching about genre in the process era, and beyond – especially as a tool for enhancing students' understanding of the ideologies implicit in the genres that they read and write. The chapter ' "Do As I Say": The Relationships between Teaching and Learning Genre', by Aviva Freedman is a response, in part, to the educational initiative undertaken by the Sydney School. Specifically, questions are raised about the possibility of students acquiring genres that are taught, out of context, through the description of formal features and explication of rules. In his essay, 'Traffic in Genres, In Classrooms and Out', Russell Hunt describes the invention and reinvention of new written genres in the classroom. These genres are not formally or explicitly 'taught', but they are acquired/created as students respond to fundamentally new pedagogic goals (based on new theories of learning), a distinctively designed syllabus, and a non-traditional distribution of power and responsibility within the class.

Notes

1 Features discussed in current US business communications textbooks.
2 Kent (1991: 425) points to a spectrum of uses of the term:

> on the one end . . . are thick formulations that depict a community as a determinate and codifiable social entity, and on the other end are thin formulations that depict a community as a relatively indeterminate and uncodifiable sedimentation of beliefs and desires.

Kent argues against the social constructionism implicit in both thick and thin formulations. His own position, based on the philosophic work of Donald Davidson, is that writing is 'a hermeneutic act that brings us in unmediated touch with the world and with the minds of others' (p. 427).

At the same time, the notion of discourse community has been subject to attack on political grounds. Fairclough worries about presenting these communities as 'static synchronic entities' in a way that makes 'contestation and struggle invisible. Yet contestation and struggle are . . . the absolutely fundamental processes out of which communities are shaped and transformed' (1992:48).

3 By composition teachers we refer to teachers of composition in United States and Canadian university departments of English; unlike high school and elementary school English teachers, these academics are expected to publish and are the majority contributors to a group of academic journals. The shifts in their intellectual allegiances are thus relatively public, explicit and documented.
4 We agree here with Morson and Emerson's (1990) distinction.
5 It remains a matter for research how some genres change in response to circumstances while others may persist to the point of becoming seriously dysfunctional in at least some respects.
6 While rarely taken up explicitly, there seems to be a common stance in North American genre studies in the treatment of agency. Given the social emphasis of this work, and the recognition of the power of context and community, it is not surprising that agents are not perceived as the autonomous Romantic individuals characteristic of earlier views of composing. Neither, however, does the notion of writer as 'subject' or 'subjected' recur. If social factors shape, they do not constrain to the extent suggested in some of Rorty's work or in that of poststructuralists like Foucault. Using Giddens's structuration theory, the social model invoked is one in which social structure is both reproduced and created through the interaction and interplay between self and society.

While few genre specialists would be familiar with his work, the model developed by the American philosopher, Donald Davidson, accounts for the position taken in their work far more comprehensively than does that of his student, and self-proclaimed acolyte, Rorty. He recognizes the irreducibly social element in what we mean and who we are: the development of individual self is always and only in terms of relations with others. Nonetheless, Davidson categorically denies the social constructionist tenet that discourse communities (or conceptual schemes) shape and control communication. Instead, Davidson posits 'a thoroughly hermeneutical and intersubjective account of communicative interaction' (Kent 1993: 2).

7 The naivety and limitations of this political and social agenda are spelled out in Luke's (1994) critique, 'Genres of Power: Literacy Education and the Production of Capital'. See the opening of Freedman's Chapter 12 for a summary.

8 The possible losses have mainly to be deduced between the lines of McCarthy's report, which Herndl rightly cites as an instance of the uncritical stance which has prevailed: 'questions of ideology and resistance are not central to her project' (Herndl 1993: 355).

9 Nevertheless, one must remember Kenneth Burke's admonition: A way of seeing is also a way of not-seeing. To see the political as primary (and the personal as political) may also entail a sacrifice of other kinds of human reality. There may, after all, be a human drive to find meaning in experience; disinterested search for truth (however small the 't', and however pragmatically and communally defined) may be a motive for some human action. Teaching and mentoring sometimes derive from disinterested impulses to nurture.

References

AUSTIN, J. (1962) *How to Do Things with Words*, Oxford: Oxford University Press.

BAKHTIN, M. M. (1981) *The Dialogic Imagination*, (ed. M. Holquist, trans. C. Emerson and M. Holquist) Austin, TX: University of Texas Press.

BAKHTIN, M. M. (1986) 'The Problem of Speech Genres', in *Speech Genres and Other Late Essays*, (ed. C. Emerson and M. Holquist, trans. V. W. McGee) Austin, TX: University of Texas Press, pp. 60–102.

BAZERMAN, C. (1988) *Shaping Written Knowledge: The Genre and Activity of the Experimental Article in Science*, Madison, WI: University of Wisconsin Press.

BAZERMAN, C. and PARADIS, J. (eds) (1991) *Textual Dynamics of the Professions*, Madison, WI: University of Wisconsin Press.

BERKENKOTTER, C., HUCKIN, T. and ACKERMAN, J. (1991) 'Social Context and Socially Constructed Text', in BAZERMAN, C. and PARADIS, J. (eds) *Textual Dynamics of the Professions*, Madison, WI: University of Wisconsin Press, pp. 191–215.

BOURDIEU, P. (1971) 'Systems of Education and Systems of Thought', in Michael F. D. Young (ed.) *Knowledge and Control: New Directions for the Sociology of Education* London: Collier-Macmillan, pp. 189–207.

BRUFFEE, K. A. (1986) 'Social Construction, Language, and the Authority of Knowledge: A Bibliographical Essay', *College English*, **48**, December, pp. 773–90.

BURKE, K. (1950) *A Rhetoric of Motives*, Berkeley, CA: University of California Press.

COOPER, M. (1989) 'The Ecology of Writing', in COOPER, M. M. and HOLZMAN, M. (eds) *Writing as Social Action*, Portsmouth, NH: Boynton/Cook Heinemann, pp. 1–13.

COPE, W. and KALANTZIS, M. (eds) (1993) *The Literacies of Power and the Powers of Literacy*, London: Falmer Press.

DEVITT, A. J. (1991) 'Intertextuality in Tax Accounting: Generic, Referential, and Functional', in BAZERMAN, C. and PARADIS, J. (eds) *Textual Dynamics of the Professions*, Madison, WI: University of Wisconsin Press, pp. 306–35.

DEVITT, A. J. (1993) 'Generalizing about Genre: New Conceptions of an Old Concept', *College Composition and Communication*, **44**, pp. 573–86.

DOHENY-FARINA, S. (1991) 'Creating a Text/Creating a Company: The Role of a Text in the Rise and Decline of a New Organization', in BAZERMAN, C. and PARADIS, J. (eds) *Textual Dynamics of the Professions*, Madison, WI: University of Wisconsin Press, pp. 306–35.

FAIRCLOUGH, N. (1992) 'The Appropriacy of "Appropriateness" ', in FAIRCLOUGH, N. (ed.) *Critical Language Awareness*, London: Longman, pp. 33–56.

FREEDMAN, A. (1990) 'Reconceiving Genre', *Texte*, **8/9**, pp. 279–92.

FREEDMAN, A. (1993a) 'Show and Tell? The Role of Explicit Teaching in the Learning of New Genres', *Research in the Teaching of English*, **27**, pp. 222–51.

FREEDMAN, A. (1993b) 'Situating Genre: A Rejoinder', *Research in the Teaching of English*, **27**, pp. 272–8.

GEERTZ, C. (1983) *Local Knowledge*, New York: Basic Books.

GIDDENS, A. (1984) *The Constitution of Society*, Berkeley, CA: University of California Press.

GOODSON, I. (1984) 'Subjects for Study: Towards a Social History of Curriculum', in GOODSON, I. and BALL, S. (eds) *Defining the Curriculum: Histories as Ethnographies*, London: Falmer.

GREEN, B. and LEE, A. (1994) 'Writing Geography: Literacy, Identity and Schooling', in FREEDMAN, A. and MEDWAY, P. (eds) *Learning and Teaching Genre*, Portsmouth, NH: Heinemann/Boynton Cook. [In press]

GROSS, A. (1990) *The Rhetoric of Science*, Cambridge, MA: Harvard University Press.

HARRIS, J. (1989) 'The Idea of Community in the Study of Writing', *College Composition and Communication*, **40**, pp. 11–22.

HERNDL, C. (1993) 'Teaching Discourse and Reproducing Culture: A Critique of Research and Pedagogy in Professional and Non-Academic Writing', *College Composition and Communication*, **44**, October, pp. 349–63.

HERRINGTON, A. (1985) 'Writing in Academic Settings: A Study of the Contexts for Writing in Two College Chemical Engineering Courses', *Research in the Teaching of English*, **19**, pp. 331–61.

KENT, T. (1991) 'On the Very Idea of a Discourse Community', *College Composition and Communication*, **42**, December, pp. 425–42.

KENT, T. (1993) 'Language Philosophy, Writing and Reading: A Conversation with Donald Davidson', *Journal of Advanced Composition*, **13**, pp. 1–20.

KNORR-CETINA, K. (1981) *The Manufacture of Knowledge*, Oxford: Pergamon.

LATOUR, B. and WOOLGAR, S. (1979) *Laboratory Life: The Social Construction of Scientific Facts*, Beverly Hills: Sage.

LUKE, A. (1994) 'Genres of Power: Literacy Education and the Production of Capital', in Hasan, R. and Williams, G. (eds) *Literacy in Society*, London: Longman.

McCARTHY, L. M. (1987) 'A Stranger in Strange Lands: A College Student Writing Across the Curriculum', *Research in the Teaching of English*, **21**, pp. 233–65.

McCARTHY, L. M. (1991) 'A Psychiatrist using DSM-III: The Influences of a Charter Document in Psychiatry', in Bazerman, C. and Paradis, J. (eds) *Textual Dynamics of the Professions*, Madison, WI: University of Wisconsin Press, pp. 358–78.

McCloskey, D. N. (1985) *The Rhetoric of Economics*, Madison, WI: University of Wisconsin Press.

Miller, C. R. (1984) 'Genre as Social Action', *Quarterly Journal of Speech*, **70**, pp. 151–67.

Morson, G. S. and Emerson, C. (1990) *Mikhail Bakhtin: Creation of a Prosaics*, Stanford, CA: Stanford University Press.

Mulkay, G. (1979) *Science and the Sociology of Knowledge*, London: George Allen and Unwin.

Myers, G. (1990) *Writing Biology*, Madison, WI: University of Wisconsin Press.

Odell, L. and Goswami, D. (eds) (1985) *Writing in Nonacademic Settings*, New York: Guildford Press.

Ohmann, R. (1976) *English in America: A Radical View of the Profession*, New York: Oxford University Press.

Olson, G. (1993) 'Literary Theory, Philosophy of Science, and Persuasive Discourse: Thoughts from a Neo-premodernist', *Journal of Advanced Composition*, **13**, pp. 283–310.

Paré, A. (1991) 'Writing in Social Work: A Case Study of a Discourse Community', PhD thesis, McGill University.

Reid, I. (ed.) (1987) *The Place of Genre in Learning*, Geelong, Victoria, Australia: Deakin University.

Rorty, R. (1991) 'Solidarity or Objectivity', in *Objectivity, Relativism, and Truth: Philosophical Papers*, Vol. 1, Cambridge: Cambridge University Press, pp. 21–34.

Schwom, B. (1993) 'The Role of Genre in Professional Discourse', paper presented at the Annual Convention of the Association for Business Communication, Montreal, 29 October.

Simon, H. W. (ed.) (1990) *The Rhetorical Turn: Invention and Persuasion in the Conduct of Inquiry*, Chicago, IL: University of Chicago Press.

Smart, G. (1992) 'Exploring the Social Dimension of a Workplace Genre and the Implications for Teaching', *Carleton Papers in Applied Language Studies*, **9**, pp. 33–46.

Smart, G. (1993) 'Genre as Community Invention: A Central Bank's Response to its Executives' Expectations as Readers', in Spilka R. (ed.) *Writing in the Workplace: New Research Perspectives*, Carbondale, IL: Southern Illinois University Press, pp. 124–40.

Swales, J. (1990) *Genre Analysis*, Cambridge: Cambridge University Press.

Toulmin, S. R. (1958) *The Uses of Argument*, Cambridge: Cambridge University Press.

Toulmin, S., Rieke, R. and Janik, A. (1979) *An Introduction to Reasoning*, New York: Macmillan.

Trimbur, J. (1993) Review of R. Ohmann, *English in America: A Radical View of the Profession (1976)* and *The Politics of Letters*, *College Composition and Communication*, **44**, October, pp. 389–92.

Young, R. E. (1976) 'Paradigms and Problems: Needed Research in Rhetorical Invention', in Cooper, C. and Odell, L. (eds) *Research on Composing*, Urbana, IL: National Council of Teachers of English, pp. 29–48.

Yates, J. (1989) *Control through Communication*, Baltimore, MD: Johns Hopkins University Press.

Part II
Genre Theory

Chapter 2

Genre as Social Action*

Carolyn R. Miller

Although rhetorical criticism has recently provided a profusion of claims that certain discourses constitute a distinctive class, or genre, rhetorical theory has not provided firm guidance on what constitutes a genre. For example, rhetorical genres have been defined by similarities in strategies or forms in the discourses (Black [1965] 1978a; Hart 1971; Campbell 1973; Raum and Measell 1974), by similarities in audience (Mohrmann and Leff 1974), by similarities in modes of thinking (Gronbeck 1978; Rodgers 1982), by similarities in rhetorical situations (Windt 1972; Ware and Linkugel 1973; Halloran 1978). The diversity among these definitions presents both theorists and critics with a problem.

While this problem is created by rhetoricians who have done work in genre theory or criticism, another problem is raised by some who do not believe rhetoricians should do such work at all. Patton (1976) and Conley (1979) have argued that genre criticism requires too much critical distance between the text and the reader and thus leads to assessments that are not fully responsible. Genre criticism, they contend, invites reductionism, rules, formalism. Patton believes that such analysis results in 'critical determinism of the worst sort' (1976: 5), and Conley that it leads to 'tiresome and useless taxonomies' (1979: 53).[1]

The urge to classify is fundamental, and although it involves the difficulties that Patton and Conley point out, classification is necessary to language and learning. The variety of critical approaches referred to above indicates the many ways one might classify discourse, but if the term 'genre' is to mean anything theoretically or critically useful, it cannot refer to just any category or kind of discourse. One concern in rhetorical theory, then, is to make of rhetorical genre a stable classifying concept; another is to ensure that the concept is rhetorically sound.

In this essay, I will address both of these concerns, the first by developing a perspective on genre that relies on areas of agreement in previous work and connects those areas to corroborating material; the second concern I will address by proposing how an understanding of genre can help account for the way we encounter, interpret, react to, and create particular texts. My effort will elaborate the approach taken by Campbell and Jamieson (1978) and support their position that genre study is valuable

*This chapter is reprinted with permission from *Quarterly Journal of Speech*, 70 (1984) pp. 151–67.

not because it might permit the creation of some kind of taxonomy, but because it emphasizes some social and historical aspects of rhetoric that other perspectives do not. I will be arguing that a theoretically sound definition of genre must be centred not on the substance or the form of discourse but on the action it is used to accomplish. To do so, I will examine the connection between genre and recurrent situation and the way in which genre can be said to represent typified rhetorical action. My analysis will also show how hierarchical models of communication can help illuminate the nature and structure of such rhetorical action.

Classifying Discourse

A collection of discourses may be sorted into classes in more than one way, as Harrell and Linkugel (1978) note in their discussion of genre.[2] Because a classification sorts items on the basis of some set of similarities, the principle used for selecting similarities can tell us much about the classification. A classification of discourse will be rhetorically sound if it contributes to an understanding of how discourse works – that is, if it reflects the rhetorical experience of the people who create and interpret the discourse. As Frye remarks, 'The study of genres has to be founded on the study of convention' ([1957] 1971: 96). A useful principle of classification for discourse, then, should have some basis in the conventions of rhetorical practice, including the ways actual rhetors and audiences have of comprehending the discourse they use.

The semiotic framework provides a way to characterize the principles used to classify discourse, according to whether the defining principle is based in rhetorical substance (semantics), form (syntactics), or the rhetorical action the discourse performs (pragmatics). A classifying principle based in rhetorical action seems most clearly to reflect rhetorical practice (especially since, as I will suggest later, action encompasses both substance and form). And if genre represents action, it must involve situation and motive, because human action, whether symbolic or otherwise, is interpretable only against a context of situation and through the attributing of motives.

'Motive' and 'situation' are Burke's terms, of course, and Campbell and Jamieson's discussion of genre leans on them implicitly, particularly the latter: 'A genre', they write, 'does not consist merely of a series of acts in which certain rhetorical forms recur . . . Instead, a genre is composed of a constellation of recognizable forms bound together by an internal dynamic' (1978: 21). The dynamic 'fuses' substantive, stylistic, and situational characteristics. The fusion has the character of a rhetorical 'response' to situational 'demands' perceived by the rhetor. This definition, they maintain, 'reflects Burke's view of rhetorical acts as strategies to encompass situations' (Jamieson and Campbell, 1982: 146).

Their explanation of genre also reflects Bitzer's (1968) formulation of the relationship between situation and discourse, perhaps more than it does Burke's. In Bitzer's definition of rhetorical situation as a 'complex of persons, events, objects, and relations' presenting an 'exigence' that can be allayed through the mediation of discourse, he establishes the demand–response vocabulary that Campbell and Jamieson adopt. Furthermore, he essentially points the way to genre study, although he does not use the term himself, in observing that situations recur: 'From day to day, year to year, comparable situations occur, prompting comparable responses'. The comparable responses, or recurring forms, become a tradition which then 'tends to function as a constraint upon any new response in the form' (Bitzer 1968: 13). Thus, inaugurals, eulogies, courtroom speeches, and the like have conventional forms because they arise in situations with similar structures and elements and because rhetors respond in similar ways, having learned from precedent what is appropriate and what effects their actions are likely to have on other people.

Campbell and Jamieson's approach to genre is also fundamentally Aristotelian. In each of three kinds of rhetoric Aristotle described – deliberative, forensic and epideictic – we find a situation-based fusion of form and substance. Each has its characteristic substance: the elements (exhortation and dissuasion, accusation and defence, praise and blame) and aims (expedience, justice, honour). Each has its appropriate forms (time or tense, proofs and style). These fusions of substance and form are grounded in the specific situations calling for extended discourse in ancient Greece, including the audiences that were qualified to participate and the types of judgments they were called upon to make. The three kinds of rhetoric seem to be quite distinct, the various aspects of each to be part of a rational whole. It is likely that an internal 'dynamic' of the sort Campbell and Jamieson postulate was at the centre of each of these three original genres. (I will comment later on the current status of the Aristotelian genres.)

Two features of this approach are of interest at this point. First, Campbell and Jamieson's discussion yields a method of classification that meets the requirement of relevance to rhetorical practice. Since 'rhetorical forms that establish genres are stylistic and substantive responses to perceived situational demands' (1978: 19), a genre becomes a complex of formal and substantive features that create a particular effect in a given situation. Genre, in this way, becomes more than a formal entity; it becomes pragmatic, fully rhetorical, a point of connection between intention and effect, an aspect of social action. This approach is different in an important way from those of Frye and Edwin Black, to which it is indebted. Although both begin by tying genre to situation, Frye ([1957] 1971: 247) with the 'radical of presentation' (a kind of schematic rhetorical situation) and Black ([1965] 1978a: 134) with the rhetorical 'transaction' (emphasizing audience effects), they base their critical analyses on form: strategies, diction, linguistic elements. For them, situation serves primarily to locate a genre; it does not contribute to its character as rhetorical action.

The second feature of interest in Campbell and Jamieson's method is that they proceed inductively, as critics. They do not attempt to provide a framework that will predict or limit the genres that might be identified. Their interest is less in providing a taxonomic system than in explaining certain aspects of the way social reality evolves: 'The critic who classifies a rhetorical artifact as generically akin to a class of similar artifacts has identified an undercurrent of history rather than comprehended an act isolated in time' (1978: 26). The result is that the set of genres is an open class, with new members evolving, old ones decaying.[3]

In contrast to Campbell and Jamieson's approach is that of Harrell and Linkugel (1978), who proceed deductively, as theorists. Their discussion illustrates one of the risks of theory, that it lends itself to the development of a closed set, usually consisting of few members – a neat taxonomic system that does not reflect rhetorical practice so much as an a priori principle. Harrell and Linkugel begin with a definition that seems similar to that of Campbell and Jamieson: 'rhetorical genres stem from *organizing principles* found in *recurring situations* that generate discourse characterized by a family of *common factors*' (1978: 263–4). The 'common factors' account for substantive and formal similarities among discourses of the same type, and the 'organizing principles', defined as 'assumptions that crystallize the central features of a type of discourse' (1978: 264), seem not unlike the 'internal dynamic' of Campbell and Jamieson. However, Harrell and Linkugel make of the organizing principle not a dynamic resulting from the interaction of situation and forms but a theoretical premise, unrelated to situation. The organizing principles are based on fundamental modes of thinking, each of which yields a principle of classification: *de facto*, structural, motivational and archetypal. The organizing principles, in fact, do not distinguish classes of discourse; they distinguish methods of classifying discourse. The structural principle yields classes based on formal similarities, the motivational yields classes based on pragmatic similarities, and the archetypal yields classes based probably on substantive similarities; the *de facto* principle apparently yields an unsystematic classification. Harrell and Linkugel suggest, however, that the motivational principle will yield more 'productive' generic groups because it better accounts for the interaction between the rhetor and situation (in this respect, it seems to be the only principle that adheres to their original definition). To define motivational genres, they adopt Fisher's (1970) formulation of four primary 'motive states' defined in terms of the possible effects of discourse upon the life of an idea or ideology (affirmation, reaffirmation, purification and subversion). Fisher's discussion relies on the Burkean conception that motives are found within or created by situations and that situations are perceived in terms of motives.

In his own discussion of genre theory, Fisher (1980) presents four levels of genre constitution. The most general level distinguishes rhetoric from other types of discourse; the second level includes classifications within rhetoric, including (among other possibilities) the four motives; the third contains the rhetorical forms that are commonly identified as genres (eulogies, apologies, nominating speeches, etc.); and the fourth consists of categories described in terms of style. Fisher's characterization is similar to Harrell and Linkugel's spectrum, for the four levels of generality require four different principles of classification.

Both of these discussions of genre are useful as ways of accounting for the variety of genre claims that have been made – indeed, they succeed better as classifications of genre criticism than as classifications of discourse. But as theories of genre they have two shortcomings. First, neither presents a single, clearly defined principle of classification that could promote critical agreement and theoretical clarity. The clearest principles that are presented lead to closed classifications, which sacrifice the diversity and dynamism of rhetorical practice to some theoretical a priori. And second, neither of these discussions grounds genre in situated rhetorical action. The closest approach is Fisher's four motives, but these operate at a level of abstraction that is too high to represent the practical rhetorical experience of those who use genres.

That is, the description of motives in terms of the possible effects of discourse on ideas does not reflect the way human motivation is engaged by particular rhetorical situations. The four motives describe more about human nature than they do about rhetorical practice. And yet the Burkean relationship between motive and situation that Fisher invokes is promising because it clearly requires an action-based (pragmatic) principle of classification. What is lacking is a connection between the motives and the kind of experience represented by Fisher's third level and by Harrell and Linkugel's *de facto* classification.

Scholars in other fields have been interested in classifying discourse, for both pedagogical and theoretical reasons, and these classifications have occasionally been adopted by rhetoricians as the equivalents of genres. But most of these systems can be dismissed here on the same points: either the classes do not represent rhetorical action or the system is not open. In the fields of literature and composition, classifications are commonly based upon formal rather than pragmatic elements. Wellek and Warren, for example, classify literary genres on both outer form (specific meter or structure) and inner form (attitude, tone purpose, as revealed in textual details) (1977: 226–37). In the field of composition, Brooks and Warren (following Alexander Bain and a long textbook tradition) describe a closed, formal system based nominally on intention but described according to form: exposition, argumentation, description, narration ([1972]1979:40).[4] Kinneavy has classified discourse on the basis of 'aim', an apparently pragmatic basis, but he also arrives at a closed system with four members: expressive, persuasive, literary, and referential discourse (1971). Aim is determined by which of the four components of a communication model a discourse 'focuses' on: sender, receiver, code, or reality. This scheme suggests a substantive rather than a pragmatic classification.[5] Linguists have also wrestled with the problem of classifying discourse, but their efforts have produced systems that are mostly formal (Frow 1980; van Dijk 1977, 1980).

In sum, what I am proposing so far is that in rhetoric the term 'genre' be limited to a particular type of discourse classification, a classification based in rhetorical practice and consequently open rather than closed and organized around situated actions (that is pragmatic, rather than syntactic or semantic). I do not mean to suggest that there is only one way (or one fruitful way) to classify discourse. Classifications and distinctions based on form and substance have told us much about sentimentalism, women's liberation and doctrinal movements, for example (Hart 1971; Campbell 1973; Black 1978b). But we do not gain much by calling all such classes 'genres'. The genre classification I am advocating is, in effect, ethnomethodological: it seeks to explicate the knowledge that practice creates. This approach insists that the '*de facto*' genres, the types we have names for in everyday language, tell us something theoretically important about discourse. To consider as potential genres such homely discourse as the letter of recommendation, the user manual, the progress report, the ransom note, the lecture, and the white paper, as well as the eulogy, the apologia, the inaugural, the public proceeding, and the sermon, is not to trivialize the study of genres; it is to take seriously the rhetoric in which we are immersed and the situations in which we find ourselves.

The problems that remain in defining rhetorical genre become somewhat more specific than those so far considered. First is the problem of clarifying the relationship between rhetoric and its context of situation; this is central to understanding genre as rhetorical action. Second is the problem of understanding the way in which a genre 'fuses' (in Campbell and Jamieson's term) situational with formal and substantive features. And third is the problem of locating genre on a hierarchical scale of generalizations about language use, in effect, of choosing among Fisher's four levels.

Recurrent Rhetorical Situations

Although Burke (1973) and Bitzer (1968, 1980) have both used the term 'rhetorical situation', Bitzer's work brought a specific version into prominence in rhetorical theory. One crucial difference between the two is Burke's use of *motive* and Bitzer's of *exigence* as the focus of situation. Although the two concepts are related, there is a tension between them that requires resolution before the relation of genre to situation can be clear. Burke's emphasis is on human action, whereas Bitzer's appears to be on *reaction*. In particular, Bitzer's use of demand–response language has made it possible to conceive of exigence as an external cause of discourse and situation as deterministic, interpretations that have been widely discussed (Vatz 1973; Consigny 1974).[6] Because these interpretations create problems for genre theory, a reconceptualization of exigence is necessary if genre is to be understood as social action.

Bitzer (1968, 1980), Brinton (1981) and Patton (1979) all emphasize the ontological status of situations as real, objective, historical events. All three describe situations as consisting of two sorts of components: Patton refers to the external and internal components, Brinton to objective and subjective, and Bitzer (1980) to the factual and interest components of exigence. All three regard the first term as fundamental, as the real part of the situation, and the second as a perceptual screen. Patton believes, for instance, that objective phenomena serve as the basis for assessing the 'accuracy' of perception. Brinton concludes that the factual component *is* the exigence and that consequently there may be 'absolute' exigences. Bitzer also describes exigence as being independent of human awareness: 'If drinking water contains a very high level of mercury, then surely an exigence exists even though no one is aware of the factual condition' (1980: 31). For him, exigence can be synonymous with danger.[7] An account of the relationship between rhetoric and situation that thus empowers external, objective elements of situation is a theory that, in Kenneth Burke's terms, features scene above any other source of motive. Such a theory he characterized as 'materialist' in a prophetic passage in *A Grammar of Motives*: 'with materialism the circumference of scene is so narrowed as to involve the reduction of action to motion' ([1945] 1969a: 131).[8] Much of the debate regarding situational theory has concerned ways of mitigating the materialist interpretation of it.

What is particularly important about rhetorical situations for a theory of genres is that they recur, as Bitzer originally noted, but in order to understand recurrence, it is necessary to reject the materialist tendencies in situational theory. Campbell and Jamieson observe that in rhetoric 'the existence of the recurrent provides insight into the human condition' (1978: 27); in the materialist account, the recurrent would lead instead to scientific generalizations. Recurrence is implied by our understanding of situations as somehow 'comparable', 'similar', or 'analogous' to other situations, but, as Stebbins notes, 'objective situations are unique' – they cannot recur (1967: 154).[9] What recurs cannot be a material configuration of objects, events and people, nor can it be a subjective configuration, a 'perception', for these, too, are unique from moment to moment and person to person. Recurrence is an intersubjective phenomenon, a social occurrence, and cannot be understood on materialist terms.[10]

Situations are social constructs that are the result, not of 'perception', but of 'definition'. Because human action is based on and guided by meaning, not by material causes, at the centre of action is a process of interpretation. Before we can act, we must interpret the indeterminate material environment; we define or 'determine', a situation. It is possible to arrive at common determinations of material states of affairs that may have many possible interpretations because, as Alfred Schutz has argued, our 'stock of knowledge' is based upon types:

> We can...imagine a type to be like a line of demarcation which runs between the determinations explicated on the basis of the 'hitherto existing' relevance structures...and the...unlimited possibilities for the determination of experience. (Schutz and Luckmann 1973: 231)

In other words, our stock of knowledge is useful only in so far as it can be brought to bear upon new experience: the new is made familiar through the recognition of relevant similarities; those similarities become constituted as a type. A new type is formed from typifications already on hand when they are not adequate to determine a new situation. If a new typification proves continually useful for mastering states of affairs, it enters the stock of knowledge and its application becomes routine. Although types evolve in this way, most of our stock of knowledge is quite stable. Schutz notes that because types are created and shared through communication, they come to reside in language:

> Whatever is typically relevant for the individual was for the most part already typically relevant for his (*sic*) predecessors and has consequently deposited its semantic equivalent in the language. In short, the language can be construed as the sedimentation of typical experiential schemata which are typically relevant in a society. (Schutz and Luckmann 1973: 234)

Schutz's account of types is useful to a theory of rhetorical genres because it shows the importance of classification to human action. It is through the process of typification that we create recurrence, analogies, similarities. What recurs is not a material situation (a real, objective, factual event) but our construal of a type. The typified situation, including typifications of participants, underlies typification in rhetoric. Successful communication would require that the participants share common types; this is possible in so far as types are socially created (or biologically innate).

The linquist M. A. K. Halliday provides a corroborating perspective on situation types:

> the apparently infinite number of different possible situations represents in reality a very much smaller number of general *types* of situations, which we can describe in such terms as 'players instructing novice in a game', 'mother reading bedtime story to her child', 'customer ordering goods over the telephone', 'teacher guiding pupils', 'discussion of a poem', and the like. (1978: 29)

Typification is possible, here again, because situation 'is not an inventory of ongoing sights and sounds but a semiotic structure' (1978: 122). Moreover, the situation type is the developmental basis for meaning. In his work on the development of language in the child, Halliday finds that the child first learns a restricted set of functions that language can accomplish: 'The child's uses of language are interpretable as generalized situation types; the meanings that he (*sic*) can express are referable to specific social contexts' (1975: 255). These original, limited uses of language expand as the child encounters and conceives a wide variety of social contexts, and 'the adult has indefinitely many uses of language' (1975: 253). Systematizing or classifying the uses of adult language would, therefore, be difficult, according to Halliday: 'the nearest we can come to that is some concept of situation type' (1978: 46).

If rhetorical situation is not material and objective, but a social construct, or semiotic structure, how are we to understand exigence, which is at the core of situation? Exigence must be located in the social world, neither in a private perception nor in material circumstance. It cannot be broken into two components without destroying it as a rhetorical and social phenomenon. Exigence is a form of social knowledge – a mutual construing of objects, events, interests and purposes that not only links them but makes them what they are: an objectified social need. This is quite different from Bitzer's characterization of exigence as a defect (1968) or a danger (1980). Conversely, although exigence provides the rhetor with a sense of rhetorical purpose, it is clearly not the same as the rhetor's intention, for that can be ill-formed, dissembling, or at odds with what the situation conventionally supports. The exigence provides the rhetor with a socially recognizable way to make his or her intentions known. It provides an occasion, and thus a form, for making public our private versions of things.

Bitzer argues that when Gerald Ford pardoned former President Nixon, Ford saw the exigence as 'protection of the national interest, which would be harmed if Watergate were not put behind us as quickly as possible', while other citizens saw the exigence as seeing justice done (1980: 30). The exigence, however, was what served as the grounds for Ford's doing anything at all – the need to establish a relationship with the previous administration, an exigence with unusual constraints in this case and one that could engage any of several particular *intentions*.

Exigence must be seen neither as a cause of rhetorical action nor as intention, but as social motive. To comprehend an exigence is to have a motive. Except in a primitive sense, our motives are not private or idiosyncratic; they are products of our socialization, as Burke makes clear: 'Motives are distinctly linguistic products. We discern situational patterns by means of the particular vocabulary of the cultural group into which we are born' ([1935] 1965: 35).[11] Schutz says much the same thing: 'Typified patterns of the Other's behavior become in turn motives of my own actions' (1971: 60). Exigence is a set of particular social patterns and expectations that provides a socially objectified motive for addressing danger, ignorance, separateness. It is an understanding of social need in which I know how to take an interest, in which one can intend to participate. By 'defining' a material circumstance as a particular situation type, I find a way to engage my intentions in it in a socially recognizable and interpretable way. As Burke put it, 'motives are shorthand terms for situations' ([1935] 1965: 29).

Blumer observed that 'the preponderant portion of social action in a human society, particularly in a settled society, exists in the form of recurrent patterns of joint action' (1979: 148). Here is a rationale for the study of rhetorical genres. To base a classification of discourse upon recurrent situation or, more specifically, upon exigence understood as social motive, is to base it upon the typical joint rhetorical actions available at a given point in history and culture. Studying the typical uses of rhetoric, and the forms that it takes in those uses, tells us less about the art of individual rhetors or the excellence of particular texts than it does about the character of a culture or an historical period. For example, Kaufer makes a telling point about classical Greek rhetoric when he observes that the 'number of definable types of rhetorical situations in Classical culture appears both curiously small and stable' (1979: 176). The three Aristotelian genres signal a particular and limited role for rhetoric, according to Kaufer, but a very important one: maintaining 'the normal functions of the state'.

By contrast, Burke observes that in an age of 'marked instablity' such as ours, typical patterns are not widely shared and hence the matter of motivation is 'liquid' ([1935] 1965: 32-33). We may not know our own motives, we cannot name them, what recurs for me does not for someone else; with a wealth of stimuli and a dearth of shared knowledge, we hardly know how to engage each other in discourse. We have many and confused intentions, but few effective orientation centres for joint action. This may be why the whole matter of genre has become problematic.

Hierarchical Theories of Meaning

If we understand genres as typified rhetorical actions based in recurrent situations, we must conclude that members of a genre are discourses that are complete, in the sense that they are circumscribed by a relatively complete shift in rhetorical situation. Thus we should recognize a lecture or a eulogy or a technical manual or a public proceeding by our determination of the typified rhetorical situation. But this does not go very far toward indicating how the genre works as rhetorical action, how we come to understand the generic meaning of 'eulogy' as fitting to the social exigence that a death produces. The 'generic fusion' that Campbell and Jamieson (1978) predicate of substantive, stylistic and situational elements is, in their view, the key to understanding the meaningfulness or 'significance' of a genre. Again using semiotic terminology, it is possible to explicate this 'fusion' and to specify how it is central to a theory of meaning.

A particular kind of fusion of substance and form is essential to symbolic meaning. Substance, considered as the semantic value of discourse, constitutes the aspects of common experience that are being symbolized. Burke maintains that substance is drawn from our 'acting-together', which gives us 'common sensations, concepts, images, ideas, attitudes' ([1950] 1969b: 21). Form is perceived as the ways in which substance is symbolized. Campbell and Jamieson adopt Burke's understanding of form as 'an arousing and fulfilment of desires. A work has form in so far as one part of it leads a reader to anticipate another part, to be gratified by the sequence' (Burke [1931] 1968: 124). Form shapes the response of the reader or listener to substance by providing instruction, so to speak, about how to perceive and interpret; this guidance disposes the audience to anticipate, to be gratified, to respond in a certain way. Seen thus, form becomes a kind of meta-information, with both semantic value (as information) and syntactic (or formal) value. Form and substance thus bear a hierarchical relationship to each other.

This hierarchical relationship is implicit in speech act theory, where meaning, according to Searle, has two elements: an utterance or proposition and the action it is used to perform, indicated as illocutionary force (1969: 16–17). But such meaning-as-action exists only within a larger interpretive context. Stephen Toulmin explains how Wittgenstein described context:

> Any expression owes its linguistic meaning (Wittgenstein taught) to having been given a standard rule-governed use or uses, in the context of such activities [language-games]. Language-games in turn, however, must be understood in their own broader contexts; and for those contexts Wittgenstein introduced the phrase 'forms of life'. (1969: 73–74)[12]

This description suggests that context is a third hierarchical level to meaning, encompassing both substance and form and enabling interpretation of the action resulting from their fusion.

But since context is itself hierarchical, as Toulmin emphasizes, we can think of form, substance and context as relative, not absolute; they occur at many levels on a hierarchy of meaning. When form and substance are fused at one level, they acquire semantic value which is then subject to formalizing at a higher level. At one level, for example, the semantic values of a string of words and their syntactic relationships in a sentence acquire meaning (pragmatic value as action) when together they serve as substance for the higher-level form of the speech act. In turn, this combination of substance and form acquires meaning when it serves as substance for the still higher-level form imposed by, say, a language-game. Thus, form at one level becomes an aspect of substance at a higher level (this is what makes form 'significant'), although it is still analysable as form at the lower level. Figure 2.1 describes this kind of progression. It is through this hierarchical combination of form and substance that symbolic structures take on pragmatic force and become interpretable actions; when

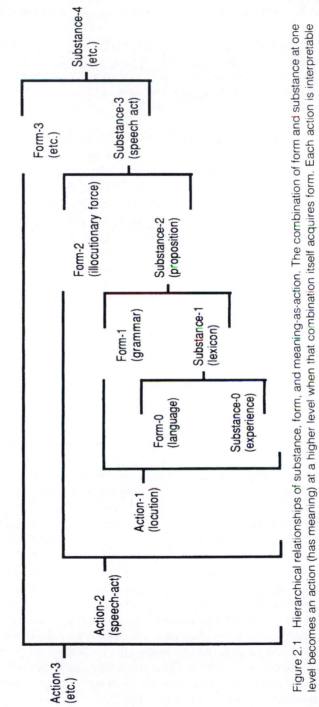

Figure 2.1 Hierarchical relationships of substance, form, and meaning-as-action. The combination of form and substance at one level becomes an action (has meaning) at a higher level when that combination itself acquires form. Each action is interpretable against the context provided by actions at higher levels.

fused, the substantive and formal components can acquire meaning in context. A complex hierarchy of such relationships is necessary for constructing meaning.

Two recent communication models instantiate this hierarchical principle in remarkably similar ways; together, they suggest a connection between rhetorical genre and the hierarchical fusion of form and substance. One model, developed by Frentz and Farrell (1976), is grounded specifically in action theory and makes explicit use of the rules approach to communication. The 'paradigm' they propose consists of three 'hierarchically structured constructs': context, episodes and symbolic acts. Context 'specifies the criteria for interpreting both the meaningfulness and propriety of any communicative event' (1976: 334). It consists of two hierarchical levels – form of life and encounters. 'Form of life', Wittgenstein's term, is used by Frentz and Farrell to refer to the cultural patterns, both linguistic and non-linguistic, that give significance to actions, both linguistic and non-linguistic. Encounters, the second level of context, 'particularize form of life through rules of propriety' (1976: 335); they are 'points of contact' in concrete locations, providing the specific situational dimension to context. The second level of the hierarchy is the episode, a 'rule-conforming sequence of symbolic acts generated by two or more actors who are collectively oriented toward emergent goals' (1976: 336). And the third and lowest level of the model is the symbolic act, the 'component' of the episode. Symbolic acts are 'verbal and/or nonverbal utterances which express intentionality' (1976: 340), characterized in much the way Searle describes speech acts.

Another hierarchical model of communication, proposed by Pearce and Conklin (1979), addresses the problem of interpreting non-literal meanings in conversation. Pearce's earlier work found that conversational coherence requires 'coordinated management of meaning' among participants and that such coordination is accomplished through rules. In the 1979 model, each level of meaning provides a context for constituents at lower levels by means of rule-governed relationships. The model consists of five levels in all: archetypes, episodes, speech acts, propositions (grammatical utterances), and the stream of behaviour that must be interpreted. Archetypes are 'those fundamental logical operations or symbolic reasoning procedures which persons use to detect or generate patterns in the sequence of events'. These are based on the common physiology that human beings share and in the common physical properties of the world they live in (1979: 78). Episodes are 'sequences of messages which have a starting and a stopping point and an internal structure'; these patterned sequences provide the context for speech acts. The hierarchical levels are connected by sets of rules that coordinate cognitive movement between them. Between the top levels are rules of symbolic identification; between the second two are rules of sociation; between the third and fourth are rules of communication; and between the last two, rules of information processing.

These two hierarchical schemes are persuasive, in part because of their comprehensiveness, in part because of their similarities, and in part because of their consistency with other social and psychological theory.[13] Although neither one has anything explicit to say about rhetorical genre, they provide a background for understanding genre as meaningful action that is rule governed (which is to say interpretable by means of conventions).[14]

A rule-based explication of genre that is consistent with these two schemes has been presented by Downey (1982); she defines genre as 'a classification of rhetorical discourses whose recurrent constitutive and regulative rules are similar in distinction and pattern'.[15] In the terms I have been using, her explanation maintains that it is constitutive rules that tell us how to fuse form and substance to make meaning and regulative rules that tell us how the fusion itself is to be interpreted within its contexts, like religion or public affairs. Seen this way, the rhetorical genre is clearly analogous to the levels of meaning of the two communication models.

Figure 2.2 proposes a hierarchy similar to these models but including genre. Genre appears at a level of complete discourse types based on recurrent situations; genres are provided interpretive context by form-of-life patterns and are constituted by intermediate forms or strategies, analogous to the dialogic episode. Because communication must rest on experience, the lowest level must be that in which symbolizing takes place. Beyond symbols, experience is idiosyncratic and incommunicable. At the other extreme, we can envision universal experience, or the biological–psychological nature of the human species, Burke's 'universal' rhetorical situation ([1950] 1969b: 146). Burke, in fact, offers a range of motives that spans both extremes of the hierarchy:

Each man's (*sic*) motivation is unique, since his situation is unique, which is particularly obvious when you recall that his situation also reflects the unique sequence of his past. However, for all this uniqueness of the individual, there are motives and relationships generic to all mankind – and these are intrinsic to human agents as a class. ([1945] 1969a: 103–4)

At the level of the locution or speech act, idiosyncratic motives (or what I earlier called intentions) predominate. At the level of human nature (or archetypes) motives of the sort that Fisher (1970) describes have their force. But at the level of the genre, motive becomes a conventionalized social purpose, or exigence, within the recurrent

Proposed Hierarchy	Frentz and Farrell's Hierarchy	Pearce and Conklin's Hierarchy
human nature		archetype
culture		
form of life	form of life	
genre	encounter	
episode or strategy	episode	episode
speech act	symbolic act	speech act
locution		proposition
language		
experience		behaviour

Figure 2.2   Proposed hierarchy of meaning, incorporating genre, compared with those of Frentz and Farrell and of Pearce and Conklin. Note the relationship of the four lowest levels in the proposed hierarchy to Figure 2.1; the higher levels would extend that figure beyond three levels of action.

situation. In constructing discourse, we deal with purposes at several levels, not just one. We learn to adopt social motives as ways of satisfying private intentions through rhetorical action. This is how recurring situations seem to 'invite' discourse of a particular type.

The exact number of hierarchical levels of meaning may not be determinable with any precision, and it may be that different kinds of communication emphasize different levels. Because monologue and dialogue pose different problems, for example, they probably operate with differing hierarchical structures. In dialogue, because the audience tends to be small and constraints managed through interactive coordination, personal intentions manifest themselves more easily. Such interaction requires elaboration of the rule structure at the lower levels of the hierarchy, to guide turn-taking, implicature and management of multiple intentions. In monologue, personal intentions must be accommodated to public exigences – because the audience is larger, the opportunity for complex statement is greater, and constraints are less easily managed; more elaborate rule structures at the upper end of the hierarchy, at the level of whole discourses, are therefore necessary for both formulation and interpretation.

As Simons observed, one of the most important problems raised by recent genre theory is that 'genres "exist" at various levels of abstraction, from the very broad to the very specific' (1978: 37). Indeed, the classifications of Fisher (1980) and of Harrell and Linkugel (1978) illustrate this problem. But if we define genre by its association with recurrent rhetorical situations, the exact hierarchical level at which the abstraction called genre occurs will be determined by our sense of recurrence of rhetorical situations; this will vary from culture to culture, according to the typifications available. Thus, the term 'genre' might under differing circumstances be applied to the class of all public addresses in a society, to the class of all inaugural speeches, or to the class of all American presidential inaugurals.

It is worth noting, in addition, that there are two kinds of hierarchies to which genre may be seen to belong, and it is helpful to keep them distinct. One kind arranges single discourses into classes and the classes into broader classes; this is the kind to which Simons refers. The other arranges constituents into units and units into larger wholes (words, sentences, speech acts, texts, etc.), in the manner of the hierarchies in Figure 2.2.[16] Genre is hierarchical in both senses, but the second has more to do with its rhetorical significance, that is, the way it works as a source of meaning.

Implications

The understanding of rhetorical genre that I am advocating is based in rhetorical practice, in the conventions of discourse that a society establishes as ways of 'acting together'. It does not lend itself to taxonomy, for genres change, evolve and decay; the number of genres current in any society is indeterminate and depends upon the complexity and diversity of the society. The particular features of this understanding of genre are these:

1 Genre refers to a conventional category of discourse based in large scale typification of rhetorical action; as action, it acquires meaning from situation and from the social context in which that situation arose.
2 As meaningful action, genre is interpretable by means of rules; genre rules occur at a relatively high level on a hierarchy of rules for symbolic interaction.
3 Genre is distinct from form: form is the more general term used at all levels of the hierarchy. Genre is a form at one particular level that is a fusion of lower level forms and characteristic substance.
4 Genre serves as the substance of forms at higher levels; as recurrent patterns of language use, genres help constitute the substance of our cultural life.
5 A genre is a rhetorical means for mediating private intentions and social exigence; it motivates by connecting the private with the public, the singular with the recurrent.

Although this perspective on genre is not precise enough to permit quantification of formal features or elucidation of a complete hierarchy of rules, it can provide guidance in the evaluation of genre claims. Specifically, it suggests that a collection of discourses (or a potential collection) may fail to constitute a genre in three major ways. First, there may fail to be significant substantive or formal similarities at the lower levels of the hierarchy. Genre claims are rarely made without this kind of first-line evidence, however. Second, there may be inadequate consideration of all the elements in recurrent rhetorical situations. A genre claim may be based on similarities only in exigence or only in audience, etc. This type of claim is sometimes made about particularly novel or subtle combinations of forms by which a rhetor addresses a situation. In such a case, however, the rhetorical situation will be differently construed by rhetor and audience. The discourse constitutes an adaption of form and substance to a private purpose, not a public exigence; the particular fusion achieved is based not on all the recurrent aspects of situation but on the unique ones. Carpenter's study of the historical jeremiad makes such a claim, based on the evidence that three works 'share salient formal characteristics' (1978: 113). But these works rather adapt the genre of historical essay to personal goals; they do not constitute another genre, because the motive that makes the discourse a social action is shared only for the historical essay, not for the jeremiad.

Another more general failure of this second sort is the attempt to use the Aristotelian types to identify contemporary genres. Although developed from recurrent situations in ancient Greece, these original genres do not describe complete situation types that recur today – they are too general. Halloran (1978) has suggested, for instance, that the public proceeding is a specialized and elaborated descendant of the epideictic genre; his analysis shows the public proceeding to be based in a recurrent situation (with several variants) and to involve elements of all three Aristotelian genres. For us, epideictic serves not as a single genre but as a form of life – a celebratory (or reaffirmative) arena of social life in which situation types develop. The original genres also persist as constituent strategies of contemporary genres. Jamieson and Campbell's (1982) discussion of the rhetorical hybrid develops this point by noting the ways critics have found the three original genres permeating each other in practice and by offering an extended critique of several hybrids in contemporary American political rhetoric. The hybrid – a transient combination of forms based in a non-recurrent (or not yet recurrent) situation – is itself not a genre but the adaption of a genre to 'the idiosyncratic needs of a particular situation, institution, and rhetor' (1982: 157). In their analysis of the deliberative eulogy, it is clear that hybridization occurs not between genres but between subforms, on the level of what I have called strategies: in their examples of the eulogies of Robert Kennedy, 'eulogistic [generic] requirements predominate and deliberative appeals [strategies] are subordinate' (1982: 150).

The third way a genre claim may fail is if there is no pragmatic component, no way to understand the genre as a social action. In a study of Environmental Impact Statements during their first five years, I concluded that this clearly defined class of documents did not constitute a rhetorical genre because it did not achieve a rational fusion of elements – in spite of obvious similarities in form and substance, and in spite of a recurring rhetorical situation that was, in fact, defined by law (Miller 1980). These documents had no coherent pragmatic force for two reasons: first, the cultural forms in which they were embedded provided conflicting interpretive contexts; and second, there was no satisfactory fusion of substance and form that could serve as substance to higher level forms and contexts. For example, the probabilistic judgments that are the substance of environmental science conflicted with the formal requirements of objectivity and quantification; further, the patterns of thinking in the context of administrative bureaucracies created a set of values at variance with the environmental values invoked by the legislation requiring impact statements. Overall, the imperfect fusion of scientific, legal and administrative elements prevented interpretation of the documents as meaningful rhetorical action. This conclusion was, of course, substantiated by the legal and administrative problems the early impact statements created and their frequent criticism in industry, government and the environmental movement.

What are the implications of the absence of a genre on the meaning hierarchy? To say that a genre does not exist is not to imply that there are no interpretive rules at that level on the hierarchy. It means that the rules do not form a normative whole that we can consider a cultural artefact, that is, a representation of reasoning and purposes characteristic of the culture. The class of discourses is just a class of discourses; the set of rules is just a set of rules. But further, the absence of a normative whole at that level poses problems of certain kinds. It means that the interpreter must have a strong understanding of forms at both higher and lower levels in order to bridge the gap at the level of genre. Similarly, in reading written discourse, we must base inferences about probable speech acts on strongly delineated propositions, at the level below, and strategies or episodes, at the level above.

The perspective on genres proposed here has implications not only for criticism and theory, but also for rhetorical education. It suggests that what we learn when we learn a genre is not just a pattern of forms or even a method of achieving our own ends. We learn, more importantly, what ends we may have: we learn that we may eulogize, apologize, recommend one person to another, instruct customers on behalf of a manufacturer, take on an official role, account for progress in achieving goals. We learn to understand better the situations in which we find ourselves and the potential for failure and success in acting together. As a recurrent, significant action, a genre embodies an aspect of cultural rationality. For the critic, genres can serve both as an index to cultural patterns and as tools for exploring the achievements of particular speakers and writers; for the student, genres serve as keys to understanding how to participate in the actions of a community.

Notes

1 See also Conley's review of Campbell and Jamieson (1978) in Conley (1978).

2 Harrell and Linkugel's essay, like this one, is motivated by the belief that rhetorical criticism suffers from the lack of a good theory of genres.

3 It should be noted that this type of induction is different from that advocated by Simons (1978). Although Simons defines a genre as a 'distinctive and recurring pattern of similarly constrained rhetorical practices' (1978: 42), a definition similar to that of Campbell and Jamieson, the method he advocates leads to quite different results. He recommends a factor-analytic examination of large numbers of texts to identify the distinctive and recurring patterns. Campbell and Jamieson, on the other hand, emphasize close examination of a single text or a small number of texts to identify the fusion of forms responsive to situation. For Simons, then, the genre just is the collection of texts; for Campbell and Jamieson, the genre is the fusion of forms exemplified by a text or texts; the genre represents 'not only...what has recurred but...what may recur' (1978: 24).

4 This system is adapted from George Campbell's classification of the ends of speaking; see Connors (1981).

5 For example, Kinneavy says, 'The language process seems to be capable of focusing attention on one of its own components as primary in a given situation' (1971: 59). The fundamental problem in Kinneavy's system is the confusion of 'aim' with 'use'. See Beale (1977) for a more complete critique of Kinneavy's work.

6 See also the exchanges among Bitzer, Patton, Tompkins, and Vatz in the 'Forum', *Quarterly Journal of Speech*, 66 (1980) pp. 85–93 and 67 (1981) pp. 93–101.

7 In an earlier statement, Bitzer seemed aware of the problem into which this example of the drinking water leads him. In the 1980 'Forum' in the *Quarterly Journal of Speech*, he wrote, 'exigences are not "objective" in the sense of being *simply factual*; nor are exigences wholly independent of human apprehension' (p. 90). Scott points out that 'Bitzer's insistence throughout on *reality* and not *sociality* is no accident in the fashion of terms' (1980: 57). He suggests a revaluation of the situational theory to recognize the intentionality of beings who act within a social reality.

8 Materialism is not an exhaustive characterization of Bitzer's discussion of situation. In Bitzer (1980), especially, there are strong elements of pragmatism, which Burke characterizes as the featuring of agency, and to the extent that Bitzer features the capacity of the rhetorical act to effect change, his work illustrates what Burke calls realism. In contrast, Vatz's (1973) emphasis on the creative power of the rhetor corresponds to the featuring of agent, which Burke characterizes as idealism.

9 See also Cox (1981).

10 As Gronbeck has observed, in a theory of communication based on social facts, 'the idea of "cause" almost disappears' (1981: 253).

11 Fisher's (1970) discussion of motives builds upon this same theme in Burke's work.

12 Recent literary theory similarly emphasizes the impossibility of interpreting a work outside of a context or framework of expectations (Culler 1975: 113–39; Fish 1978; Michaels 1979).

13 Van Dijk, for example, says that the tasks involved in language, perception, complex planning, and action 'cannot possibly be accounted for at the level of linear processing of micro-information, but . . . hierarchical rules and categories and the formation of macro-structures are necessary' (1977: 159).

14 A likely reason for this failure to connect is that the hierarchical models and the study of genres come from different research traditions. Genre has been useful in discussions of literary art, written rhetoric, and public address, all of which are forms of monologue. The hierarchical models draw from work in interpersonal communication, which relies on dialogue. It seems reasonable to suppose that monologue and dialogue do not 'mean' in different ways and that a hierarchy of rules and interpretive contexts might be as applicable to monologue as to dialogue. The constituents of each model do not preclude such an assumption, being for the most part terms common to rhetorical analysis.

15 An important difference between Downey (1982) and my discussion here is that she does not distinguish between form and action.

16 In this type of hierarchy, one can deal either with instances or with types. Searle (1975) has proposed a classification of speech act types, but these types could not be further clustered into text types – that would mix the two kinds of hierarchies.

References

BEALE, W. H. (1977) 'On the Classification of Discourse Performances', *Rhetoric Society Quarterly*, **7**, pp. 31–40.

BITZER, L. F. (1968) 'The Rhetorical Situation', *Philosophy and Rhetoric*, **1**, pp. 1–14.

BITZER, L. F. (1980) 'Functional Communication: A Situational Perspective', in WHITE, E. E. (ed.) *Rhetoric in Transition: Studies in the Nature and Uses of Rhetoric*, University Park, PA: Pennsylvania State University Press, pp. 21–38.

BLACK, E. ([1965] 1978a) *Rhetorical Criticism: A Study in Method* (reprint) Madison, WI: University of Wisconsin Press.

BLACK, E. (1978b) 'The Sentimental Style as Escapism, or the Devil with Dan'l Webster', in CAMPBELL, K. K. and JAMIESON, K. H. (eds) *Form and Genre: Shaping Rhetorical Action*, Falls Church, VA: Speech Communication Association, pp. 75–86.

BLUMER, H. (1979) 'Symbolic Interaction', in Budd, R. W. and Ruben, B. D. (eds) *Interdisciplinary Approaches to Human Communication*, Rochelle Park, NJ: Hayden, pp. 135–53.

BRINTON, A. (1981) 'Situation in the Theory of Rhetoric', *Philosophy and Rhetoric*, **14**, pp. 234–47.

BROOKS, C. and WARREN, R. P. ([1972] 1979) *Modern Rhetoric*, 4th ed, New York: Harcourt Brace Jovanovich.

BURKE, K. ([1931] 1968) *Counter-Statement*, (reprint) Berkeley, CA: University of California Press.

BURKE, K. ([1935] 1965) *Permanence and Change: An Anatomy of Purpose*, (reprint) Indianapolis, IN: Bobbs-Merrill.

BURKE, K. ([1945] 1969a) *A Grammar of Motives*, (reprint) Berkeley, CA: University of California Press.

BURKE, K. ([1950] 1969b) *A Rhetoric of Motives*, (reprint) Berkeley, CA: University of California Press.

BURKE, K. (1973) 'The Rhetorical Situation', in THAYER, L. (ed.) *Communication: Ethical and Moral Issues*, New York: Gordon and Breach, pp. 263–75.

CAMPBELL, K. K. (1973) 'The Rhetoric of Women's Liberation: An Oxymoron', *Quarterly Journal of Speech*, **59**, pp. 74–86.

CAMPBELL, K. K. and JAMIESON, K. H. (1978) 'Form and Genre in Rhetorical Criticism: An Introduction', in CAMPBELL, K. K. and JAMIESON, K. H. (eds) *Form and Genre: Shaping Rhetorical Action*, Falls Church, VA: Speech Communication Association, pp. 9–32.

CARPENTER, R. (1978) 'The Historical Jeremiad as Rhetorical Genre', in CAMPBELL, K. K. and JAMIESON, K. H. (eds) *Form and Genre: Shaping Rhetorical Action*, Falls Church, VA: Speech Communication Association, pp. 105–17.

CONLEY, T. M. (1978) 'Review of *Form and Genre* by Campbell and Jamieson', *Communication Quarterly*, **26**(4), pp. 71–75.

CONLEY, T. M. (1979) 'Ancient Rhetoric and Modern Genre Criticism', *Communication Quarterly*, **27**(4), pp. 47–53.

CONNORS, R. J. (1981) 'The Rise and Fall of the Modes of Discourse', *College Composition and Communication*, **32**, pp. 444–55.

CONSIGNY, S. (1974) 'Rhetoric and Its Situations', *Philosophy and Rhetoric*, **7**, pp. 175–86.

COX, J. R. (1981) 'Argument and the Definition of the Situation', *Central States Speech Journal*, 32, pp. 197–205.

CULLER, J. (1975) *Structuralist Poetics*, Ithaca, NY: Cornell University Press.

DOWNEY, S. D. (1982) *The Evolution of Rhetorical Genres*, Louisville, KY: Speech Communication Association.

FISH, S. (1978) 'Normal Circumstances, Literal Language, Direct Speech Acts, the Ordinary, the Everyday, the Obvious, What Goes Without Saying, and Other Special Cases', *Critical Inquiry*, **4**, pp. 625–44.

FISHER, W. R. (1970) 'A Motive View of Communication', *Quarterly Journal of Speech*, **56**, pp. 131–9.

FISHER, W. R. (1980) 'Genre: Concepts and Applications in Rhetorical Criticism', *Western Journal of Speech Communication*, **44**, pp. 288–99.

FRENTZ, T. S. and FARRELL, T. B. (1976) 'Language-Action: A Paradigm for Communication', *Quarterly Journal of Speech*, **62**, pp. 333–49.

FROW, J. (1980) 'Discourse Genres', *Journal of Literary Semantics*, **9**, pp. 73–81.

FRYE, N. ([1957] 1971) *Anatomy of Criticism: Four Essays* (reprint) Princeton, NJ: Princeton University Press.

GRONBECK, B. (1978) 'Celluloid Rhetoric: On Genres of Documentary', in CAMPBELL, K. K. and JAMIESON, K. H. (eds) *Form and Genre: Shaping Rhetorical Action*, Falls Church, VA: Speech Communication Association, pp. 139–61.

GRONBECK, B. (1981) 'Qualitative Communication Theory and Rhetorical Studies in the 1980s', *Central States Speech Journal*, **32**, pp. 243–53.

HALLIDAY, M. A. K. (1975) 'Learning to Mean', in ROGERS, S. (ed.) *Children and Language*, New York: Oxford University Press.

HALLIDAY, M. A. K. (1978) *Language as Social Semiotic: The Social Interpretation of Language and Meaning*, Baltimore, MD: University Park Press.

HALLORAN, M. (1978) 'Doing Public Business in Public', in CAMPBELL, K. K. and JAMIESON, K. H. (eds) *Form and Genre: Shaping Rhetorical Action*, Falls Church, VA: Speech Communication Association, pp. 118–38.

HARRELL, J. and LINKUGEL, W. A. (1978) 'On Rhetorical Genre: An Organizing Perspective, *Philosophy and Rhetoric*, **11**, pp. 262–81.

HART, R. P. (1971) 'The Rhetoric of the True Believer', *Speech Monographs*, **38**, pp. 249–61.

JAMIESON, K. H. and CAMPBELL, K. K. (1982) 'Rhetorical Hybrids: Fusions of Generic Elements', *Quarterly Journal of Speech*, **69**, pp. 146–57.

KAUFER, D. (1979) 'Point of View in Rhetorical Situations: Classical and Romantic Contrasts and Contemporary Implications', *Quarterly Journal of Speech*, **65**, pp. 171–86.

KINNEAVY, J. L. (1971) *A Theory of Discourse: The Aims of Discourse*, Englewood Cliffs, NJ: Prentice-Hall.

MICHAELS, W. B. (1979) 'Against Formalism: The Autonomous Text in Legal and Literary Interpretation', *Poetics Today*, **1**, pp. 23–34.

MILLER, C. R. (1980) 'Environmental Impact Statements and Rhetorical Genres: An Application of Rhetorical Theory to Technical Communication', doctoral dissertation, Rensselaer Polytechnic Institute, Troy, New York.

MOHRMANN, G. P. and LEFF, M. C. (1974) 'Lincoln at Cooper Union: A Rationale for Neo-Classical Criticism', *Quarterly Journal of Speech*, **60**, pp. 459–67.

PATTON, J. H. (1976) 'Generic Criticism: Typology at an Inflated Price', *Rhetoric Society Quarterly*, **6**(1), pp. 4–8.

PATTON, J. H. (1979) 'Causation and Creativity in Rhetorical Situations: Distinctions and Implications', *Quarterly Journal of Speech*, **65**, pp. 36–55.

PEARCE, W. B. and CONKLIN, F. (1979) 'A Model of Hierarchical Meanings in Coherent Conversation and a Study of Indirect Responses', *Communication Monographs*, **46**, pp. 76–87.

RAUM, R. D. and MEASELL, J. S. (1974) 'Wallace and His Ways: A Study of the Rhetorical Genre of Polarization', *Central States Speech Journal*, **25**, pp. 28–35.

RODGERS, R. S. (1982) 'Generic Tendencies in Majority and Non-Majority Supreme Court Opinions: The Case of Justice Douglas, *Communication Quarterly*, **30**, pp. 232–6.

SCHUTZ, A. (1971) *Collected Papers I: The Problem of Social Reality* (ed. M. Natanson) The Hague: Martinus Nijhoff.

SCHUTZ, A. and LUCKMANN, T. (1973) *The Structures of the Life-World* (trans. R. M. Zaner and H. T. Engelhardt, Jr) Evanston, IL: Northwestern University Press.

SCOTT, R. L. (1980) 'Intentionality in the Rhetorical Process', in WHITE, E. E. (ed.) *Rhetoric in Transition: Studies in the Nature and Uses of Rhetoric*, University Park, PA: Pennsylvania State University Press, pp. 39–60.

SEARLE, J. (1969) *Speech Acts: An Essay on the Philosophy of Language*, London: Cambridge University Press.

SEARLE, J. (1975) 'A Taxonomy of Illocutionary Acts', in GUNDERSON, K. (ed.) *Language, Mind and Knowledge*, Minneapolis, MN: University of Minnesota Press, pp. 344–69.

SIMONS, H. W. (1978) ' "Genre-alizing" About Rhetoric: A Scientific Approach', in CAMPBELL, K. K. and JAMIESON, K. H. (eds) *Form and Genre: Shaping Rhetorical Action*, Falls Church, VA: Speech Communication Association, pp. 33–50.

STEBBINS, R. A. (1967) 'A Theory of the Definition of the Situation', *Canadian Review of Sociology and Anthropology*, **4**, pp. 148–64.

TOULMIN, S. (1969) 'Concepts and the Explanation of Human Behavior', in MISCHEL, T. (ed.) *Human Action: Conceptual and Empirical Issues*, New York: Academic Press, pp. 71–104.

VAN DIJK, T. (1977) *Text and Context: Explorations in the Semantics and Pragmatics of Discourse*, New York: Longman.

VAN DIJK, T. (1980) *Macrostructures*, Hillsdale, NJ: Lawrence Erlbaum.

VATZ, R. (1973) 'The Myth of the Rhetorical Situation', *Philosophy and Rhetoric*, **6**, pp. 154–61.

WARE, B. L. and LINKUGEL, W. A. (1973) 'They Spoke in Defense of Themselves: On the Generic Criticism of Apologia', *Quarterly Journal of Speech*, **59**, pp. 273–83.

WELLECK, R. and WARREN, A. (1977) *Theory of Literature*, 3rd edn, New York: Harcourt Brace Jovanovich.

WINDT, T. O., JR. (1972) 'The Diatribe: Last Resort for Protest', *Quarterly Journal of Speech*, **58**, pp. 1–14.

Chapter 3

Anyone For Tennis?*

Anne Freadman

[. . .]

Part 1

My father put a hex on me, one day, when he was trying for the nth time to teach me to hit tennis balls against the back lav. He told me I had no ball sense. What he meant, of course, was what we nowadays call hand-eye coordination, and I've since learnt to separate the issues. But it's had untold consequences. One is that tennis can never be more, or less, for me than a metaphor. Or maybe I mean a simile. Or an allegory.

Imagine a game of tennis, preferably, of course (if you have any ball sense), singles. The players are not exchanging balls, they're exchanging shots. The ball, like the rackets, the players themselves, the court with its markings, and the rules of the game, is one of the things that make the shots possible. Without the ball, and with everything else, the shots are possible but not realized. Even this problem has been solved for board games, such as chess, but only by means of the ingenious invention of material substitutes for the board and the men (men, in chess, includes the queen). As Saussure said, any substitute for the piece will work exactly like the piece, if the rules governing its piece-hood (its manhood?) are spelled out. The material determinants of tennis balls are more intractable: you need another tennis ball, though children make do with almost anything.

Let us take the distinction between exchanging balls, and exchanging shots, as something like the distinction between 'exchanging meanings' and 'exchanging signs', respectively. I expect you thought I should have made an equivalence between 'ball' and 'sign', and 'shot' and 'meaning'. This shot is about why I didn't. Imagine hard little pellets of meaning travelling towards you like a Mandlikovan serve. Then duck. Michael Reddy (1970) calls this 'the Conduit Metaphor'.

If we said, about tennis or any ball game, that what we were exchanging was the ball, scoring would not be possible. The game would be posited on the absolute

*This chapter is a condensed version of the essay which appeared in *The Place of Genre in Learning: Current Debates*, Ian Reid, ed. (Geelong, Australia: Deakin University, Centre for Studies in Literary Education, 1987), 91–124. [1994 Update: additional notes have been added to this version, clearly identified with square brackets and the date.]

symmetry of the players, and its objective, if objective there were in such circumstances, would be its maintenance. There are games in which the confirmation of balance is the only stake, and the loss of balance a sign that the match should not have taken place. I heard, for instance, of a betrothal ritual from the Cameroons. In it, the fathers of the prospective couple enter into an intellectual joust, where they match their respective funds of cultural knowledge and skill. They argue for as long as they are well-matched, and a ritual ending marking neither victory nor defeat proclaims that the match is a good one. Winning becomes important in a situation such as this only if one of the protagonists, with his seconds, begins to lose respect in a systematic or protracted way, for his opposite number; then he must win, to demonstrate publicly that inequality was the proven outcome; the marriage, then, will not take place. This is not unlike the system of 'seeding' in championship tennis: any one match between top seeds may be won or lost, where the understanding is that the result could reverse at the next round. The contrast with the single singles match is not, after all, so great: in any given match, winning is what the players are trying to do, though they must be well-matched for the game to be worth playing. While in the most ritual of jousts and the most equal of display games, equality, no less than winning and losing, depends on scoring. Scoring depends on shots, not on balls.

Player A plays a shot; player B plays it back. What is this 'it'? It is not useful to say ' "it" is the ball'; and it is manifestly inaccurate to call it the same shot. Player B is, let's say, the 'receiver', but to *receive* a shot s/he must return it, play, that is to say, another. The same shot, then – Player A's serve – has a *different value* for each of the two players: a 'good shot' may win a point for its player, but, well-received, it may turn against her/him, its speed, its turn, or its angle enabling an unexpected return.

If I return, now, to the silent comparand, you may well wish to object that we have always known this, that words or texts have differrent meanings for any two interlocutors, that it's what we do with them that counts. So I'd best not return, just yet. If tennis is to be a simile, it had better pay off better than that.

[...]

To suppose that discursive interaction is the giving and receiving of *meanings* is like describing a game of tennis as the giving and receiving of balls. To suppose, on the contrary, that it is the playing of shots is to allow the value of those shots to be subject to play, and the meaning of the interaction to be the upshot of the perpetual modification of each shot by its return.

Each shot, in this analogy, produces value in two ways: in what it enables, or prevents; and to either player. Each shot is formally determined by the rules of the game, and materially determined by the skill of the players, and each return shot is determined by the shot to which it is a response. Responses, then, are not 'freed', or bound even by what is loosely known as pragmatic circumstance as if this latter were 'outside' the text. Returns, and readings, work within certain clearly marked conventions, and *with the material at hand*. They are both enabled, and constrained, by the formal-material determinants of the signs they read and the signs they will write.

Our signs, then, our semiotic artefacts, bid for value in a field of like and unlike; and their value as objects resides neither 'in' them nor in their owners. Rather, using the analogy of the marketplace, the extent to which they are kept in play – the number of times they are bid for, the changes they effect around them, the bids they make of place and function within this field – they have no value if they are not constantly renegotiated. Priceless, they say, of paintings, and of conversation-stopping jokes.

So...maybe...then...too...(if I go on)...(allons, Gogo, il faut me renvoyer la balle de temps en temps)...a metaphor, a simile, or an allegory, is just this: the play of a sign between two systems of values, itself an allegory, of what it is to play ball, or to make sense.

Part 2

What is the value of this very elaborate metaphor? – you may well ask. It seems to have worked well enough as a way of writing about Communication, or Discourse, and it is tempting to take the metaphor of a *game* to correspond with the notion of 'genre'. The authority for this usage is Wittgenstein (1953: sec. 23).[1] Yet there is little evidence in his use of the metaphor of the 'language game' that it designates in his writings a concept commensurate with that conventionally associated with 'genre'. The kind of thing meant by 'language game' might be, for example, 'referring', or 'asking questions', and could be said to *overlap* with that of 'genre' to the extent that 'genre' is either modelled on, or thought through, the concept of the *speech act*. Literary theorists, and linguists concerned with discourse, have been led, quite fruitfully, to consider genre as an extension of speech acts, and have, accordingly, attempted to construct *theories of genre* that extend the *theory of speech acts*.[2] Historians of what we are wont to call ideas argue that there is a great deal in common between the Wittgensteinian notion of the 'language game' and the theory of speech acts deriving from Austin (1967). Both, they would say, are strategies to contest the dominance of the formal models used by logic to describe meaning. They would also say that this move in philosophy is paralleled by the move in literary theory, which has adopted pragmatic notions of *discourse as social action* to contest formal models of textuality (cf. Pratt 1977), or the more traditional notion that the meaning of a text resides solely in its 'referential function', i.e., what it can be said to represent. In all these places, discourse is thought in terms of 'doing things with words' and terms like 'perform', 'function', 'act', 'action', 'moves', 'strategies', 'tactics'...figure large in such theories. Since a lot of this vocabulary is common to the ways in which we talk about playing games and those in which we talk about our engagement in social forms and forces, it is tempting to talk about a *genre* as if it were a *game*. It seems to suggest a combination of the serious and the playful, and to authorize the use of the model of constitutive rules (as in the description of games) with the need to talk about individual action in relation with regulative rules (as in the description of social facts). The authority for this combination is Searle (1978), who in many ways combines Wittgensteinian notions (e.g., taking 'referring' as an act) with the impetus given to speech act theory by Austin.

However, 'the game' – or rather *a* game – may be a misleading metaphor for genre. It may require some adjustment. It suggests that once you have learnt the rules – implicit and explicit, and including rules such as those that constitute the basis of skill (e.g., one's grip in golf or tennis) – the playing of a correct game follows automatically, like the output from a simple algorithmic programme in a computer. Obviously individual variables such as actual skill, mental and physical agility, and so on, play a part, but they are not an issue if what is at stake is whether what you are doing *counts* as the playing of that game. To use this metaphor for genre suggests that a text is the output of a set of rules. This is what I call the 'recipe theory' of genre. We have known for many years that a very wide range of 'texts' – far beyond what usually pass for 'literary', 'artistic' or 'creative' texts – fail to be usefully described as conforming with a generic recipe; we have also known for many years that it is this kind of genre theory with its failures that has caused the discrediting of the very notion of genre, bringing about in turn its disuse and the disrepair many of us found it in, within the last, say five to ten years, when we attempted to apply it in the emerging set of problems in literary and semiotic theory. What constitutes a game as distinct from other games is its rules, their rules, and the difference between them. This is important. But we need to adjust our metaphor to accommodate the idea that these rules are *rules for play.*

In the description of the game I have given in Part 1, I have described the playing of a shot in terms that converge in the notion of 'uptake'. This may be said to correspond to the 'tactical' level of game playing; on this analogy, the 'strategic' level corresponds to the attempt to determine the terms in which the interaction – the game – is set up. 'Update' is a term from speech act theory, and it is said that kinds of speech acts (requests, commands, invitations . . .) determine a, or a set of, appropriate uptake(s). The strategic level of game-playing is that level where a (set of) medium-term goal(s) is established, and the tactics planned in accordance with this. It is the relation between strategy and tactics that suggests that genre might be a generalization over speech-acts, or an extension of the notion. But it is also this relation that shows us that we are no longer talking about a game and its rules; we are talking about the playing of a game. In the very elaborate discussion of chess strategies, so formalized that they take on the status of *kinds of games*, there is no discussion of the relating of these strategies with the tactics of the play at any given point, except in the detailed descriptions of particular matches. You might just as well substitute 'particular texts', in the previous sentence. Now the playing of a game is a *ceremony* which involves a great deal more than the game itself. There are the preparations, the choice of partners, occasion and venue. There is the warm-up, the toss, and, at the end, the declaration of the winner and closing down rituals – showers, presentations, or the drink at the bar.

There may be no important ethnographic or sociological difference between the notion of a ceremonial and that of a game, but I need to retain the two terms for tactical purposes. Ceremonies are games that situate other games: they are the rules for the setting of a game, for constituting participants as players in that game, for constituting participants as players in that game, for placing and timing it in relation with other places and times. They are the rules for playing of a game, but they are not the rules of the game. Games, then, are rules for the production of certain acts in those 'places'. To the extent that the grammatical rules of my language permit me to make this distinction, I could say that where ceremonies are rules for playing, games are rules for play. That there be 'play' at both these levels is important: knowing the rules is knowing how much play the rules allow and how to play with them. I want to suggest, then, that each of the moments, phases, stages or 'places' in a ceremonial is a genre, and that speech-acts might have the function of the opening or closing of the ceremony, the marking of the passage from one phase to another, as well as of tactics 'within' any genre. If this is the case, the notion of genre and the notion of speech-act are not coextensive, and are not usefully thought of as deriving one from the other.[3] I also want to suggest that it will be useful to think of most of our talking and writing as ceremonial, and that what we can mean, in the semiotics of discourse, by 'social setting' can be usefully explored by means of this series of analogies.

There are points of similarity between the framework I am setting up and the Hallidayan model of register.[4] Schematically, on the assumption that games are formalized symbolic structurings of interlocutory relations, then field:tenor::ceremonial:game. My terminology has the advantage of declaring the kind of relation that might hold between the two 'levels' but this may not be a difference worth fighting over. On the other hand, there are significant differences between the two models. Mine is a model in general semiotics, which starts from the postulate that 'texts' are the product of the interaction of a variety of 'languages', or semiotic systems, none necessarily homologous with any other. The Hallidayan model and its derivates arise from the postulate of a functionalist linguistics, which maps social structures onto the single semiotic system we call 'natural language' or 'human discourse'. The argument for the general semiotics position is that it is practically impossible to find a text that mobilizes only one language: the relation of speech and gestures is the most immediately available example of this claim; the relation of typesetting and other publishing conventions with the 'written' forms of language is another. In this perspective, film is not an exception to this semiotic rule, but a particularly rich exploitation of it. The limitations of linguistic models of, or premises for, a theory of discourse arise quite naturally from the theoretical and methodological enterprise of linguistics itself. The argument against the linguistic model is, then, that if we are to account for what it is to make a text, we are unlikely to find out a great deal from studying the properties of only one of its languages.

There is another difference between me and the linguists with respect to the more precise question of genre; but the problem I wish to raise is not in this case a direct product of the premises of linguistics. Rather, I am taking issue with the whole tradition of genre theory as it derives from literary studies. Most unfortunately, it seems that the linguists have taken over some tacit assumptions from this tradition and have fallen into the 'traps for young players' that recent literary theory has attempted to undo. Briefly, these assumptions are:

1 that a text is 'in' a genre, i.e., that it is primarily, or solely, describable in terms of the rules of one genre;
2 that genre is 'in' a text, i.e., that the features of a text will correspond to the rules of the genre.[5]

If, as I am suggesting, a genre is a game, then it will be more useful to think of it as consisting, minimally, of two texts, in some sort of dialogical relation. For example,

- theoretical debate;
- brief and report;
- play and audience response;
- essay question, essay, feedback.

Some of these will be in the same ceremonial, and others will be in distinct ones, for example,

- a recipe and its making, and the meal.

Sometimes the insertion of a text into an inappropriate ceremonial will make a parody (as Malcolm Muggeridge is said to have said, 'how better could you parody this letter [which appeared in *The Times*] than by reprinting it verbatim in *Punch?*'), but at other times, such as misappropriation just makes nonsense, or at best restates, or recuperates the borrowed text in the terms of the borrowing ceremonial. For example, the use of simulation techniques in the ceremonial frame of 'straight' classroom practice subverts the simulated game: its stakes are no longer at stake; the stakes of playing are those of playing the usual work for marks and teacher's feedback game. What has gone wrong is that the pairing of the text produced by the simulation with its appropriate uptake has been broken. It has simply become another assignment.

If genres are usually described as pairs or groups of texts, certain implications follow:

1 texts, like speech acts, are tactical;
2 the rules of a genre, and the formal properties of a single text, will not correlate; but rather
3 the two texts of a generic pair will have different properties, like question and answer, theory and refutation;
4 one of the things a text will do is to play its partner, whether or not that partner is 'present'. In order to do so, it must *represent* its partner – previous, current, future, fictional or ideal. The rules for such representations are an integral part of any genre in precisely the same way as the rules of a game include the rules of the interaction of the partners.[6] But texts may, and frequently do, play several games – and thus, several partners – at once.

The rest of my discussion will dwell on the level of genre, not of text. This is because I think there's a need for working over what we mean by this term. Discussions of genre usually take the form of discussions of 'classes of text', or 'text types', and proceed on the basis of the assumption that a classification is constructed by a series of descriptions of similarity and difference. I shall start by doing just that, and go on to show how statements of similarity and difference require to be construed through the notion of ceremonial place. Tennis will recur, but only fleetingly. To discuss how a text plays its game(s) requires close readings – another genre.

'Like-statements'

'Like-statements' are statements which we use to classify things, either to establish the class, or to include something apparently different within it. Frequently they are strategies for sorting out what might count as salient properties, understanding something unfamiliar by asking whether it shares this or that feature with something familiar. To claim that items x, y and z form a class is to make certain features salient above others, and to claim that these features go someway towards describing how each member functions, or is placed, in relation to others not sharing these features. In the description of genres, or of texts in terms of generic classifications, 'like-statements' look like this:

You could say that
- an architect's plan is like a recipe,
- and that a doctor's prescription is a recipe that can only be made by a qualified pharmacist,
- preparing an article for publication in such-and-such a journal,
- writing sonnets

are also like recipes; but do we get good sonnets and good science reports from instructions in this form? Recipes are a genre; but genres are not recipes.

'Not-statements'

Most theories of genre concentrate on 'like-statements'; most descriptions of individual texts in terms of generic generalizations concentrate on 'not-statements'. I want to propose a way of thinking about genre theory that takes 'not-statements' as its starting point.

Doors are like windows, but they are not windows.

It is important for us to know the difference between an architect's plan and a recipe, and it may be that this is best described in terms of social setting. Saying that we have something like the *same genre* turning up in different settings may be important for genre theory, in order to avoid the social determinist position, which might claim:

1 that genres are specific to social (e.g., disciplinary or institutional) setting and
2 that social relations such as class and institutional hierarchies determine genre.

Such claims can be refuted by linguistic and discursive analysis of textual features.[7]

It is also important for us to know, and to be able to describe, the differences between a doctor's prescription and a doctor's referral letter to another doctor. Being able to describe this difference is the business of genre theory, and knowing it in practice matters for getting on with the business of getting the right professional advice from the right 'person'. These two kinds of text are strategies for doing two things:

1 dealing with a diseased and suffering body;
2 asserting the structural and functional relations that make a profession more than a collection of trained workers. This assertion needs to be made in order to make the profession work as such, and it also needs to be addressed to the patient, in order that s/he use it as a profession. Not to do so is equivalent to misusing it, or using it incorrectly; it makes the system dysfunctional in respect of that case.

Let us suppose, then, that a 'medical consultation' is a ceremony, consisting of several genres: greeting, the eliciting of presenting symptoms, examination, decisions for treatment. Within each of these genres, different tactical moves are made by both players, and these moves can be described as speech acts: commands, requests, complaints, advice, reassurance...as well as the less formal acts that structure the relationship of doctor and patient. The question then arises whether there is any tactical leeway in the writing of prescriptions or referral letters. In the former case it is minimized and regulated as much as possible, to guard against possible mistakes, but I am certain that if the doctors would allow us to collect a corpus of their referral letters, a considerable range of variation would be discernible. In particular, I would wager my professional integrity on the following hypothesis: that they have all sorts of ways of indicating to one another not only their medical judgments, but their assessments as to the patient's supposed character, his/her way of handling suffering, and specifically, his/her tactical manoeuvres in medical consultations. This latter, of course, neither in detail nor as such: I suspect the patient's game-playing abilities are what provide the 'evidence' for assessments as to character and personality.

We should also note that the fact that prescriptions are not typewritten, and that doctors by and large give bad handwriting the status of a characteristic of their profession, are both able to be described as tactics designed to preclude the patient from the position of addressee of this kind of text. However, the exclusiveness of the language used in prescriptions, though it may have this effect in a secondary way, is generic, rather than tactical, since this language defines the professional relationship of doctor and pharmacist, and mediates their professional difference.

A medical consultation is not the same as a consultation with a lawyer: this is a difference of institution, but the ceremonial may be usefully described as similar. The consultation (patient to doctor, client to lawyer) is the ceremonial that situates the genre we call 'referral' in the one case and 'brief' in the other, but 'referral' and 'brief' may be similar, and when we say so, we can make some sense of the variety of situations in which we find 'briefs'. A brief fulfils a certain function within a profession, mediating two functionally and hierarchically different places, such that one can request work from the other. It is frequently the case that the person to whom the brief is addressed is placed *by the brief* in the position of specialist, but this does not necessarily correspond with hierarchical superiority. A government, for example, briefs an expert, or a committee, from a position of uncontested authority, by contrast with the professional hierarchiziation which places an instructing solicitor 'below' the barrister s/he briefs. Briefs may also be addressed to and by colleagues who are formally or informally equal, as requests to intervene in a debate or meeting 'from a different point of view'. A brief, in effect, mediates a highly complex network of different social placings, addressing a request where a simple hierarchy would address a command. Nevertheless, it does seem to be a rule that briefs cannot go from below to above; nor can they be addressed from a specialist to a place of authority. Like a command, a brief places boundaries, or states parameters, defining the substantive form of the text that will be its uptake, and that text will respond by restating these, giving the brief as the site and source of its informing intentions. Tactics within the brief include requests for advice, the provision of information describing the case in such a way as not to pre-empt specialist opinion, but so as to justify the choice of this, rather than another, specialist. In a medical system such as that which obtains in Australia, where all consultations of a specialist are mediated by a generalist, the manners of a referral letter include the request for advice and impose the obligation on the specialist to respond accordingly. That is, though the specialist may take over the effective treatment of the patient, s/he will inform the generalist of the diagnosis and decisions for treatment, thereby maintaining the fiction that s/he is acting on behalf of the generalist, and that the patient is the generalist's patient.

The manners of a referral letter and the response that it elicits are not those of a formal or informal discussion between the same two doctors about the same case. Such a discussion may occur before the writing of a referral letter, after that but before the patient's visit to the specialist, or at any time after this, during – or indeed following – treatment. What is different is certainly not the concepts deployed, but the uptake expected in that place. Sometimes, indeed, the same information must be reproduced in a different place in order to take on a different function.

'Not-statements' are useful in precisely this sort of situation. The point of a not-statement is to make a distinction between two terms – kinds of texts – which in other respects are described by a like-statement. Starting from the class of all texts, or discourse, the not-statement is the first move establishing a generic classification. Indeed, it is the first move establishing the very postulate of genre. Nevertheless, typical genre descriptions take the form: 'like...but not...' The 'like' part of the generic description establishes the domain of pertinent comparisons; the 'not' part establishes a boundary, not in the sense of a limitation, or a limit on possibilities, but in the sense of locating 'this kind' of text in a space, and *vis-à-vis* other kinds. The not-statement gives this kind of place among other places.

The strategy I use to describe the genre of a text is contrastive: it starts from a not-statement. This is by contrast with the recipe, which starts from the ingredients. To be effective, such negative descriptions rely on strategically chosen contrasting genres. For example, a recipe book is like:

1 manuals, and other how-to books;
2 menus.

It is also unlike both in crucial respects, particularly because menus are not like manuals.[8] The characteristic inclusion of handy hints, household advice, and personal anecdotes, marks it off and allies it with still other genres.

'Not-statements' are not just made by genre-theorists about texts: they are frequently made by texts themselves as a self-situating strategy. But they need not be in the explicit propositional form of a negative description. It is useful to note some examples of this explicit form before finding what might count as equivalents:

> This work is an essay in Peirce's epistemology, with about an equal emphasis on the 'epistemology' as on the 'Peirce's'. In other words our intention *has not been to write exclusively a piece of Peirce scholarship* – hence the reader will find no elaborate tying in of Peirce's epistemology to other portions of his thought, no great emphasis on the chronology of his thought, etc. Peirce scholarship is a painstaking business. His mind was labyrinthine, his terminology intricate, and his writings are, as he himself confessed, 'a snarl of twine'. This book *rather* is intended perhaps even primarily as an essay in epistemology, taking Peirce's as the focal point. The book *thus addresses a general philosophical audience and bears as much on the wider issue as on the man.* (Davis 1972: vii; my emphasis)

Notice that the not-statement precedes the positive description, but that even were they are in the reverse sequence, the positive description would not be specified without the negative. Without the not-statement, the sentence 'The book is intended primarily as an essay in epistemology, taking Peirce's as the focal point' would tell us no more than the title: alone, the title sets up two possibilities – that this is an author study ('Peirce scholarship') – and that this is a topic study ('epistemology'). When the not-statement is made, it distinguishes these as two genres of philosophic writing. The question of genre is tied to the question of audience, and thus to the question of expectations and predictions: a topic study is addressed to philosophers, whereas a book 'on Peirce' might well find that it had relatively few readers who defined themselves as philosophers, and relatively many from such fields as semiotics and literary theory. Peirce is in this respect something of a special case; yet were we to put, say, Kant in the place of the proper name of this title, the specification would still hold, distinguishing for instance historians of ideas from philosophers in the technical sense.

This book is nominally an abridgement of the *Concise Oxford Dictionary, but has in fact* cost its compilers more labour, partly because the larger book was found *not to be easily squeezable*, and partly owing to changes in method *un*connected with *mere* reduction in quantity. The one merit, however, that they feel entitled to claim for the C.O.D. has been preserved to the best of their power in the abridgement – that is, they have kept to the principle that *a dictionary is a book of diction, concerned primarily with words or phrases as such, and not*, except so far as is needed to ensure their right treatment in speech, *with the things those words and phrases stand for*. This principle, while it *absolves* the dictionary-maker *from encumbering his pages with encyclopaedic information, demands on the other hand that he should devote much more space than that so saved to the task of making clear the idiomatic usage of words*. (Preface, *Pocket Oxford Dictionary*, 1955; my emphasis)

It appears that the important not-statement is the one that contrasts the *Concise* with the *Pocket Oxford*, but they are more 'like' than 'unlike' in that they share a not-statement that sets all dictionaries in contrast with another genre. The crucial contrast that constitutes the definition of a dictionary is that a dictionary is 'not an encyclopedia'. This opposition, which plays out in a special way the 'words vs. world' dichotomy, has needed to be made since the first encyclopedias, dating from the eighteenth century, jostled for position in the space occupied by the much older, traditional genre which took on its conventional features in the age of Humanism. The history of the Encyclopedia as genre is a most interesting question, which goes, I'm afraid, beyond my present brief. What I do wish to dwell on for a moment is the fact that 'a dictionary is not an encyclopedia' seems to be a more important or urgent statement to make than, for example, 'a dictionary is not a grammar'. We might find this latter statement in treatises of linguistics. The former statement is found in those places where there is possible confusion that arises as a result of a like-statement: the layouts of dictionaries and encyclopedias are very similar. They both have columns dividing their pages, and each column consists of an entry, having the *form of a word*, followed by explanatory information about the 'word'. Dictionaries, however, define them as the names of things. The convention whereby encyclopedias illustrate their information with images – diagrams, photographs, maps, portraits and the like, has as its function to demonstrate the distinction between the 'word' and what it names by showing the thing named in a form other than verbal. The convention whereby dictionaries illustrate their explanations as to usage by *uses* (quotations) demonstrates their fundamental claim, that the conventions of a language explain that language, that the rules of usage do not lie outside the language, but within it. When Ferdinand de Saussure (1986) defined a language as 'something like a dictionary', he was relying on the generic conventions of dictionaries to make this analogy. When, furthermore, he defined a sign by its place within the rules of usage, *rather than* as the name of a thing, he was relying on the not-statement whereby dictionaries and encyclopedias are contrasted, and he was saying that the generic conventions of dictionaries provide a better analogy than those of encyclopedias for a linguist concerned with the problem of how a language determines meaning. (Since then, semioticians have done loads of interesting things with the [generalized] notion of the encyclopedia. But all this, too, lies beyond my brief.)

Let me return briefly to my earlier statement, that there is a difference between saying 'a dictionary is not an encyclopedia' and 'a dictionary is not a grammar'. Each of these not-statements serves as a particular purpose. The former, as I have said, plays out the words vs. world dichotomy; the latter serves to distinguish two kinds of information that linguists provide in the descriptions of languages. Both, however, are statements as to genre. This seems to suggest that a genre cannot be defined by a single not-statement, but rather, that a generic definition ('definition' is, literally, 'the tracing of boundaries' rather than the discovery of an essence) arises as (or 'from') a series of contrasts which position 'this' kind in amongst other adjacent kinds of texts. Think, for instance, of the public transport tickets available in your town or city: there may be:

- single passes (for a one-way trip);
- day passes (for travel between given hours on one day, using any number of vehicles and kinds of vehicles, in any direction);
- weekly passes (similar to the above, but valid over a longer period);
- monthly passes (ditto).

The difference between the tickets giving you these rights will be marked in a variety of ways: they may be colour coded, and a difference made between those that must last (printed on card), and those that *must not* last (printed on flimsy paper). Single fares will be identified by the amount paid, but passes for longer periods will be identified with dates and times. They may also be personalized. It is useful to recall from this example that although we may be inclined to believe that the genre is marked inherently on each kind of ticket, those markings only work because they are correlated with *places in a system of contrasts*. To rely on the inherent features of each is the 'recipe theory of genre'; to take into consideration the system of contrasts is the alternative that I am proposing.

> What you will be reading here are the results of my research. *They are not intended as a biography* in the usual sense, *but as a kind of casebook*, told in the words of those who were closest to the individual at the time. (Buzacott 1987: 8)

Think about who writes casebooks, and for what purposes. Buzacott's claims (for his fiction, NB!) is not only that it is 'true'; it uses the documentary mode to contest the coherent narrative form that makes the subject of a biography a hero. The subject of this study is a 'case', appearing on 'documents' independent of the story-telling proclivities of a narrator.

> This form is *not* to be completed by people who propose only a visit to Australia for a period of temporary *rather than* permanent settlement. *Separate forms* are available for these purposes.[9]

The not-statements in this text distinguish forms for prospective immigrants from forms for tourist visas and temporary settlement visas. This distinction is crucial for the work of the Immigration Department, but it may be far less crucial for a theorist of discourse whose brief, is, for instance, to describe the genres in use in Australian Government offices. S/he might be tempted to group all 'forms' together; questions of layout, printing, kinds of purpose, and the function of spaces on the form, are common to all forms. We 'know' a form when we see one,[10] and although an immigration form might ask for a certain amount of information that you would also find, for instance, in a curriculum vitae, nevertheless we know the difference between these two genres. On the other hand, having made the statement I have just made, it occurs to me that it may be useful to group together c.v.s and forms, and to say that the crucial difference between them is in the social settings in which they function. Both work to identify a person in a 'liminal' situation, attempting to pass from one space into another, and both present the information that might be necessary for that passage to be authorized. However, here I am discussing the curriculum vitae as if it were coextensive with a job application, whereas in fact it is only a part of it; in isolation, a curriculum vitae is more like a biography whose events are listed rather than narrated. Job applications and visa applications are by and large the same ceremonial, used in different institutions.

This discussion illustrates a statement I made earlier, about different classificatory statements making different features salient. It also demonstrates that different like-statements and different not-statements are used for different purposes. This suggests that 'genre' is not absolute (let alone 'primitive', as some linguistic uses of the term need it to be): it is pragmatic. This does not mean, however, that it is merely whimsical, or subjective. It means that:

1 generic descriptions are a genre; and
2 this genre turns up as a game in a variety of social settings:
  – filing systems,
  – library classification systems,
  – publishing and bookselling,
  – institutional administration,
  – the construction of school syllabuses,
  – any theoretical activity designed to describe the pragmatics of discourse,
  – etc.

It also has a great deal to do with how we separate the learned disciplines from one another.

I have suggested above that not-statements can be made in a variety of ways, and are not restricted to explicit negative descriptions. Two of my examples illustrate this point: the transport tickets make their not-statements by means of the variety of contrastive codings that I have sketched out. Forms make not-statements with black lines, and code these lines as 'heavy' or 'light' in order to group bits of information and separate them off from other groups. Just as two kinds of typeface are used in dictionaries and encyclopedias, to distinguish 'word' and 'explanation' within the entry, and paragraphing and columns, to distinguish entries, so do these sorts of typographical techniques provide ways of saying 'not that, but this', in other kinds of printed objects. Columns do not, but boxes do, distinguish articles in a newspaper or magazine, and conventions of paging as well as boxing organize such objects into ordered collections of genres. The system of titles that override headlines makes these classifications explicit where this is necessary. The same news item may occur twice in the same issue of the same newspaper, working to 'mean something different' depending on the genre with which it is grouped. Such things as an event in the business community may count as 'news' on page 1 or 2, and be repeated as useful information for investors in the business pages. The death of a famous person may count as news, and then be repeated, for instance as an obituary somewhere else (some papers have quasi-permanent obituary columns). If the famous person is a woman, the obituary may be printed on the women's pages (which are generically distinguished in most Australian newspapers), or these same pages may carry a general article about the woman and her work, using the death as pretext and occasion. Women's pages in newspapers function to make the statement 'women count as news, too'; which is precisely a way of saying that we don't – or at least, that it's not the same kind of news!

It may be argued that such considerations on newspaper and magazine layout are too mechanically formal to count as genuine genre descriptions. I wish to argue the contrary, but of course, the lines and squares do not in and of themselves count as generic descriptions. They are the not-statements that are tied to the like-statements. They work to say 'this is like news' and it is also 'like other articles of interest to the girls'. Then we need to find out what is implied by such a grouping. 'News' makes the death of Simone de Beauvoir 'like' any news item involving an internationally famous person; but the locating of an article about her life and work on the women's pages makes the *salient feature* the fact that she was a woman. The not-statement suggests that classifying might always be *re*classifying, that it is useful to think of it as an act, and a strategy; it also suggests that the 'place' of the text in some sense *precedes* the features that we take to be characteristic of it.

The Metaphor of 'Place'

The metaphor of place is not a mere convenience in genre theory. Its tactical usefulness goes back for centuries, and is one of the generic markers of the treatises on 'Poetics' following the authorial example set by Aristotle. Indeed, it may well be the case that the metaphor of place is more than a tactic; there are good reasons for thinking that it is actually germane to the problems of doing classifications in general, and generic classifications in particular. It may not, then, be an accident that we so often use diagrams to repreent taxonomical and other classificatory forms, that we talk about 'borderline cases' when we are not sure whether something fits in this, or another, class, or that when we describe the genres of television and radio we use the notion of the 'time slot'. I shall return to this last non-accident shortly.

[. . .]

Place and Time

All generic descriptions rely on a more or less explicit 'filing system', and it is said that the earliest attempts to formlize genre theory arose from the need to rationalize the classifications and systems of location of the collections in the great libraries of the ancient world. It is clear in this example that 'place' must be taken quite literally, and the same is true of newspaper layout. Taking the index, always to be found on one of the outside pages of a newspaper, certain rules as to the location of given kinds of items can be discerned. This is not to say that the television programmes and meteorology reports will always be found on page 10; rather, they will never be found on the first or last page. Similarly, it is not helpful to think of library locations as corresponding to particular shelves in particular rows: rather, PN books come before PQ books, and after B books. This suggests that the notion of place that we need to discuss in such questions is relational, rather than absolute, and that such systems have a time, or a sequence built into them such that they impose a pattern of use which determines what counts as first and last, before and following, front and back. The rules for the use of the system are rules for mapping together actual spaces, such as library buildings, with systemic places, such as the Library of Congress classification. They are set out in indexes, guides to classifications and locations, tables of contents, and these are necessarily sequential. Television and radio programmes do the same sort of thing with actual times.

Another sense in which the notion of place must be taken quite literally in the description of genre is this: some kinds of texts occur necessarily, or always, in kinds of places, between participants defined by their social roles. The briefs and referral letters I mentioned earlier are a case in point; so would be the rulings of an administrative tribunal or a judge. Office memoranda, lectures, board meetings and a million other examples must be defined in this way, and it is clear that what gets said, and the kinds of interlocutory relationships that are produced, are largely determined by this notion of place. I might tell a story about how someone jostled me in a queue, or how someone pulled rank to be promoted ahead of me, or seen out of turn at the doctor's. If I tell this story to my neighbour over a drink, it is a story about the other person, or about social injustice; but if I tell the same story to my psychiatrist, it is a story about me, my lack of personal confidence, and my failure to self-assert. [. . .] This [. . .] leads me to suggest that when we are talking about genre, and ceremonials, it may be useful to talk about 'the manners of a text'. If the rhetorical rules of a genre are thought of as an etiquette, rather than as fixed laws, it is easier for us to think of them as being to do with how people get on with one another. In some cases, etiquette is best thought of as rules appropriate to a pre-existing situation, but this is far less often the case than we might suppose. Manners are instrumental in organizing and determining role-relations, and thus in forming settings. They 'make' the person, in more senses than one. Etiquette may be written as an immutable code, and expressed in the form of dogmatic deontics; when it is, we tend to find it ridiculous and out of date. But this does not mean that we don't observe an etiquette appropriate to whatever occasion, and social groups continually renegotiate the forms of acceptable behaviour in relation with an implicit or explicit criterion of appropriateness. We take for granted that such rules are pretty arbitrary, and we may be more comfortable with the fiction that our rules are not real rules, and need not be spoken. But even this fiction is 'good manners' in a group that thinks of itself as unregulated by anything but spontaneity and fellow-feeling. Such rules, like the rules of genre or of a ceremony, are there to 'make things work'.

Nevertheless, manners are never a matter of simple conformity with a normative model. They can be used for the purposes of an interaction, not just followed; they are good or bad shots, productive or not of situations requiring inventive uptakes.

The identification of time-slots in television programming is a particularly interesting case, which shows, among other things, that the 'place' precedes the 'internal' features of a given genre. The identification of kinds of audiences by the times of the evening at which they might watch the box is also a factor in the determination of those audiences: 'children', 'family viewing', 'late night' and so on are slots in rather the same way as in a printed form which organizes bits of information into different places on a sheet of paper, and thereby creates groupings and ways of relating those bits of information. They may even create, or determine, that information. Given the economics of TV programming, it is an important fact about televisual genres that they are written for, produced for, and bought for slots, and not the other way around. But these slots are not just empty spaces: they are spaces in a relational system that is organized around key points – before and after the early and mid-evening news, to take the obvious example (this is called 'the hook') – which have the function of marking boundaries, and thus making the not-statements, that produce the major differentiations (see Paterson 1980). It is an interesting fact that it is the news programmes that have this crucial function: this is the genre that makes explicit the major generic distinction in Australian television – the differentiation of 'information' from 'entertainment'[11] – and at the same time shows the extent to which the patterns of television programming are derivative of the patterns of arrangements of texts that make up newspapers and magazines.

A recent survey of television violence is of some interest here. It has long been an assumption of most work in the sociology of television that there is 'more violence' in the 'late night' slot than in the 'family viewing' or 'children's' slots, but, using explicit criteria for the identification of violence, this was shown not to be the case. There is a great deal more violence in, for instance, cartoons, than in the genres where we might expect to find it – police series, thrillers, horror movies and the like. What seems to be at issue here is that it doesn't count as violence in sports casts, cartoons, and soap operas: what counts as television violence for the sociologist is what counts as socially dangerous. It is 'not dangerous' to show a crocodile mauling a body, not dangerous to show a punch-up on a football field; not dangerous to show a character zapping another beyond all recognition in a cartoon. This is because what counts as violence for the viewer is governed – 'made intelligible' – by generic criteria. It is these that rationalize it and make it acceptable. To be the viewer of a cartoon is to know the difference between fantasy and the real; to be the viewer of a sports cast is to be on a side; to be the viewer of the news is to do your duty, knowing what's going on in the world, however nasty it might be. The moral dimension of 'realism' has its full force here. It may well be that the violent content in such programmes is more worrying on some criteria than the conventional struggle of marginal characters with each other and the forces of law and order, but the point is not, for the moment, there. The 'content' of victors and victims is the same; it just works differently, has a different status, and thus means something different depending (a) on its relation with other generic conventions, and (b) on its slot and the production of viewing habits in a type-audience. This is the same point as that made in speech–act theory, according to which 'the same propositional content' functions differently, and thus means something different, according to its performative setting. Meaning is not content; it is place and function.

Place and Function

Let me retrieve my problem of games and ceremonials. In, for example, court proceedings, the important stages or phases of the event can be said to be places (or times) marked out and occupied by different kinds of texts. The clerk of the court reads what counts as the title of the hearing, the proper names in a conventional order that shows which is defendant and which prosecution. There is the choice and swearing in of the members of the jury, where appropriate, and the judge's instructions to them, the opening addresses of the counsel, calling of witnesses and cross-examination, addresses to the jury, the jury's deliberations, their recall and the pronouncement, the judge's address and passing of sentence. Each of these moments is a genre, though it may be occupied by several texts, and each of the texts will deploy a range of tactics. It is, of course, quite possible to isolate, say, all the texts pronounced by the prosecution counsel, or the judge, or a witness, and there are certain purposes – for instance, for the jury's deliberations – which make this a useful thing to do. Anybody studying the career or personality of one of these participants would likewise need to make this set of choices, rather than the choices governed strictly by generic criteria. Yet it would be misleading to overlook the generic place of the texts, even in such a study, for to do so would be to neglect the question of strategy – what is said, not said, and how represented – for the particular purposes dictated by a given 'place' in the proceedings. To understand the rules of the genre is to know when and where it is appropriate to do and say certain things, and to know that to do and say them at inappropriate places and times is to run the risk of having them ruled out. To use these rules with skill is to apply questions of strategy to decisions of timing and the tactical plan of the rhetoric.

The same sorts of considerations bear on the decision to use, for instance, the place of a speech at a graduation ceremony to make a statement about the funding of graduate study, or an after-dinner speech to pull the rug from under a beset and beleaguered politician. All sorts of things may be said on such occasions: the genre of the after-dinner speech is not set by its inherent features so much as by the range of uses to which this place can be put. Nevertheless, it must be stressed that 'place' in this sense is not empty, neutral, or uninformed. Just as with the television audiences, the roles of the two interlocutory participants, their predictions and the kind of behaviour that is appropriate to them, are set by the occasion. These may indeed determine features inherent to the modes of address, and a text can be fruitfully studied for the way it constructs its audience positions. These may well be genre-specific, but a lot of work remains to be done before we find the most useful ways of describing them. What we can say, however, is that it is place, in the complex of meanings I have attempted to sketch out for this term, that determines the reading of linguistic or other formal features. It is most unlikely, however, that any linguistic feature taken in isolation could be held to be characteristic of a genre; rather, what we might expect is that combinations of features might count as the conventional markers of a genre. It is a quite other question whether such combinations of features count as *constitutive* of a genre in the same way that the use of performative verbs in the first person, present tense indicative mood indicate the typical cases of many speech acts. My argument leads me to suggest that it is place, rather, that constitutes genre, and that the functions and roles entailed by place determine the interlocutory structure of a genre. Conversely, if one of the tasks of a text is to mark itself generically in relation with others in order to get its partners to play ball in the appropriate manner, this can be said to constitute at least some of the parameters of its place.

Place and Framing

The notion that our texts arise within ceremonials, and that their form is determined by their ceremonial place and function, can be restated to say that the ceremonial frames a time and space, setting it apart from others, and marking its specificity. The distinction I made earlier, between 'a game' and 'the playing of that game', can also be made between a piece of music and its performance, and a play and its performance. The performance in either case is not restricted to the players: it includes the constitution of the audience, their assembly in particular time and place, and the rituals whereby that assembly marks the audience *as* audience, rather than as a collection of discrete units, setting them in position to make the playing possible. Reading a book, attending and giving lectures, dinner conversations, filling in forms, interviews. . .and a host of others are all ceremonial frames and/or the genres that occur within them. On this view, it is not stretching the point to argue that the publishing conventions that makes books the way they are – with covers, titles, bibliographical and cataloguing information, title pages, tables of contents, acknowledgements, prefaces by series editors, footnotes, indexes, glossaries, etc. – are notational frames for the ceremonies of reading. The variety of liminal and closing texts, their arrangement, and their formal features, have a great deal to do with the business of setting the genre of the text they enclose. A book is a material space, like an office or a classroom. Like books, the material arrangement of the space in which a text occurs has a bearing on the sense of that text and has a lot to do, necessarily, with the briefs we give the architects of the institutional, industrial, commercial and domestic spaces that design our signs. A discussion between two executives, one slightly superior in the company hierarchy to the other, will work differently, depending on whether the piece of furniture between them is a desk or a lunch table, and depending on whether the desk is the superior's or his subordinate's. The piece of furniture together with the other 'props' define a space and the ceremonial appropriate to it. It may well be that the participants might try to have 'the same' discussion in both places, but the choice of one or another ceremonial alters the conditions of speech and understanding. We might be inclined to say that the choice of lunch for such business conversations is 'more relaxed', or a way of getting away from the formal rituals of the office with its hierarchies; but I think this is misleading. We never leave the space of rituals for a space of non-rituals: we choose one ritual instead of another.

It is clear in this example that the notion of 'genre' and that of 'ceremonial' are effectively coextensive; but it is equally clear in the example of the court proceedings that this is not the case. Neither would it be useful to make 'genre' and 'ceremonial' coincide when talking about the theatre, or about music. A sonata has formal properties which make it recognizable as a sonata in the printed score, differentiating it crucially from a concerto, in much the same way as this latter is differentiated from a symphony. Criteria such as solo vs. orchestral playing, the relation of soloist to the orchestra (outside the orchestra or within it), as well as the formal harmonic properties associated with instrumental arrangements such a these, are important here. Some musical genres have effectively lapsed with the virtual disappearance of home entertainment, and in this case, too, it is important to specify both the generic and the ceremonial criteria. Some genres, on the other hand, subsist in different ceremonials from the ones in which they conventionally arise. In such cases, they take with them the signs of the lost ceremony, connoting that ceremony and the social relations it governs. For all these reasons, the problem of the formal properties of a genre will not go away.

In the history of genre theory, it is a remarkable fact that we have not, by and large, felt the need to theorize or otherwise make explicit the features of those genres which are so thoroughly specified by their ceremonial places that they seem self-evident. With the recent interest shown by linguists of discourse in these questions, this is changing. Discovering the implicit rules for the self-evident is the very project of the linguist and the sociolinguist. But traditional genre theory rarely asked what the consitutive form of a prayer or a sermon was,[12] and although certain questions about the rhetoric of preaching, pleading, and other forms of public speaking were indeed the stock-in-trade of the treatises of oratory, these were broached as questions of etiquette and of tactics, as if the question of generic specificity was unproblematical. It seems that genre theory has only been concerned to differentiate those genres that can occupy the same, or very similar places. So we have worried about the differences among the genres of the theatre, but not about the difference between novels and plays. Within the history of philosophy, and library cataloguing, we had to worry about the difference between psychology and the philosophy of mind, placing considerable distance between them to signify that difference. And since the Renaissance, we have come to worry about the generic specificity of what we call 'poetry', because the ceremonials defining the place of lyric verse (e.g., accompanied recitation) have been lost. Verse itself has been said to be not constitutive of poetry, and following the loss of a musical setting, the typesetting conventions have also been disturbed: poetry has 'broken bounds' as it has come to be read under material and ceremonial conditions very similar to those appropriate to the reading of prose fiction. The continual debate about 'prose' and 'poetry' is a debate about a contested boundary; but it is also the play for generic specificity *within the same space*. My very strong suspicion is that we can generalize from this case: the question of the constitutive status of formal features arises when, and only when, there is more than one game possible in a single ceremonial setting.[13]

[. . .]

Finish

The ceremonial of a game marks its ending: 'game, set and match'; applause; home; or 'back to square one'. I could attempt to maintain the fiction – ring the bell, propose the toast, or close the proceedings with a wave of the hand and an anthem. Yet there is a very important sense in which that would be inappropriate. My text is not a game, but a move in a game. It expects an uptake.

In this place, this uptake could come from two apparently distinct, but effectively convergent quarters – the genre-theorists, or the curriculum developers and teachers. I have remarked previously that generic classifications can arise in a variety of settings, of which theories of discourse and the writing of a syllabus are only two. It is not only the classifications that can find themselves in these places. More importantly, the principles adopted for taking 'genre' or 'a genre' as object and focus of an investigation both arise from the place of that investigation, and themselves have a bearing on the use that can be made of the classifications arising from them. It is in terms of the principles underlying the very notion of genre that I have been playing my game.

In the debate between the process-writing theorists and the linguists (see Sawyer and Watson 1987) and responses (Martin *et al.* 1987), the question is whether genre is called 'primitive', i.e., whether it is basic to the form of a text, or peripheral. This cashes out in the debates about pedagogical strategy as to whether it can be taught as a set of rules, and practised in writing exercises, or whether on the contrary it is most appropriately added in during this process of refining the final drafts of a text. I agree with neither of these views. On the one hand, the assumptions that appear to underlie the process theory mobilize an effective separation of 'form' and 'content'; apparently, we could learn the 'content' of science, for instance, and thereafter learn the appropriate expository forms. We do not, however, learn the 'content' of a game – whatever that could be – and then learn its rules. A game – and likewise a genre – is *constituted* by its rules and the techniques for implementing them. It is only for the special purposes of psychology that a game is thought of as a personal expressive activity; such things as chess and basketball are not usefully thought of as spontaneous behaviour regulated in a second phase by rules of the do and don't variety.

To this extent, I agree with the linguists: my game analogy makes genre a central concept in the theory of discourse, and an informing concept in the constitution and processing of texts. But – I now play my other hand – I cannot agree with them if their position is that it is *linguistic forms* that are constitutive of genre, and that teaching these forms will result in appropriate texts. I have introduced the notion of the ceremonial and its attendant notion of 'place' in order to make the point that language interacts with other semiotic systems to form texts, and the conventions that mark a genre derive from all of these. I would concede that in texts that are predominantly verbal, it is frequently the linguistic forms that secure uptake *once the 'receiver' is positioned in the right game.* But the genre – the game of the text – is constituted by its ceremonial place, and this is appropriated by the full range of semiotic systems available as strategies or enablement conditions to that genre. It follows from this position that if we are to teach the effective practice of genres as the basis for writing and speaking skills, it would be wise to teach the full range of 'languages' – their rules, and the rules of their interaction – that form any genre. This would vastly expand the list of ingredients, and may even go some way in the direction of expounding the 'method' as well. Even so, it would also be wise not to confuse the recipe with the rules of place and appropriateness, nor constitutive rules with regulative rules.

My text expects an uptake; but it is also, itself, an uptake – albeit a mite disobedient. I was asked to draw out the implications of this way of thinking about genre for the practical purposes of curriculum design and classroom practice. I decline this clause of my brief, insofar as I can claim no competence in these fields. I have chosen instead to repeat in this place what we know so well in others: that we don't learn to write until we can read. Here, I mean 'read' in the very strongest sense.

If writing is a craft (and there is no other definition of any strategic use to a teacher), then perhaps we should think about apprenticeship. An aspiring carpenter learns the job, acquiring a practice of tasks, tools and techniques. Particular techniques and tools are geared to kinds of tasks and materials. Poets and painters in the Renaissance taught their arts in just this way, delegating big toes and drapery to their pupils, and studying with them, in the work of their peers and predecessors, effects and the strategies for achieving them.

Whether in the traditional academic disciplines, or the vocationally oriented genres, doing the task effectively is the operative criterion. Not doing it effectively is, by contrast, socially disempowering. The understanding of the task is surely crucial: what is its place, what are the interlocutory positions defined by this place, what are the functional requirements in the interchange of each of the interlocutory roles? If writing – or speech – involves discovering the practical difficulties likely to arise each time that kind of job is to be done, and acquiring an arsenal of tricks to deal with them, then 'reading' is part of the apprenticeship.

Knowing a genre is also knowing how to take it up: the manners are reciprocal. What do you *do* with a form, if you've never been taught to fill one out? What do you do with theoretical writing, if all you have learnt to read with is narrative? How do you take a parody, if you've never met parody or the genre that it spoofs? Using a text is primarily a matter of understanding its genre and the way it plays it – recognizing it, certainly, but also reading its tactics, its strategies, and its ceremonial place. Learning to write, equally, is learning to appropriate and occupy a place in relation to other texts, learning to ensure that the other chap will play the appropriate game with you, and learning to secure a useful uptake: the rules for playing, the rules of play, and the tricks of the trade.

The questions start when you ask why – and how – you would play tennis in the classroom. Come to think of it, the wall of the back lav was a very wooden partner.

Acknowledgement

I wish to thank the following people for their comments and suggestions in response to an earlier draft of this paper; Jennifer Craik and Frances Oppel, of Griffith University; and John Macarthur and James Wheatley, of Queensland University; Laurie Gafney, of Curriculum Services, Queensland Department of Education – great tennis players, all.

Notes

1 The notion has been taken up and its use extended by Lyotard (1984).

2 Cf. Todorov (1978), Bakhtin/Volosinov (1973). Derrida assumes the continuity of the two notions in his critique, 'The Law of Genre' (1980).

3 [1994 update: On this argument, I had gone on to suggest in the original article that 'genres' and 'speech acts' were *therefore* not coextensive. I have modified my position on this. It may be that it is on the distinction between the formulaic and the non-formulaic that the class of 'speech acts' is established in practice; but it does not follow that this practice is well or usefully theorized as a distinction between genre and speech act. Clearly, the formulaic and the non-formulaic define a range, not a clear-cut distinction; and equally clearly, a rhetoric of genre worked out, for example, in terms of *topoi*, makes the distinction untenable.]

4 Halliday (1978); cf. the use made of Halliday's work by Frow (1980); and more recently by Kress (1985a, 1985b). Cf. also Martin and Rothery (1980). Halliday, as distinct from some of his followers, does invoke the notion of 'the semiotic system that constitutes the culture' (in Frow 1980: 73), but the assumption that this is a *single* system, coupled with the failure to investigate its operations, results in a reduction of this notion to those of 'context' and 'situation'. This is a simple text/context model, where 'text' is the output of two sets of rules, linguistic and social. To name this latter 'social semiotic' changes very little in practice. For a critique of the notion of 'register' in terms of its inadequacy to deal with 'genre', see Reid (1987b).

5 [1994 update: Jean-Marie Schaeffer (1983) has explored the ramifications of this issue in a significant article, 'Du texte au genre'.]

6 Note that this requirement is not included in the notion that the rules of a game are the rules governing the pieces (e.g., of chess) and the uses to which they can be put; cf. Lyotard (1984: 10; glossing Wittgenstein).

7 This claim is made on the basis of arguments contesting the place of 'discourse' in a model of the generation of texts, but *mutatis mutandis* holds for genre as well. See Lee (n.d.).

[1994 update: I now wish to nuance this statement in respect of 'being specific to a social setting': no genre is exclusive to one institutional or disciplinary setting. But it is clear that a genre might have a 'home' setting, and that it can be adapted or cited in others; the home setting might be a factor in the interpretability of the cited genre, while its citability is an assumption from the oldest tradition of genre theory, and is elaborated as a principle by

Derrida (1972). There is also the question of disciplines, which do develop their own rhetorics and behave like genres; see John S. Nelson *et al.* (1987), in particular the study therein by Charles Bazerman of the style manual of the American Psychological Association. It is consistent with Lyotard's argument (in *Le Différend*), and with the logic of classification that I go on to expound in the following pages, to consider disciplinary distinctions as coming under the same set of problems as generic distinctions. The error, then, would consist in counting disciplines as sociological phenomena enjoying a distinct ontology that would permit them to 'cause'/'determine'/'explain' discursive phenomena in some way. They may, however, like ceremonials, organize genres into sets or fields which would account for (some of) the relations of uptake mentioned above.]

8 [1994 update: Alistair Fowler (1982) draws fruitfully on Wittgenstein's notion of 'family resemblances' to deal with this aspect of generic classes.]

9 Department of Immigration and Ethnic Affairs, application for entry for settlement. Form M 47 (8-78) 14, Attachment 1, Chapter 12, front of form.

10 [1994 update: Well, we may 'know' a form, depending on our previous training. Teachers of English as a Second Language to migrant groups in Australia address this as one of the primary practical literacy needs of their clients.]

11 [1994 update: Latterly (1994) 'infotainment' has made its appearance in media commentary, showing that the 'mixed genre' occurs at the boundary marking a crucial differentiation. See my argument concerning 'mixed doubles' in Freadman and Macdonald (1992).]

12 Such genres are, however, included in Frow's categorization of discourse genres (1980: 75).

13 [1994 update: A detailed argument along these lines is made in respect of the historical emergence of 'prose' as a formal practice of writing, in Kittay and Godzich (1987). The historical argument concerning the forms of written French in the Middle Ages is the reverse of the story of reading practices in the post-print age where, I suggest, the distinction documented by Kittay and Godzich is partially collapsed; but the theoretical implications of the two stories are similar. Prose emerges as a distinct category with the demise of the *jongleur* in medieval Europe, his loss of the socio-institutional place of his power, and the rise of distinct rhetorical practices to guarantee the authority and the stability of the text. Although Kittay and Godzich argue that this distinction 'exceeds the scope of genre' (p. xiii), I am inclined to think that the classificatory mechanisms, and the relation of semiotic practices with them, are parallel and demonstrate the same paradoxes.]

References

AUSTIN, J. L. (1967) *How to Do Things with Words*, Cambridge, MA: Harvard University Press.

BALZAC, H. DE (1972) *Le Père Goriot*, Paris: Livre de Poche.

BERGER, J. (1987) 'Imagine Paris', *Good Weekend, the Sydney Morning Herald Weekend Magazine*, 28 February, pp. 42–45.

BUZACOTT, M. (1987) *Charivari*, Sydney: Picador.

DAVIS, W. H. (1972) *Peirce's Epistemology*, The Hague: Martinus Nijhoff.

DERRIDA, J. (1972) 'Signature événement contexte', *Marges de la Philosophie*, Paris: Minuit, pp. 365–93.

DERRIDA, J. (1980) 'The Law of Genre', *Glyph*, 7, pp. 176–201.

ECO, U. (1984) *The Name of the Rose*, (trans. W. Weaver) London: Picador.

FOWLER, A. (1982) *Kinds of Literature: An Introduction to the Theory of Genres and Modes*, Oxford: Clarendon Press.

FREADMAN, A. (1987) Paper read to the Architecture School, University of Queensland, 3 March.

FREADMAN, A. and MACDONALD, A. (1992) *What is this Thing Called 'Genre'?*, Brisbane: Boombana Publications.

FROW, J. (1980) 'Discourse Genres', *Journal of Literary Semantics*, 9(2), pp. 73–81.

GRACE, H. (1982) 'To the Lighthouse', in COVENTRY, V. (ed.) *The Critical Distance*, Sydney, Australia: Hale and Ironmonger, pp. 112–9.

HALLIDAY, M. A. K. (1978) *Language as Social Semiotic*, London: Edward Arnold.

KITTAY, J. and GODZICH, W. (1987) *The Emergence of Prose*, Minneapolis, MN: University of Minnesota Press.

KRESS, G. (1985a) *Linguistic Processes in Sociocultural Practice*, Geelong: Deakin University Press.

KRESS, G. (1985b) 'Socio-Linguistic Development and the Mature Language User: Different Voices for Different Occasions', in SELLS, G. and NICHOLLS, J. (eds) *Language Learning: An Interactional Perspective*, London: Falmer Press.

LEE, D. (n.d.) 'Discourse: Does It Hang Together?' unpublished ms.

LYOTARD, J.-F. (1984) *The Postmodern Condition: A Report on Knowledge*, (trans. G. Bennington and B. Massumi, foreword F. Jameson) Minneapolis, MN: University of Minnesota Press.

MARTIN, J. R. and ROTHERY, J. (1980) *Writing Project Report*, No. 1, Working Papers in Linguistics, Linguistics Department, University of Sydney, Australia.

NELSON, J. S. *et al.* (eds) (1987) *The Rhetoric of the Human Sciences*, Madison, WI: University of Wisconsin Press.

PATERSON, R. (1980) 'Planning the Family: The Art of the Television Schedule', *Screen Education*, **35**, Summer, pp. 79–85.

Pocket Oxford Dictionary ([1924], 1955) Preface to the 1st edition (revised), Oxford: Oxford University Press.

PRATT, M.-L. (1977) *Towards a Speech–Act Theory of Literary Discourse*, Bloomington, IN: Indiana University Press.

PRENDERGAST, C. (1986) *The Order of Mimesis*, Cambridge: Cambridge University Press.

REDDY, M. (1970) 'The Conduit Metaphor', in ORTONY, A. (ed.) *Metaphor and Thought*, Cambridge: Cambridge University Press, pp. 284–324.

REID, I. (1987a) 'Reading Frames for Literary Learning', *Australian Reading Conference on lang'gwag and ler'ning, Gosford, New South Wales (July), Conference Proceedings*, Sydney, Australia: Ashton Scholastic.

REID, I. (1987b) 'A Register of Deaths?', in BURTON, T. and BURTON, J. (eds) *Linguistic and Lexicographical Studies: Essays in Honour of G. W. Turner*, London: Boydell and Brewer, pp. 103–14.

SAUSSURE, F. DE (1966) *Course in General Linguistics*, (trans. W. Baskin, ed. C. Bailly and A. Sechehaye, in collaboration with A. Reidlinger) New York: McGraw-Hill.

SCHAEFFER, J.-M. (1983) 'Du texte au genre', *Poétique*, **53**, pp. 3–18.

SEARLE, J. ([1969] 1978) *Speech Acts*, Cambridge: Cambridge University Press.

STEIN, G. (1985) *Three Lives*, New York: New American Library (Signet Classics).

TODOROV, T. (1978) *Les Genres du discours*, Paris: Seuil.

VOLOSINOV, V. N. (1973) *Marxism and the Philosophy of Language*, (trans. L. Matejka and I. R. Titunik) New York: Seminar Books.

WELTY, E. (1983) *The Ponder Heart*, London: Virago.

WITTGENSTEIN, L. (1953) *Philosophical Investigations*, (trans. G. E. M. Anscombe) Oxford: Basil Blackwell.

Chapter 4

Rhetorical Community:
The Cultural Basis of Genre

Carolyn R. Miller

In my essay 'Genre as Social Action', I claimed that a genre is a 'cultural artefact' (Miller 1984: 164; corrected version Chapter 2, this volume) that is interpretable as a recurrent, significant action. At the time I didn't think very carefully about what I meant by 'cultural artefact'. I was, in part, trying to emphasize that a rhetorically useful notion of genre should be grounded in the conventions of discourse that a society establishes as ways of 'acting together' (in Kenneth Burke's phrase), that we should look to ethno-categories of discourse rather than to the theoretically neat classifications that seemed to control most discussions of genre at the time. I was also, in part, groping toward an understanding of the problematic relationship between action and structure that, I now realize, has engaged many others in a variety of disciplines.

I haven't written much about genre since then, although my convictions about it organize much of my teaching; I think, for example, that there is something specifically *generic* to be learned about what it means to write a progress report, or an application letter, or a research article, or even an essay. As I said, in 1984,

> what we learn when we learn a genre is not just a pattern of forms or even
> a method of achieving our own ends. We learn, more importantly, what
> ends we may have . . . ; for the student, genres serve as keys to understanding
> how to participate in the actions of a community. (1984: 165).

I don't necessarily know how to *teach* these things very directly, although I've learned a lot from people like Charles Bazerman, Tom Huckin, Leslie Olsen, and John Swales. Since 1984 I've also come to appreciate the effect that our understanding of genre has on the structure of curricula and, in particular, how the failure to understand genre as social action afflicts the typical first-year college writing program in the United States; it turns what should be a practical art of achieving social ends into a productive art of making texts that fit certain formal requirements (Miller and Jolliffe 1986: 378).

But the opportunity for 'rethinking genre' at this point is an especially welcome one, for two reasons. First, I find that I can now clarify or at least contextualize better some issues I left unresolved in the earlier essay. And second, the concept of genre can help us think through some other issues I've recently become interested in, specifically those having to do with participation in a community. What I'll be doing here, then, is to rethink parts of my earlier work on genre and to connect it to some of my more recent writing about rhetorical community.

One aspect of 'Genre as Social Action' that now strikes me as naively prescient is the emphasis it places on middle-level phenomena, on a sense of genre as somehow located *between* what I've learned to call the micro-level and the macro-level of analysis. My speculative suggestion that cultural-linguistic phenomena could be arrayed on a hierarchy from the micro-level of natural-language processing to the macro-levels of 'culture' and 'human nature' placed genre somewhere toward the middle, connected to levels above and below by a semiotic system of constitutive and regulative rules; in this model pragmatic social action is constructed out of syntactic form and semantic substance in a neat, cumulative array. I still find this a persuasive image, and it does have some corroboration from theorists and researchers in other areas.[1] But it remains merely a nifty hypothesis at best. In the lower levels of the hierarchy, from language up through genre, I relied on the pretty firm foundation of pragmatic linguistics and conversational analysis, and it is here that the triple nature of each level is comprehensible; that is, each level is interpretable in its pragmatic aspect as action, in its syntactic aspect as form, and in its semantic aspect as the substance for the next higher level of meaning. At the higher levels I can't demonstrate that this is the case, and whether the semiotic relationships pertain in any analytically useful way at levels higher than the genre I don't know. I did claim that 'genre serves as the substance of forms at higher levels', and that 'as recurrent patterns of language use, genres help constitute the substance of our cultural life' (1984: 163), and it's this claim that I'd like to explore a bit further here.

What is a culture and how is it constituted? Are genres at least some part of that constitutive substance? This is an extremely complex issue; Raymond Williams (1976) has called 'culture' one of the two or three 'most complicated' words in the English language, with three main senses. I'll take as a working definition Williams's second sense, developed in the nineteenth century and underlying the work of anthropology: culture as a 'particular way of life' of a time and place, in all its complexity, experienced by a group that understands itself as an identifiable group (1976: 80). It surely is the case that in different times and places different sets of genres appear. It is probably also the case that a genre that seems to occur in two rather distinct times and places will not really be 'the same' in an important sense, although to support this notion rigorously you'd have to be a better comparative anthropologist of discourse than I am. To take a familiar example, however, the Athenian polis had a genre set consisting of (at least) deliberative, forensic and epideictic speeches. Undoubtedly, the ancient Athenians had many additional recurrent situations in which discourse was used – in education, for example, or in business transactions, or in diplomatic relations or religious ritual – and the traditional restriction to these three may tell us more about Aristotle than it does about Athens. It does not serve us very well to characterize discourse that takes place in our courtrooms as a 'judicial' genre in the same sense that Aristotle did, however; there are too many substantive and procedural differences – the laws, the decision-making procedures (the size of the juries, the distinction between judge and juries), the rules of evidence, the definitions of crimes, the possible punishments are all quite different. We might want to refine further our judicial discourse into such genres as opening and closing arguments, cross-examination, *amicus curiae* briefs, *voir dire* of witnesses, and the like. These all constitute courtroom discourse, which we might want to conceive of on a higher level than genre, as a form of life. But surely we would also find that courtroom discourse in North American democratic culture in the late twentieth century bears recognizable resemblances to courtroom discourse in fourth century BC Athenian culture, through an evolutionary heritage. What is similar or analogous is the general social functions being served. Although these cultures are related and although they comprise many similar social functions, they are far from the same, at both micro and the macro-levels.

I'll mention several other brief examples of how genre and culture have been understood together. Bazerman (1988) has shown that the nature of the experimental research article has changed over the past 300 years – its function within the scientific enterprise, or form of life, has evolved, as have its characteristic modes of representation, its topoi, its appeals. It is not exactly the same genre as it once was; the genre and the scientific form of life have evolved together within the changes in western culture at large. Jamieson (1975) has discussed this evolutionary process in her work on antecedent genre as rhetorical constraint, noting that Roman imperial documents are evolutionary ancestors to the contemporary papal encyclical and that the King's Speech to the parliament gives rise to the early presidential inaugural addresses in the United States. Finally, 'new historical' work in literary studies has begun to understand genres as cultural constructions that reflexively help construct their culture. In one of the earliest programmatic statements about such work, Greenblatt introduced a special issue of the journal *Genre* devoted to cultural forms and power in the Renaissance by claiming that 'the study of genre is an exploration of the poetics of culture'. By problematizing the traditional distinctions between literature and political power, for example, new historicism understands aesthetic forms and their relationships to 'the complex network of institutions, practices, and beliefs that constitute the culture as a whole' as themselves 'collective social constructions' (1982: 6), that is, as cultural artefacts.

Calling a genre a 'cultural artefact' is an invitation to see it much as an anthropologist sees a material artefact from an ancient civilization, as a product that has particular functions, that fits into a system of functions and other artefacts. Thus, much of what we know about ancient Greek culture we have learned from recurrent patterns – in the pottery, sculpture and architecture as well as in the discourse; and not only in the extant judicial, political and epideictic discourse but also the ways the Greeks had of telling their own history, the nature of the drama and rhapsodic poetry, the treatises and dialogues on intellectual matters. As bearers of culture, these artefacts literally *incorporate* knowledge – knowledge of the aesthetics, economics, politics, religious beliefs and all the various dimensions of what we know as human culture. As interpreters – historians, anthropologists – we in the twentieth century must try to reconstruct the knowledge that it takes to see these patterns as significant and as interrelated. We make inferences from specific artefacts, or from specific actions, to culture as a whole. Thus, it seems that we might characterize a culture by its genre set – whether judicial, deliberative and epideictic or experimental article, grant proposal, poster, peer review and the like. The genre set represents a system of actions and interactions that have specific social locations and functions as well as repeated or recurrent value or function. It adumbrates a relationship between material particulars, instantiations of a genre in individual acts, and systems of value and signification.

The general issue here is how to understand the relationship between, on the one hand, the observable particular (and peculiar) actions of individual agents and, on the other, the abstract yet distinctive influence of a culture, a society, or an institution. Do speech acts, moves, episodic encounters – the micro-discursive levels – somehow cumulate, as I implied, and 'add up to' culture, to the Athenian polis, the scientific community, the Renaissance court? And if so, how? And exactly how do the macro-levels (genre, form of life, culture, etc.) contextualize the micro-levels? To put the matter most broadly, what is the relationship between the micro-levels and the macro-levels? How *can* we bridge 'the gap between action theory and institutional analysis', as social theorist Anthony Giddens put it (1981: 161)? What *is* the relationship between minds and institutions, as anthropologist Mary Douglas put it (1986: 7)? As I noted earlier, this issue has been a focus for much social theorizing recently, and it is these perspectives that are missing from my earlier work, which focused more carefully on the micro-levels. As several social theorists have noted, this issue became more prominent with the collapse of positivist empiricism in the social sciences, for 'covering laws' can no longer be invoked causally and determinately to connect action and structure (Giddens and Turner 1987; Knorr-Cetina 1981). The general issue has been represented in many ways and taken many forms: micro vs. macro-sociological analysis, subject vs. society, action vs. institution, innovation vs. regularity, subjectivism vs. objectivism, private vs. public, cognitive vs. social.

Giddens's solution lies in what has come to be called 'structuration theory'.[2] 'Structuration' describes our experience that social relations are structured across time and space. The structures of social relations consist of rules and resources; rules, as in linguistics, are both constitutive and normative (1984: 17–21); resources are the means by which rules are actualized – they are 'capabilities of making things happen' (1981: 170). These structures are largely tacit, matters of practical knowledge that are mutually held by members of a society (1984: 4); in another formulation, Giddens calls structure a 'virtual order', meaning that structure exists 'only in its instantiations in . . . practices and as memory traces orienting the conduct of knowledgeable human agents' (1984: 17). The traditional 'dualism' of action theories and institutional theories is avoided by what Giddens calls the 'duality of structure', a phrase used to mean that structure is 'both medium and outcome' of the social practices it recursively organizes (1984: 25); structure, in other words, is both means and end, both resource and product. The analogy to linguistic rules and structures applies; uttering a grammatical and meaningful sentence requires drawing upon a set of mostly tacit semantic, syntactic and pragmatic rules, and the instantiation of these rules in an utterance reproduces them – reinforcing them and making them further available.

Structuration thus serves as the explanatory nexus between individuals and collectivities, between, that is, the concreteness and particularity of action and the abstractness and endurance of institutions. Two features are important here. One is that although structure has only a virtual existence, out of space-time, it yet must be instantiated in space-time, in the actual flow of material existence. Hence, actors must *create* structure, for themselves and for others, must schematize existential situations, must interpret or 'indexicalize' the 'inherently equivocal' confusion of possibilities in which they find themselves (Cohen 1987: 292). They do this, of course, by relying, recursively, on already available structures, on shared classifications and interpretations, which necessarily are social. Substituting duality for dualism thus enables Giddens to moderate the postmodern dilemma of whether the human 'subject' can be a centre of conscious control or must be decentred into oblivion (1984: xxii). He also shows how social and institutional power is wielded. As Douglas notes, although institutions do not have purposes or 'minds of their own' (1986: 9), they do have immense power: 'Institutions systematically direct individual memory and channel our perceptions... They fix processes that are essentially dynamic, they hide their influence, and they rouse our emotions... they endow themselves with rightness' (1986: 92).

The second important feature in Giddens's structuration theory is that the instantiation of structure must also be the *reproduction* of structure; as he says, 'the conduct of individual actors reproduces the structural properties of larger collectivities' (1984: 24). Reproduction is thus a stronger way to characterize what rhetoricians have called 'recurrence'. As I used the term in my earlier essay, it seemed to be a matter primarily of intersubjective perception: 'Recurrence is implied by our understanding of situations as somehow "comparable", "similar", or "analogous" to other situations' (Miller 1984: 156). What the notion of reproduction adds is the action of participants; social actors *create* recurrence in their actions by reproducing the structural aspects of institutions, by using available structures as the medium of their action and thereby producing those structures again as virtual outcomes, available for further memory, interpretation, and use.

What I want to propose, then, is that we see genre as a specific, and important, *constituent* of society, a major aspect of its communicative structure, one of the structures of power that institutions wield.[3] Genre we can understand specifically as that aspect of situated communication that is *capable of reproduction*, that can be manifested in more than one situation, more than one concrete space-time. The rules and resources of a genre provide reproducible speaker and addressee roles, social typifications of recurrent social needs or exigences, topical structures (or 'moves' and 'steps'), and ways of indexing an event to material conditions, turning them into constraints or resources. In its representation of and intervention in space-time, genre becomes a determinant of rhetorical *kairos* – a means by which we define a situation in space-time and understand the opportunities it holds.[4]

To see genre in this way as a mid-level structurational nexus between mind and society suggests the specific contribution rhetoric makes to the problem in social theory; this derives from the nature of rhetoric as 'addressed'. The practical need to marshal linguistic resources for the sake of social action connects the micro and macro-levels. In his discussion of 'speech genres', Bakhtin, for example, emphasizes what he calls 'addressivity' as a 'constitutive feature of the utterance' (as contrasted with the sentence); hence 'the various typical forms this addressivity assumes and the various concepts of the addressee are constitutive, definitive features of various speech genres' ([1852] 1986: 99).[5] Similarly, Thomas Farrell has recently suggested that the 'goods' internal to rhetorical activity 'are necessarily relational' (1991: 187), that is, that the qualities 'actively cultivated through excellence in rhetorical practice' require other persons; such goods include civic friendship, a sense of social justice, strategic imagination, competitiveness, empathy and the like. My point is that this addressivity, or relational quality, provides a specific mechanism by which individual communicative action and social system structure each other and interact with each other. The individual must reproduce patterned notions of others, institutional or social others, and the institution or society or culture must provide structures by which individuals can do this. The mutual, cultural knowledge that enables individual actors to communicate as competent participants includes structures of interaction, of exigence, of participant roles, and of other rules and resources. Genres, as Douglas might have put it, help do our rhetorical thinking for us.[6]

I do not mean by my emphasis here on Giddens's notions of structure and structuration to revise my claim that genre is social *action* to the claim that genre is social *structure*. I would still maintain that structure, or form, is a constituent aspect of action and that action is primary. Giddens claims that 'the structural properties of social systems do not exist outside of action' (1984: 374). Although structures are what is recognizable as constituents of society, for it is structure that is reproducible, action is what is significant, and it is in action that we create the knowledge and capability necessary to reproduce structure. The primacy of action is a strong theme in social theory. As Blumer noted, 'human group life consists of, and exists in, the fitting of lines of action to one another by the members of the group' (1979: 147). Burke put it this way (and I believe that Blumer would concur): in acting together, we have 'common sensations, concepts, images, ideas, attitudes'. These make us 'consubstantial' ([1950] 1969: 21), they give us a common substance, which, reciprocally, enables and enhances our common actions. Giddens's 'duality of structure' also captures this reciprocity.

This brings me to my second major agenda here. We cannot fully understand genres without further understanding the system of commonality of which they are a constituent, without exploring further the nature of the collectivity. As Swales has insisted, 'genres belong to discourse communities, not to individuals' (1990: 9). Of the many terms for collectivity – society, institution, culture, community – it is the last that has recently become an important and contested term in a variety of social disciplines – in science studies, literary studies, composition theory, linguistics, political theory, and probably in sociology as well. It was a powerful but hidden undercurrent in classical rhetoric, acquired prominence from the social construction-ism of the early part of the twentieth century, but is still not well conceptualized, politically or rhetorically. It is a troublesome concept, one that seems to devalue individual rights and capabilities, to privilege the domination of a majority or an orthodoxy; it is a concept that makes it difficult to account for change, a notion that can be – and has been – vague, comforting and sentimental. I have explored elsewhere the resources that classical rhetoric offers us for conceiving of community and the recent debate in political theory and postmodernism (Miller 1993a; 1993b). Here, however, I'd like to focus on what it takes to make a community a specifically rhetorical one, as distinct from a speech community, a political community, a discourse community.

In his contribution to an essay collection on the micro/macro-problem, Harré explores what he calls the 'metaphysical status of collectives' (1981: 140). He suggests that there are two sorts of collectives, which he calls 'taxonomic' and 'relational' (1981: 140, 147). Members of taxonomic collectives have similarities, perhaps even shared qualities or beliefs, but these are shared only in the sense of being common to the members, who have no real interrelations with each other. The collectivity exists in the mind of the classifier (1981: 147). Members of relational collectives, in contrast, have real relations with each other, by means of which active sharing occurs, and the collective itself has a structure: it is differentiated. Harré believes that social research often identifies taxonomic collectives (such as the group of British passport holders) about which little more of 'sociological interest' can be said:

> merely showing that a taxonomic group exists... is no ground for concluding that that group has any other, more elaborate, structure. And if it is the case that inductive sociological methods can establish no more than the fact of taxonomic groupings when the scale is greater than that of institutions and the like, there is a clear limitation to the empirical employment of macro-social concepts. (1981: 148)

It might be interesting to examine various rhetorical and linguistic treatments of community to see whether they yield taxonomic or relational groups; I suspect, for example, that some definitions of speech community tend toward the taxonomic, since it is common linguistic behaviour that is being examined, not relational actions or structures; although members of a speech community, by definition, are capable of interacting with each other, Nystrand points out that they 'are not ever required, either by rule or definition, to actually interact with each other' (1982: 15). Swales notes several reasons why speech community is not a sufficient notion for socio-rhetorical purposes, all of them tied to the fact that a socio-rhetorical discourse community must be relational in the way that speech community is not (1990: 24). But I want to suggest that there's a kind of community that has yet a third metaphysical status, in contrast with both taxonomic and relational collectives, a status that Giddens might call 'virtual', rather than material or demographic. A rhetorical community, I propose, is just such a virtual entity, a discursive projection, a rhetorical construct. It is the community as invoked, represented, presupposed, or developed in rhetorical discourse. It is constituted by attributions of characteristic joint rhetorical actions, genres of interaction, ways of getting things done, including reproducing itself. Like Giddens's structures, rhetorical communities 'exist' in human memories and in their specific instantiations in words: they are not invented anew but persist as structuring aspects of all forms of socio-rhetorical action. Like genres, rhetorical communities 'exist' on a discourse hierarchy, not in space-time; they exist, however, at a much higher level of cumulation than genres. I believe that many rhetoricians have committed a category fault analogous to that of the sociologists whom Harré chides: they have been looking for community demographically and geographically – in classrooms, civic task forces, hobby groups, academic conferences.

How does a rhetorical community *operate* rhetorically? It works in part through genre, as we have said, as the operational site of joint, reproducible social action, the nexus between private and public, singular and recurrent, micro and macro. It operates more generally, however, as a site where centrifugal and centripetal forces must meet (to use Bakhtinian terms). If we look carefully, for example, at the Greek city-state as a rhetorical community, what we see is not primarily comfortable agreement or a dominating majority: what we see most of all is contest, the *agon*. As I elsewhere characterized the polis, the ur-rhetorical community, it is

> most centrally a site of contention. Certainly it was a site disputed by the sophists and the aristocrats. More generally it is the site of political debate between citizens, a locus of self-defining communal action [as well as a site of suppressed contest between citizens and non-citizens]. Because there are many citizens, there are differences; because there is one *polis*, they must confront those differences. (Miller 1993a)

Farrell makes similar observations about what he calls the rhetorical forum:

> What is critical to the power and constraint of the forum is that two very different sorts of loci may always intersect there: first, is the cumulative weight of customary practice: convention, commonplace and *communis sensus* associated with the forum's own history; and second, the inevitably uncertain fact of otherness. (1991: 198)

It is this inclusion of sameness and difference, of us and them, of centripetal and centrifugal impulses that makes a community rhetorical, for rhetoric in essence requires both agreement and dissent, shared understandings and novelty, enthymematic premises and contested claims, identification and division (in Burke's terms). In a paradoxical way, a rhetorical community includes the 'other'.

So rather than seeing community as an entity external to rhetoric, I want to see it as internal, as constructed. Rather than seeing it as comfortable and homogeneous and unified, I want to characterize it as fundamentally heterogeneous and contentious. The centrifugal forces of difference are important, and I do not want to seem to minimize their power, which derives in part from the multiplicity of communities in which and by which any given person can be engaged. Before concluding, however, I would like briefly to identify some centripetal forces that are rhetorically available to keep a virtual community from flying apart (or dissipating). The first is genre, of course; genre's power to structure joint action through communal decorum should be apparent from all I've said so far. Another is metaphor, or figurality in general. This dimension of language provides us a wealth of ways to create similarity out of difference, to wheedle, as it were, identification out of division (Miller 1993b: 19). Another is narrative. Several writers have recently emphasized this unifying, community-building function of narrative, among them Rouse (1990), as well as MacIntyre (1984). Rouse notes, for example, that 'membership in . . . communities is . . . constituted in substantial part by sharing [a] past as a basis for further action, and by our accountability (to ourselves and others) for the intelligibility of those actions in terms of that past' (1990: 184). In effect we must be able to tell ourselves, and others, stories about that past and our location in it:

> the intelligibility of action, and of the things we encounter or use in acting, depends upon their already belonging to a field of possible narratives. On my view, we live within various ongoing stories, as a condition for our being able to tell them, or for doing anything else that can count as an action. (Rouse 1990: 181)

Furthermore, Rouse suggests that narrative has specifically the function of holding heterogeneity together:

> Sharing a situation as a narrative field thus makes possible meaningful differences along with convergence. The need to make differences intelligible and a common project possible compels an ongoing struggle to keep in check the divergence of versions of the community's story . . . This struggle takes the form of a shared concern to construct, enforce, and conform to a common narrative which gives common sense to everyone's endeavor. (1990: 185)

Social order, continuity and significance are effects of structuration; structuration is accomplished through the actions of individual actors, and some of their actions are rhetorical. Rhetoric provides powerful structurational resources for maintaining (or shoring up) social order, continuity and significance. Figures make connections that otherwise can't be made; narrative imposes intelligibility on past events; genres impose structure on a given action in space-time. There may be others, as there are undoubtedly non-rhetorical resources. Genre, however, I want to maintain, is the only one of these three resources that has specifically pragmatic power as social action. Narration and figurality are structural and semantic capabilities that become socially and rhetorically meaningful only within pragmatic activities like speech acts or genres. Narration, for example, can be used within many genres, from simple story-telling to scientific reporting to eulogizing. Genres, then, in their *structural* dimension, are conventionalized and highly intricate ways of marshalling rhetorical resources such as narration and figuration. In their *pragmatic* dimension, genres not only help real people in spatio-temporal communities do their work and carry out their purposes; they also help virtual communities, the relationships we carry around in our heads, to reproduce and reconstruct themselves, to continue their stories.

Acknowledgement

Carl G. Herndl and Michael C. Leff provided helpful comments at crucial points in my revision of the original conference paper. I would also like to thank

Aviva Freedman and Peter Medway for inviting me to the 'Rethinking Genre' conference and thereby introducing me to what was for me a new community of research on genre.

Notes

1 I would now also point to work by Sinclair and Coulthard (1975), who develop a system of discourse analysis for classroom talk using a 'rank scale', or hierarchy in which 'each rank can be expressed in terms of the units next below' (p. 20); the ranks they identify are lesson, transaction, exchange, move and act (p. 24). Coulthard (1985) provides a table (similar to my Figure 2.1 in this volume) comparing categories of analysis used by several discourse analysts, with ranges similar to those used by Sinclair and Coulthard. In a somewhat similar vein, Freadman (1987: 100; condensed version Chapter 3, this volume) suggests that genres consist of moves, or speech acts, and that several genres together comprise a 'ceremony', such as the consultation (medical or legal).
2 Giddens acknowledges that this is an 'unlovely term at best' but disclaims personal responsibility for it (1984: xvi).
3 Giddens admits the 'central significance of the "linguistic turn"' in social theory (1984: xxii) and the 'fundamental role' of language in social life (1984: xvi).
4 For recent discussions of *kairos* see Kinneavy (1986) and my essay on *kairos* in science (Miller 1992). Freadman's (1987) discussion of genre emphasizes the importance of place and time in understanding the appearance and significance of genres.
5 I should note here that Bakhtin does not seem to distinguish, as I wish to, the generic speech act (a reproducible schematic action that can be as short as a single word or as long as a Dostoyevsky novel), whose boundaries are 'determined by a change of speaking subjects' ([1952] 1986: 71), from the genre as a macro-unit of discourse that is built up from smaller units such as speech acts and patterned sequences of speech acts; its boundaries are determined by a relatively complete change in the complex called the rhetorical situation, with a socially identifiable exigence at its core.
6 What she did say was that institutions 'do the classifying' (Douglas 1986: 91).

References

BAKHTIN, M. M. ([1952] 1986) 'The Problem of Speech Genres', in *Speech Genres and Other Late Essays*, (ed. C. Emerson and M. Holquist, trans. V. M. McGee) Austin, TX: University of Texas Press, pp. 60–102.

BAZERMAN, C. (1988) *Shaping Written Knowledge: The Genre and Activity of the Experimental Article in Science*, Madison, WI: University of Wisconsin Press.

BLUMER, H. (1979) 'Symbolic Interaction', in BUDD, R. W. and RUBEN, B. D. (eds) *Interdisciplinary Approaches to Human Communication*, Rochelle Park, NJ: Hayden, pp. 135–53.

BURKE, K. ([1950] 1969) *A Rhetoric of Motives*, (reprint) Berkeley, CA: University of California Press.

COHEN, I. J. (1987) 'Structuration Theory and Social Praxis', in GIDDENS, A. and TURNER, J. H. (eds) *Social Theory Today*, Stanford, CA: Stanford University Press, pp. 273–308.

COULTHARD, M. (1985) *An Introduction to Discourse Analysis*, 2nd edn, London: Longman.

DOUGLAS, M. (1986) *How Institutions Think*, Syracuse, NY: Syracuse University Press.

FARRELL, T. B. (1991) 'Practicing the Arts of Rhetoric: Tradition and Invention', *Philosophy and Rhetoric*, **24**, pp. 183–212.

FREADMAN, A. (1987) 'Anyone for Tennis?' in REID, I. (ed.) *The Place of Genre in Learning: Current Debates*, Deakin University, Australia: Centre for Studies in Literary Education, pp. 91–124.

GIDDENS, A. (1981) 'Agency, Institution and Time-Space Analysis', in KNORR-CETINA, K. and CICOUREL, A. V. (eds) *Advances in Social Theory and Methodology: Toward an Integration of Micro- and Macro-Sociologies*, Boston, MA: Routledge and Kegan Paul, pp. 161–74.

GIDDENS, A. (1984) *The Constitution of Society: Outline of the Theory of Structuration*, Berkeley, CA: University of California Press.

GIDDENS, A. and TURNER, J. H. (eds) (1987) *Social Theory Today*, Stanford, CA: Stanford University Press.

GREENBLATT, S. (1982) 'Introduction to Special Issue on The Forms of Power and the Power of Forms in the Renaissance', *Genre*, **15**(1, 2), pp. 3–6.

HARRÉ, R. (1981) 'Philosophical Aspects of the Macro–Micro Problem', in KNORR-CETINA, K. and CICOUREL, A. V. (eds) *Advances in Social Theory and Methodology: Toward an Integration of Micro- and Macro-Sociologies*, Boston, MA: Routledge and Kegan Paul, pp. 139–60.

JAMIESON, K. M. (1975) 'Antecedent Genre as Rhetorical Constraint', *Quarterly Journal of Speech*, **61**, pp. 406–15.

KINNEAVY, J. L. (1986) 'Kairos: A Neglected Concept in Classical Rhetoric', in MOSS, J. D. (ed.) *Rhetoric and Praxis: The Contribution of Classical Rhetoric to Practical Reasoning*, Washington, DC: Catholic University of America Press, pp. 79–105.

KNORR-CETINA, K. D. (1981) 'Introduction: The Micro-sociological Challenge of Macro-sociology: Towards a Reconstruction of Social Theory and Methodology', in KNORR-CETINA, K. and CICOUREL, A. V. (eds) *Advances in Social Theory and Methodology: Toward an Integration of Micro- and Macro-Sociologies*, Boston, MA: Routledge and Kegan Paul, pp. 1–47.

MACINTYRE, A. (1984) *After Virtue: A Study in Moral Theory*, 2nd edn, Notre Dame, IN: University of Notre Dame Press.

MILLER, C. R. (1984) 'Genre as Social Action', *Quarterly Journal of Speech*, **70**, pp. 151–76.

MILLER, C. R. (1992) '*Kairos* in the Rhetoric of Science', in WITTE, S. P., NAKADATE, N. and CHERRY, R. D. (eds) *A Rhetoric of Doing: Essays on Written Discourse in Honor of James L. Kinneavy*, Carbondale, IL: Southern Illinois University Press, pp. 310–27.

MILLER, C. R. (1993a) 'The Polis as Rhetorical Community', *Rhetorica*, **11**, pp. 211–40.

MILLER, C. R. (1993b) 'Rhetoric and Community: The Problem of the One and the Many', in ENOS, T. and BROWN, S. C. (eds) *Defining the New Rhetorics*, Newbury Park, CA: Sage, pp. 79–94.

MILLER, C. R. and JOLLIFFE, D. A. (1986) 'Discourse Classifications in Nineteenth-Century Rhetorical Pedagogy', *Southern Speech Communication Journal*, **51**, pp. 371–84.

NYSTRAND, M. (1982) 'Rhetoric's "Audience" and Linguistics' "Speech Community": Implications for Understanding Writing, Reading, and Text' in NYSTRAND, M. (ed.) *What Writers Know: The Language, Process, and Structure of Written Discourse*, New York: Academic Press, pp. 1–28.

ROUSE, J. (1990) ' The Narrative Reconstruction of Science', *Inquiry*, **33**, pp. 179–96.

SINCLAIR, J. M. and COULTHARD, R. M. (1975) *Toward an Analysis of Discourse: The English Used by Teachers and Pupils*, Oxford: Oxford University Press.

SWALES, J. M. (1990) *Genre Analysis: English in Academic and Research Settings*, Cambridge: Cambridge University Press.

WILLIAMS, R. (1976) *Keywords: A Vocabulary of Culture and Society*, New York: Oxford University Press.

Chapter 5

Systems of Genres and the Enactment of Social Intentions

Charles Bazerman

'*A theory of language is part of a theory of action*'.

(John Searle)

In this chapter I want to build upon what we already know about genres and connected sets of genres, what we know about intertextuality and systems of intertextually-linked documents, what we know about speech acts and writing as forms of social action, and what we know about individual micro-acts and social macro-structure. I want to do this to present a vision of how people create individual instances of meaning and value within structured discursive fields and thereby act within highly articulated social systems. The action is accomplished through performance of genres that have highly specific, systematically contextual requirements and well-defined consequences for further generically-shaped social acts.

That is, I wish to present a vision of systems of complex located literate activity constructed through typified actions – typified so that we are all to some extent aware of the form and force of these typified actions. As we become more informed and involved with these typified literate actions, we come to share a more precise set of functional meanings and consequential relations through the kinds of texts. By using these typified texts we are able to advance our own interests and shape our meanings in relation to complex social systems, and we are able to grant value and consequence to the statements of others.

From the viewpoint of the mythical outside observer, I want to present a system of a complex societal machine in which genres form important levers. From the viewpoint of the participant in society, which we all are, I want to identify how the genres in which we participate are the levers which we must recognize, use and construct close to type (but with focused variation) in order to create consequential social action. This machine, however, does not drive us and turn us into cogs. The machine itself only stays working in-so-far as we participate in it and make our lives through its genres precisely because the genres allow us to create highly consequential meanings in highly articulated and developed systems.

I will pursue this project through the example of the patent, choosing particulars from the latter half of the nineteenth century; this choice of materials is a consequence of historical work I am currently doing on Edison's light. Despite major rewritings of the US patent law since then, the outlines of the patent system and the genre remain largely the same.[1] Further, although the legal system and regulatory network of government organizes, institutionalizes, regulates, and creates compelling exigencies for the production and use of explicit characteristic genres in perhaps a more determined and articulate way than in other domains of life, it gives insight into the way other less explicit socio-textual systems work.

What We All Know About Patents

As a textual form we all can recognize a patent, despite some minor adjustment of the form over time. A patent, usually a printed document, describes an invention, identifies its inventor and declares particular aspects of the invention as original (the claim); it further carries some official designation of the patent granting body, a patent number and a date from which the patent right begins. In late nineteenth-century United States, the patent typically opened with one or more technical drawings, signed by the inventor and two witnesses. The first page of text was headed by 'United States Patent Office', with subheadings identifying the inventor and the name of invention, followed by the formula 'Specification of Letters Patent xxxx, dated xxxx'. The text then opens in the form of a letter 'to all whom it may concern', followed by the boilerplate formulaic opening paragraph:

> Be it known that I, xxxx, of xxxx, have invented a new and improved xxxx; and I do hereby declare that the following is a full and exact description thereof, reference being had to the accompanying drawing and to the letters of reference marked thereon.

A general elaboration of the invention and its improvements over prior art is followed by a detailed description of the invention and its operation, typically introduced by a formula such as 'To enable those skilled in the art to fully understand and construct my invention, I will proceed to describe it'. The description is usually cross-indexed to the illustration through reference letters. The patent then ends with precise claims of novelty, prefaced by some such language as 'I claim as new, and desire to secure by Letters Patent . . .' The signature of the inventor and two witnesses again appears at the end.

One obvious feature of this genre in the nineteenth century is that the body of the text is in the first person in the form of a legal petitionary letter, although the patent, as indicated by the heading and opening formula, is presented as already granted. Indeed the patent adopts directly the specification from the application, which it only amends by adding the designations of official approval by the Patent Office. Currently the specification is written in the third person, without the markers of individual petition, but the practice remains of wholesale transport of the language of the application into the language of the grant. Then, as now, the reigning patent law identifies the specific elements to be put into the patent application, and thus the elements that will appear in the final patent. Title LX, Sections 4888 and 4889 of the 1874 patent law read:

> Sec. 4888. Before any inventor or discoverer shall receive a patent for his (*sic*) invention or discovery, he shall make application therefor, in writing, to the Commissioner of Patents, and shall file in the Patent Office a written description of the same, and the manner and process of making, constructing, compounding, and using it, in such full, clear, concise, and exact terms as to any person skilled in the art or science to which it appertains, or with which it is most nearly connected, to make, construct, compound, or use the same; and in case of a machine he shall explain the principle thereof, and the best mode in which he has contemplated applying the principle, so as to distinguish it from other inventions; and he shall particularly point out and distinctly claim the part, improvement, or combination which he claims as his invention or discovery. The specification and claim shall be signed by the inventor and attested by two witnesses.
>
> Sec. 4889. When the nature of the case admits of drawings, the applicant shall furnish one copy signed by the inventor or his attorney in fact, and attested by two witnesses, which shall be filed in the Patent Office; and a copy of the drawing, to be furnished by the Patent Office, shall be attached to the patent as a part of the specification. (Scientific American 1881)

Thus the law suggests the content, organization and even some of the phrasing of the patent.

All of us can also give a brief description of the system the patent is part of. The patent is a legal document that has been approved by the patent office, under authorizing and regulating legislation from the US Congress in fulfillment of constitutional provisions. The patent application is reviewed by a patent examiner who takes action to approve or disapprove the patent according to particular criteria, established by the enabling law and interpreted through the courts. The patent grants economic ownership to the invention claimed therein for a specified number of years (17 in the late nineteenth century and today). Thus through legal means the patent realizes a policy of trading temporary monopoly privileges for the encouragement of new arts and the public dissemination of these arts with the end of general improvement of the national economy. The patent provides a mechanism for the inventor to turn a concept into economic value – it is the means by which you 'turn your ideas into money' as the ads for patent brokers say. It is part of the system of economic property, as Oliver Wendell Holmes points out in *The Common Law* (1881).

The account of patents I have just given and the analysis to follow is consistent with standard public beliefs about patents. Indeed genres rely on our being able to recognize them and to some degree understand the meanings they instantiate within the systems of which they are part. A textual form which is not recognized as being of a type, having a particular force, would have no status nor social value as a genre. A genre exists only in the recognitions and attributions of the users. The formal features, let us say, of 14 lines, iambic pentameter, certain stanzaic patterns, and corresponding rhyme schemes, only gain generic force of the kind sonnet in-so-far as they are recognized and then attached to that tradition. The same text, of course, also may be attached to other kinds, superordinate or subordinate or independent of the kind sonnet, that may be recognized prior to or after or totally independently of the attribution of sonnetness (e.g., poem, rhymed stanzaic verse, lyric, Petrarchan, polemic, compliment).

Since what I say about patents will contain no scandal about patents, it will only elaborate further and lay out the consequences of what we already know in recognizing a particular text as a patent, and will thereby help us understand the force of genre and its place within structured human activities.

Genre as Typified Utterance and Intention

Genre theory as elaborated by Carolyn Miller (1984), John Swales (1990) and myself (1988) has been concerned with the development of single types of texts through repeated use in situations perceived as similar. That is, over a period of time individuals perceive homologies in circumstances that encourage them to see these as occasions for similar kinds of utterances. These typified utterances, often developing standardized formal features, appear as ready solutions to similar appearing problems. Eventually the genres sediment into forms so expected that readers are surprised or even uncooperative if a standard perception of the situation is not met by an utterance of the expected form.

Moreover, the genres, in-so-far as they identify a repertoire of actions that may be taken in a set of circumstances, identify the possible intentions one may have. Thus they embody the range of social intentions toward which one may orient one's energies. The existence of a patent system and the existence of recognized forms of patent applications are preconditions for the intention to obtain a patent, and therefore to apply for one. The existence of a recognized patent system and typified forms of communication as actions within that system are also necessary for others (such as patent examiners, patent judges, competing inventors and manufacturers) to recognize your intentions in filing a written application and to respond appropriately. That is: the intention, the recognition of the intention, the achievement of that intention with the coparticipation of others, and the further actions of others respecting that achievement (that is treating the realized intention as real and consequential) all exist in the realm of social fact constructed by the maintenance of the patent system and the communicative forms (genres) by which it is enacted.

Patent History: The Nexus of System, Genre and Intentions

The mutual development of the patent genre, patent intentions, and the social system of patent grant can be seen historically. Patents in Renaissance England were simply a designation of a monopoly privilege granted by the Crown, for any benefit or favor to the state embodied in the monarch. Thus a king might grant a patent for the importation of salt, or the colonization and exploitation of a newly discovered or conquered piece of the Americas. Thus earliest patents were realized textually through the traditional forms of petition to the Crown and royal grant.

Such Crown privileges were of course open to abuse arising from the conflation of the royal pleasure and the good of the state and its citizens. In England during the middle of the seventeenth century, in repugnance against the widespread abuses of James I and Charles I, all forms of state granted monopoly were outlawed by Parliament except for the single temporary monopoly granted to the inventor of a new good, under the belief that invention would advance the economic well-being of the country. A temporary monopoly was thought to encourage both invention and the sharing of knowledge to be exploited by all once the short monopoly period expired. Moreover, since invention created new value, a monopoly was not sequestering a previously open part of the economy, but was only granting temporary privilege for a value that would not have existed without the invention. Thus the association of invention with the idea of national economic well-being and with the granting of limited privileges developed together within a newly emerging belief in market economy. Copyright then emerged as a subset of patents as a way of protecting the interests of printers (only later of authors).

Once the idea of privilege dependent on specific value to the state emerged, it became necessary to create a mechanism whereby individuals might request this privilege and present their claim to it for evaluation. In England this led to a registration procedure followed by litigation in the courts when the patent was contested. This system remained in effect until 1852. In the Anglo-American colonies patents were granted on an individual basis by courts and local legislatures. The framers of the United States Constitution were concerned to regularize and limit this practice, so they made patents and copyrights a federal responsibility under Article 1, section 8 granting Congress the power 'to promote the progress of useful arts by securing for limited times to authors and inventors the exclusive right to their respective writings and discoveries'.

The first patent bill was signed by President Washington in April 1790, placing responsibility for approving patents on three cabinet members: Secretaries of State and War, and the Attorney General. They were charged with determining that the 'invention or discovery [be] sufficiently useful and important'. The application was to include a specification and drawing, and if possible a model. However, the form of the application was not further determined by the law.

Because of an 1836 fire in the patent office, we only have a limited number of reconstructed files of the earliest patents. The earliest application that is currently in the patent records dates from 1790, and consists of a petitionary letter from William Pollard addressed directly to Secretaries Jefferson and Howe and Attorney General Randolph. The letter gives a detailed account of Pollard's difficulties in obtaining a model of Awkright's spinning machines and his failure to create a working model of it until he determined certain improvements which he wishes to patent. He also provides many financial details of the spinning industry in Britain to establish the value of the machine. The details of the machine and its operation appear to be only present in a drawing that was attached, but is no longer in the patent record. Thus in this earliest extant application, the rhetorical emphasis was on the deserving character of the petitioner and the great economic value to befall the United States; the specific technical improvement is purely secondary and unargued. That is the presentation follows the legally designated criteria of usefulness and importance rather than novelty.

The actual patent, from the example of the one granted Francis Bailey in 1791, is a signed certificate with a seal of the United States and signed by both the President and the Attorney General. It looks much like a traditional diploma. The specifics of the invention are mentioned only in a single sentence which also identifies Bailey as the inventor and attests that 'the said Invention appears to be useful and important'. The rest of the document consists of reference to the law, the date of issuance, testimony of the act of approval and signing, certification of the document etc. The meeting of criteria and that of granting the privilege remain at the forefront of the document.

During the three years this law was in operation 55 patents were approved, but the burden of evaluating the applications was too much a drain on the time of the cabinet officers. In 1793 the law was revised to become simply a registration system with no evaluative procedures. The application, from the examples on file, turned to a description of the invented object, cross-referenced to a drawing. Models (not necessarily working) were also to be provided to the patent office. The grant consisted only of official testimony that the papers were filed and the fees paid. Since no check was made of prior art and the putative inventor had to make no case beyond presenting the object and paying fees, many lawsuits developed. Apparently within the litigation, two crucial issues emerged – the identity of the actual inventor and what exactly was being claimed as novel in the patent. Thus, in order to provide legal standing for these issues, by 1830 patent applications typically had two new elements – the formulaic opening identifying the putative inventor and a closing statement identifying the claim.[2]

In 1836 a new patent law was passed, reintroducing examination and establishing a patent office with examiners to carry out this task. This law establishes the system still in effect in the US, with some modifications from later law, most extensively in 1870 and 1952. The form of the patent in effect at Edison's time both was first specified in the 1836 legislation and was followed in practice. Moreover the procedures and criteria for examination (aimed at preventing excessive litigation) were established both by the law and the practices of the newly-formed patent office. These examination procedures and criteria focused the task of the application, which rhetorically was aimed at passing through procedures and criteria to gain approval.

Patent Applications and Grants as Speech Acts

The two related and evolving genres we have been considering (the patent application and the patent grant, or letters patent) may be seen as classic speech acts as described by Austin and Searle. These documents have recognized a stable illocutionary force within the legal system as directives (requesting or applying is an attempt to direct another's behaviour) and declarations (announcing or declaring a thing is so, makes it so – that is why the early patents looked like diplomas or marriage certificates); moreover, they are surrounded by rules of proper utterance. The movement towards formalization of language and textual appearance as well as of the rules surrounding their adequacy only reinforce the recognition that they are aimed at achieving certain acts, are surrounded with particular conditions which must be fulfilled for their perfection or achievement, and that they attempt to meet those criteria by making explicit and easily locatable precisely how they attempt to meet each of the conditions or criteria of perfection.

Indeed speech acts of the most familiar sort are frequently carried out by the most formulaic of utterances: 'I bet you'; 'With this ring I thee wed'; 'I hereby declare this bridge to be open'. Although many of the rules surrounding such acts as betting are left informal and implicit, except to the linguistic analyst, many other speech acts are surrounded by formal regulations: making contracts, changing names, requesting a rebate for electric batteries.

Searle derives these rules from an analysis of the conditions that must surround the utterance of the speech act for the act to be successful. Austin initially called these felicity conditions. The contextual conditions identify such things as timing of the utterance; authority of the utterer; relationship between speaker and hearer; psychological state of speaker and hearer towards the act, the utterance and each other; the speaker and hearer's perception of the situation of utterance; the conventions of language through which the utterance is enacted, and the kinds of particulars (propositions and predications) included, guide the creation of a successful utterance.

Thus one's success in having one's assertion of a sentence accepted as a scientific truth depends on who one is, who hears, the hearer's perception of the speaker and utterance, the channel of communication, the relationship of the utterance to certain other accepted scientific claims of others, the relationship of the statement to material events that are represented (and that can be affirmed on challenge) to have occurred in the utterer's laboratory and that others have experienced and will experience in their labs, and so on. These conditions of success can be transformed into a set of constitutive, regulatory and advisory rules for making successful scientific assertions (also perceived as scientific method, values and practice).

Concerning patents, we can most simply see that if one's application for a patent meets all the conditions for a patent, then one's application for a patent will be a success, and a patent should be granted, as the illocutionary force will be complete, and the patent examiner will be compelled to approve the application. If not you can take the examiner to the appeals board or court. The appeals board or court can then enforce that the illocutionary force of a perfected application will be met by the perlocutionary effect of the issuance of a grant – unless the 'course of justice is perverted', which only the courts themselves can determine. That is, the courts and surrounding legal bodies and procedures are engaged in interpretive actions; the identification and certification of all conditions of success or felicity conditions require *interpretation – but patents are one instance in which there are procedures and institutions to match illocutionary force to perlocutionary effect –* thus bringing the interpretive procedures to the surface and making participants accountable for their interpretations. This makes patent and other similar legal procedures different from most speech acts. In many instances illocutionary forces are not even linked to an anticipated perlocutionary effect (asserting you are happy does not direct how your listener might respond); in any event, perlocutionary effect is usually up to the free choice of the hearer (as a call for help may be ignored).

Difficulties with Speech Act Theory

Before we continue with our analysis of the conditions which a patent application must meet for its success, we must first deal with several related difficulties concerning speech act theory and its application to long, complex written documents.

The first difficulty is the importance of local circumstances in the identification, interpretation and realization of speech acts. For example, what I take the force of the statement 'We have coffee, milk and juice' to be depends very much on who I am, who I am speaking to, what my relationship is with them, whether I am about to go shopping or I have expressed thirst or I am sitting at a dinner table. Simply to put such equivocal cases in the category of indirect speech acts is inadequate for several reasons: first, unless we are total strangers to a situation, we always use our knowledge of local circumstances to confirm or extend or modify our view of the explicit statement; second, most statements are not fully explicit or universally univocal in their illocutionary intent; third, there are many subtle distinctions among acts and the way acts are taken that only emerge out of the interpretation of situation; and fourth, there are many kinds of acts that are only conceivable within highly defined circumstances, such as undermining the credibility of a scientific argument by mentioning a piece of apparatus used in producing the result, thereby invoking a disciplinary understanding of the inappropriateness of that apparatus to the experimental problem. Although speech acts may potentially be reduced to a few abstract categories with certain abstract guidelines, they are thereby stripped of the locally significant aspects of their meanings – just those aspects which go into constructing the local event as distinctive from others and which provide individuals with the subtle tools necessary to successfully respond to and negotiate events as they unfold in local circumstances.

Austin's awareness of the importance of local circumstances in the interpretation and enactment of speech acts, both locutionary and illocutionary, led him to withdraw from absolute formalizations in the closing two lectures of *How to Do Things with Words* (1962), to qualify his conclusions as only abstractions, and to caution us to examine local circumstances. In Lecture 11 in particular he examines a number of examples where local factors are essential for interpretation, and winds up making such statements as 'Reference depends on knowledge at the time of utterance' (p. 144) and 'The truth or falsity of a statement depends not merely on the meanings of words but on what act you were performing in what circumstances' (p. 145).

Searle, however, in *Speech Acts* (1969) and subsequent works (1979, 1984; Searle *et al.* 1980), took on the project of pursuing the formalizations to obtain an abstract calculus of meaning which incorporated reference and illocution in a logically contained interpretive scheme. Local circumstances are only included as conditions that must be met for the successful completion of a speech act. For example, a person conducting a marriage ceremony must be legally qualified to do so, and the event must be carried out in a legally appropriate place and time, between people legally qualified to marry, if the events are to count as a legal marriage. In so doing, Searle helped identify some features of speech acts as they often emerge in institutionally structured settings, and we will call on that analysis later. However, this analysis of general rules and conditions for speech acts is accomplished at the expense of suppressing analysis of the particularity of institutional settings within which individual acts arise and of obscuring the interpretation of acts in less well defined settings.

The second difficulty is the polysemousness of speech acts. Any speech act may be uttered and interpreted with a variety or multiplicity of intentions and frameworks for attributing meaning. Any utterance may serve different functions for different utterers and different auditors, and these multiplicities of functions and meanings may be operating simultaneously. Moreover, the conditions of success for the utterance may become multiple, depending on the functions and meanings attributed to the utterance. In stating at a dinner party that I like vanilla ice cream, I may be placing an order, expressing delight in anticipation, revealing personal character, defending my food against the predatory habits of a dessert-loving child, making small talk, or all of the above simultaneously. The host, my child, my neighbours who served me chocolate last week, and other guests I have just met that evening, may each interpret the remark in a variety of ways, as they may evaluate the effect and effectiveness variously according to how they understand the situation and act.

In a more subtle example, when an intimate friend tells me a dream, is it a personal revelation, a request for an interpretation, an invitation for commiseration, a step in the coconstruction of a communal imagination, a reproach, or an invitation for me to tell my own dreams? The person telling the dream may have no single or clear intent, nor may inform us of what kind of response would be invited. Perhaps no particular force is attributable to the dream telling until after the conversation has unfolded, and even then the two parties to the conversation are likely to walk away with rather different perceptions of what has happened.

The nature of the speech act, or the series of speech acts, is manifold and indeterminate. This indeterminacy, multiplicity and interpretive complexity may present substantial difficulties in our most spontaneous and close relations, difficulties which we sometimes only resolve by providing some simple, determinate and benign after-the-fact explanation that excludes some of the more troublesome interpretations triggered by the situational indeterminacy and multiplicity. Although such reductions to primary interpretations of actions and intentions may be fostered in highly institutionalized settings with highly typified actions, as we will examine below, that still does not fully exclude multiple secondary intentions and uses packed into or pulled out of the utterances. Thus formalizations of speech acts can at best characterize a dominant appearance in a multiple act, and only in those circumstances where that dominant appearance is well-marked and supported in institutionalized circumstances.

Speech Acts are not Generally a Langue

These first two difficulties point to the power of the concept of a speech act even as they point to limitations in trying to specify the exact meaning of any particular speech act by using a generalized understanding of speech acts. The difficulties examined serve to illuminate the richness of the activity embodied by utterances within circumstances. Events are alive with new forms of life growing in the unfolding of both typified and novel utterances. Every utterance itself exists at the intersection of the typified and novel, as perceived by the participants coming to terms with each new moment. In Saussurean terms, speech acts exist precisely where *langue* and *parole* meet, at the alive utterance. Any attempt to reduce speech acts to a speech system removes the activity from the act and reduces complex, interpretive, intelligent, motivated human behaviour to a static set of signs, no longer responsive to human needs and creativity. When speech acts are reduced to a system of *langue*, the typifications – employed as resources by humans attempting to relate through signs – are taken as the definition and rules of the utterance. The typified speech acts then become superordinate to the activity, rather than the speech acts being embedded parts of the overall activity. A less distorting understanding of speech acts requires constant attention to events unfolding in particular circumstances with local definition and interpretation of successful activity. Perceivable regularities in speech acts, whether perceived and acted upon by the participants or the late-comer analyst, need to be seen as historically evolved resources of typified interpretation, in relation to other social regularities and institutions that help identify the nature of each social moment as enacted by the participants.

As analysts of speech activity, our task is simplified and stabilized when we look to behaviours in highly regularized or institutional settings that help enforce recognizable and socially agreed upon characters to particular moments. Since the institutions and social understandings set the stage and define the game, it is much easier to see what is going on, and we can make plausible connections among various moments or acts if participants see and treat those moments or acts as similar. We should not, however, confuse a reasonably stable set of linguistic practices evolved within a particular strand of socio-historical circumstances with an absolute understanding of speech acts.

Below, we will examine a highly developed set of typified practices, which even surpass Searlian rigour in their compulsivity, but that does not mean the rigour extends beyond any particular set of typifications. Law, on the face of it, is a rigorous practice, but it is a different rigorous practice in medieval France and the nineteenth-century United States. And twentieth-century plain language philosophy is, at least some would claim, also a rigorously typified practice, but again a different one. Each, nonetheless, evolves with novel utterances and moves, as do less tightly typified systems with wider ranges of freedom for novelty and multiplicity, such as contemporary literary theory, which nonetheless operates under its own set of recognizable understandings and interventions. Finally, in each of these cases, no matter how rigorous the typifications that guide the enactment any single moment may be, the dynamics of the moment grant new meaning and life to the typifications, and we must look to the dynamics of the moment to understand what is happening.

Long, Complex Written Documents as Speech Acts

The final difficulty with speech act theory, particularly for this study, is its application to long, complex written documents. Speech acts as envisioned by Austin and Searle are short utterances carrying out single acts. For the sake of analytic clarity Searle explicitly excludes from consideration any but the most simple utterance (1969: 22).

Written texts characteristically contain more than one sentence. A text contains potentially many acts. Moreover, it is unclear whether middle sentences of extended discourses embody speech acts of specific illocutionary force in the way isolated sentence utterances do. At best we can imagine in a highly compulsive, closed text with a compliant reader that the text attempts to push the reader down a certain path of reaction through a series of related acts. Nonetheless, what the sum of the various acts of a text amounts to is unclear.

However, if the text is distinctly identifiable as of a single genre, it can gain a unified force, for it is now labelled as of a single kind instantiating a recognizable social action. That is, the text effects a law (a declaration), or makes application (a directive), or contractually binds you (a commissive), or presents a scientific claim (an assertive), or conveys outrage at a governmental action (an expressive).[3] The various smaller speech acts within the larger document contribute to the macro-speech act of the text, and each of the subacts must carry its weight. In fact the expectations of generic form are such that any missing or weakly instantiated feature of the genre may weaken the generic force. Particularly if the genre is responsive to formal regulation, a defect in any of the subactions may be reason for the failure of the work of the genre. A patent application without a representation of the object, or a declaration of originality, or a specification of claim is not a valid application and will not achieve the purpose of gaining approval. Thus a defective specification will never appear as an officially approved patent, distributed in reprints by the patent office. We will examine in a moment how perfection of each of a patent's sections may also be related to the satisfaction of specific conditions of success.

In a contract many acts are fulfilled, but the overall effect is to bind parties to mutual obligations and rights, including all the stipulations that are part thereof. The stipulations are meaningless – both in the sense of being non-binding and in the sense of being purposeless and unmotivated and perhaps unintelligible – without the perfection of the overall contractual act. Seductions, sales, all other events that end with a bottom line, a mutual agreement and focused conjoint action among parties would have the effect of a macro-action and give to the entire proceedings the shape of the single act. Indeed the minor actions that go into it would be hard to understand, hard to attribute intention to, hard to see as effective acts, without the frame within the macro-act.

Many written genres seem to resolve themselves into single acts. A patent application, a tax form, a mail order for a pair of shoes, or a final examination in English Lit 202 once it has completed its work to gain the patent grant or shoes, to satisfy the IRS, to demonstrate one's competence in the subject, can be filed away purely for the record unless someone wants to call the perfection of the document or consequent actions into question. The text becomes dead or a black box and exists only in its consequences. Much of scientific writing is of this character as articles only have a short shelf life (or citation life) and then gather only dust; they live through their consequences or lack thereof, unless someone wants to open up the black box of dusty research. This indeed is a central premise of Latour's *Science in Action* (1988).

Other texts, however, to have force must constantly be reread, for they have multiple forces that are created only by the reader's interaction with the texts. When we read a novel or a book of philosophy many things are done to us. It is clearly reductionist to characterize these multiple effects under a single macro-act, such as being entertained or enlightened. We recall the poem or work of philosophy not just as having a single overall force (as scientific citations sometimes become symbols for single concepts), but as a collection of moments and gestures as well as an overall structure of arguments or feelings or imaginative moves. These texts live not in any sense of unified consequences, but in their multiplicity of effects on the readers' minds, arising from the complex of actions realized through the text. If you were to leave such texts in a file or on a dusty library shelf they would not do their work; nor would they if we were to reduce them to simple slogans which we were to carry around in our heads. At the risk of oversimplifying, we may say that such genres exist more for the process of their interaction with the reader or the details that go into the act, rather than for the overall act itself or the after-the-fact consequences. Plays may stir up passions that lead to confessions, poems can aid in romance, theories can bring about new forms of government, and medical textbooks may provide information that will save lives; nonetheless, the *Wakefield Mystery Plays*, Donne's *Poems*, *The Communist Manifesto* and *Diseases of the Liver* remain as complexes of prompts for cognitive and affective activity – and when successful have multiple and complex effects on our beliefs, understanding and perception.

Yet even though multiplicity of action remains in these texts, attribution of genre still helps to limit the domain and focus the character of the multiplicities offered by, or to be read out of, the text – that is, genre recognition usually limits interpretive flexibility. Genres that must be constantly reread to have continuing force, although they encompass all the traditional literary genres (which was the first concern of genre theorists) as well as many theoretical and informational genres, present special problems that extend beyond the scope of this chapter and I will exclude them from further consideration here. I do wish to point out, however, that this distinction between reducible and non-reducible genres may provide a fundamental puzzle for genre theory to address. It is also interesting to note that, at first pass, such non-reducible genres seem to fall primarily into Searle's classes of assertives and expressives. Nonetheless, many assertive and expressive texts can be reduced to a dominant primary force when enacted within defining typifications.

Directive to Declarative: Transforming Application to Patent

To return now to the consideration of patent applications and grants as documents having single recognizable overriding illocutionary force, let us examine some of the conditions that must be met by a successful application and how the various parts or features of the text may be related to that success.

To obtain a patent you must have an idea for an object or process. This object or process must be useful. It must be novel. You must have invented it. Thus all these items must be asserted in the specification. As we have seen in Edison's time, the text of the patent opens with an identification of the inventor and the assertion of invention which is new and useful. A description of the invention follows, supported by an illustration. The object need not be working or in manufacture or profitable in the marketplace. Indeed patents are obtained early in the process before working prototypes, investments in manufacture, or marketing efforts; in the US system the patent is usually a precondition for substantial investment and publicity – a kind of insurance policy that you own the idea, will get the rewards from the investment, and do not have to worry about others finding out and competing with you in the market. However, since you do not yet have the patent, the patent requiring approval, you must cast the application in the form of a petitionary letter, closing with some petitionary language like 'I claim as new and wish to secure by letters patent. . .' This petitionary format would be further framed by a cover letter, a standard form of which is given in the *Scientific American Reference Book* of 1881:

> To the Commissioner of Patents:
> Your Petitioner, a resident of xxxx, xxxx, prays that letters-patent be granted to him (*sic*) for the invention set forth in the annexed specification.
> > signed

These petitionary features clearly identify that the person intends the document as a request, that the petitioner intends the receiver to understand this as a request, that the petitioner desires the receiver do what is requested, that the text is communicated to the receiver who is capable of interpreting the text, that the petitioner believes that the person receiving the request (the Commissioner of Patents) is able to grant such a request, that the request is for something that the receiver would not already have done in the normal course of affairs, and all the similar social and psychological conditions that must be met for a request to be granted, of the sort that Searle spells out for the act of promising (1969: 57–61, 66). Within the particular regulated and typified context of the legal system, a request can become not only recognizable, but compulsorily must be taken as such by certain people structurally employed to receive requests.

The nature of the request, however, is special, a product of the particular system of which these texts are part. The request is that the receiver declare that your representation of an object or process be considered a patent. That is, the petitioner must assert that his or her idea meets the criteria of a patent so that the receiver will then declare the representation to be a patent protecting the idea. Therefore we must look into the propositions or representations embodied in the patent.

Reference and Predication Acts in the Patent Application

Searle points out that every speech act has a propositional content, and that proposition consists of acts of reference and acts of predication. This observation, which attempts to recover general truth criteria for statements within a situational and action oriented analysis of language, may well be faulted in its attempt to hold all discourse accountable to the language practices of a small group of contemporary philosophers, rather than to consider the complexity of representation making and use in the infinite variety of circumstances and interpretive procedures through which it is enacted. Nonetheless, the observation is useful when applied and given a specific interpretation in relation to a regularized discourse such as patents which is embedded within a set of referential practices, enforced both by inspection and by application of those representations to the world. That is, particular inspection procedures invoked at various points in the process hold the text accountable to certain kinds of states of affairs outside the text and then certain new states of affairs in the world beyond the text are established by application of textual definitions. Moreover, the referential accountability is held tighter when the text concerns itself with only a limited set of states of affairs, when the text is expressed so as to conform with general assumptions about the way things are outside the text, and when the inspection of states of affairs produces certain representations that can be directly correlated with the textual representations. To apply this most simply with respect to patents, patents describe certain things in specialized ways, and the truth of these descriptions is tested and contestable through well defined procedures. Thus within the patent system there is a complex apparatus supporting the Searlean propositional act, giving it a specific interpretation, consequentiality and procedural mechanism for validation enforced through bureaucratic institutional rules, practices and procedures.

On one level, the act of reference of the application is to the commissioner declaring a patent and the predication is that the commissioner will do it. That would be the standard propositional content of a request. However, the commissioner's declaration is based on an evaluation (to be performed by a patent examiner) of the object or process represented in the specification and the claims predicated of that object or process. Thus the key propositions refer to the item for which patent status is sought. Because there is an examination process done by the receiver that extends beyond the representation created by the petitioner, we must consider the propositional acts in two stages – as represented and as received, and what conditions must be met in each instance for success of the patent application.

The patent refers to the self, the act of invention and the object or process which represents the invention. Thus the patent opens with the identification of the applicant, a representation of the act of invention, and details of the object. The largest part of the patent is given over to the representation of the object in the form of illustrations, description of the parts of the object in relation to the illustrations, and a description of its operation, use, and/or construction. From the point of view of the writer, these representations rely on the writer indeed believing that these represent himself or herself, his or her actions in inventing, and most importantly the object or process he or she has conceived. The inventor need not have brought this idea to working perfection, so the reference is to an imaginative construction that the inventor is in the process of bringing into physical realization. These representations share information about the idea seeking patent status not only with the patent examiner for the purposes of evaluation, but (after the patent is granted) with others, allowing them to use the idea after the period of protection.

The propositional act, however, also consists of predications as well as of reference. It is not enough to represent yourself as having invented or conceived of the object, but you must also claim that the object is new, it is useful, and it instantiates some particular forms of useful novelty. Thus the patent of the 1870s typically had some such language near the beginning as appears in patent number 98, 469:

> This invention relates to certain improvements in chandeliers designed for use in public and private apartments.

> The object of this invention is to obtain a chandelier, which will cause the light emitted from its jets to be more generally diffused throughout the apartment than hitherto, and at the same time...and the means by which this object is accomplished, are –
>
> First, by the use of two or more burner-rings specially arranged in relation to a series of reflectors...

Then the patent closes with a specification of the claim:

> I do not claim, broadly, or irrespective of the ring or hoop j, the double reflector...
>
> I do claim as new, and desire to secure by Letters Patent –
>
> 1 The burner rings B C, two or more, having different diameters, and placed one above the other...

From Speaker's Sincere Statement to Examiner's Approval

The inventor in making a patent application represents himself or herself, therefore, as having of a certain date the idea for a particular kind of device or process, that he or she believes this idea is workable and useful, and that it is an improvement of a substantial kind and therefore is an invention; and that moreover the novel improvement can be characterized within specific claims. The applicant may always be in bad faith concerning any of these representations, but in forwarding the application the inventor must present himself or herself as sincere in these representations. It is up to the patent examiner to evaluate these representations as accurate and inaccurate, and therefore give public, legal approval to the validity of these representations, turning the individual's belief about his or her ideas into a form of public certification and knowledge.

The procedures for evaluation, whereby illocutionary force (embodying intent to obtain a patent) is converted to a state of belief on the examiner's part that will legally compel the desired perlocutionary effect (of actual issuance of that patent), however, are quite specific and limited and only attend to certain aspects of the representations of the application. The inventor's representation of name and geographical location are accepted on the oath of the inventor. The date of filing is a matter of record of receipt and a matter again of oath of signing. There is no procedure for determining whether the idea is workable, beyond obvious violations of physical laws (so that perpetual motion machines are not patented); the workability is left to the future of the product development. Indeed, if the idea is unworkable the patent will be of no financial value and will be abandoned, making the patent monopoly moot and insignificant.

This is an important point. The patent is a monopoly only of a potential. The reference is only to an idea, a projection of a future product. The patent is of no meaning or value if that potential does not become realized or is not realizable. The patent examiner has no way of knowing and no obligation to determine the future prospects of this idea. Similarly the question of the usefulness of the patent is left unexamined, because that is left to the marketplace. Since the patent monopoly will be moot if no one wishes to use or purchase the patent, there is no reason to examine the usefulness - nor is there any prior-to-the-fact way of determining it.

Since we are not dealing with actual already-produced objects the representation is only of an idea. The idea itself is embodied in the patent description, so that there is no further examination of whether there is an idea here or whether this is the idea the inventor had. This situation provides a loophole that left open the possibility of submitting defective or incomplete representations of the object to stymie competitors, because the examiner would have no way of knowing the completeness of the idea. This is also the loophole that tempted the possibility of emendation and reissue of corrected patents, under the notion that the inventor actually had the correct or full idea, but the representation on paper was not fully clear or accurate. The only usual rejection or evaluation of patents on the description of the idea is on the grounds of lack of clarity or specificity, that is, that it remains vague as to what the patent-seeking idea is.

The forms of examination in patent office practice are actually only intertextual. The patent descriptions and claims are compared to the file of existing patents and to other representations of the current state of the art, such as textbooks and encyclopedias. Thus only the novelty of the claim is examined, leaving agnostic even the question of whether this novelty is an improvement (for improvement is equivalent to the usefulness of the novelty). The most sensitive item for novelty is the claim - specifically how broad it can be given the object or process described in the application and given the history of prior claims. This claim, however, in terms of ownership is precisely the most crucial matter, for it will define the extent of the rights that the inventor will own as a result of the issuance of the patent.

Intentions and Intersubjectivity

The intentions to obtain a patent monopoly require the fulfillment of the genre of application through meeting in appropriate textual form (primarily of a representational kind) the success conditions of that speech act of request for a status. That is, the inventor has to represent the idea as patentable. The actual grant of the patent requires the intention of the examiner to fulfil his or her duty by applying appropriate examination procedures to determine the success of these representations of the idea as meeting the criteria of patentability. Only certain aspects of the representation come under systematic scrutiny, however, and even that is a kind of scrutiny that is contrary to the kind of scrutiny by which the patent is conceived (except of course that the inventor and surrogates – patent agent and/or attorney – try to anticipate the examination procedure by patent searches and clever formulation of claims). That is, the inventor tries to solve problems and claim turf. The examiner is not concerned about the solution of problems, but examines whether turf is already occupied, and tries to limit turf claimed to those specific novelties instantiated in the idea representation.

What the inventor and examiner do agree on is that what is sought is patent status with its monopoly privileges. If and when the patent is approved, they both have collaborated in the creation of the patent and they both agree on the kind of thing, or status that has been achieved. They have created new value, a new property to be owned – and that property is a licence to attempt to make money from a particular technology. Intentions meet over this status which is created by the speech act of declaration.

Multiple Participation in the Creation of the Patents

Thus we have a clarification of the curious multivocality of the patent text which we discussed earlier; that is, that the patent consists of text written by the applicant before the grant as though the patent were already granted and text by the patent office validating this before-the-fact text as an after-the-fact accomplishment. There is a collaboration and most obvious heteroglossia in the text. And there is a conflation of two contiguous speech acts of directive and declarative into a new act of assertive. That is, when we read patents as made available in the archives, we read them as informational – that x patent exists, that y idea counts as an invention, and that it was invented by person z at time t.

This creation of the status of invention (and inventor, as the person to own the patent and receive the benefit of the patent) has a curious historical effect in that it reinforces the folk belief that inventions are discrete acts occurring at discrete times by discrete people. The history and sociology of technology have been trying to disabuse us from this belief in heroic isolated individuals and isolated eureka moments creating true and unanticipated novelty. Most detailed examinations of cases and experiences of people involved in the creation of novelties indicate a much murkier, more fluid and interactive situation among multiple actors and multiple ideas. Nonetheless, the legal framework, because it must assign ownership of discrete ideas to discrete individuals based on priority, requires that these discrete items be declared as a result of the patent process. Having created and assigned discrete ownership of discrete property, the law then prepares the individual to take that value into other discourse circulation systems within which property provides an important counter or playing chip, such as the financial or industrial worlds. Thus, having a patent, Edison or any other inventor can begin to negotiate with investors to back the development of a product or with corporations to produce or licence or purchase the patent.[4]

Indeed much of the work of legal procedures is to declare that some murky real world event has a certain technical legal status, so that it can then have standing in the technical symbolic procedures of law and regulation. The legal proceedings when finished will then be consequential for other spheres of endeavour in which one participates. Thus court proceedings serve to define a sequence of events leading up to an exchange of physical violence as a case of third-degree assault committed by *a* upon *b*, so as to distribute legal blame, legal punishment and financial liability, with consequences for one's residence and one's financial standing. Similarly, zoning laws define different classes of land and zoning boards become sites of contention over how a particular parcel should be labelled and therefore how it can be used. Since law and government are primarily realms of symbolic exchange following special communicative and adjudicative rules, all events that come under the purview of law and regulation must be translated into that realm and assigned values, rights and statuses – the legal consequences of which in turn become translated back into other kinds of activities.

Legal Systems and Systems of Genres

Of course, legal activity entails far more than a single document or even just a small cluster of documents. Every court ruling requires cartons of documents and statements. Every law requires volumes of proceedings, negotiations, letters, studies. Every patent requires a thick file of correspondence, forms, documents, appeals and possibly court judgments with all the documents and texts that are part of that. These documents are all in well defined genres which are closely related to each other. Each letter to the Commissioner of Patents is responded to by a potentially limited range of responses in well defined generic forms. Each court proceeding is constituted out of a limited range of utterance types that must be in appropriate form at the appropriate time. When you have a serious legal matter you must hire a lawyer not so much to tell your story as to know the sequence and timing of various utterances, to help you navigate the welter of genres – to file the right papers at the right time, to object at a particular moment, to know when you are wasting your breath – that is to know the legal moves or manoeuvres. In turn, the moves of others, whether examiners, judges, legislators or opponents in a court case can be met with only a limited number of appropriate moves by yourself. Moreover, each of these moves or acts or generic utterances has identifiable conditions of success, so an objection or application or appeal can be ruled on (accepted or rejected) by the appropriate official.

What we have, in essence, is a complex web of interrelated genres where each participant makes a recognizable act or move in some recognizable genre, which then may be followed by a certain range of appropriate generic responses by others. The sequence of generic responses results at particular junctures in certain laws, rulings, declarations, etc. that offer stabilized meanings that can then be used to assign values, punishments, obligations, etc. with impact on extra-legal life. Unless these rulings, laws, etc. are challenged in some legally appropriate way, the judgments will stand.

The challenge to the judgment, if it comes, is likely to come in a form that questions whether some aspect of the performance of the speech act of the judgment does not meet a condition of success. Thus a law may be challenged as unconstitutional, for one of the conditions of success is that all laws of the land must be in conformity with the supreme law of the land. A deed may be challenged if clear title to the land has not been ascertained through the records of ownership. A patent may be challenged on the grounds that the claim is improperly formed, that the representation of the inventor is inaccurate, that the presumptive novelty was not novel, but rather essentially instantiated in earlier patents, that fraud was involved in the original application, etc. That is, the challenge attempts to undo the speech act which has resulted in the declaration.

Patent litigation is a highly specialized discourse domain with specific moves and specific rules governing the success of those moves. The maintenance of a valuable patent (remembering that low value patents are of interest to few and certainly not to the court) requires navigating one's way through all the challenging discourses to maintain the integrity of the patent declaration. In the wake of the extensive litigation over patents, not only have the court procedures become typified, but new rules have been adopted to clarify procedures and rule out certain forms of inappropriate challenges, thereby focusing the discourse even further.

In late twentieth-century United States, the speech/symbolic acts that constitute participation in the legal system (and particularly the subculture of patent law) are highly regularized and regulated, but these acts are also recreated every time they are re-enacted within our current understandings. Lawyers never stop looking for new angles, new strategies, new interventions that transform the acceptable moves to unexpected outcomes, that cut out opposing moves by the other side and open pathways to more favourable lines of actions. Thus the participations that constitute legal practice continue to evolve. Yet every potential lawyer, in order to play the game, must learn the forms of currently available moves through extensive education and apprenticeship activities. The United States has a legal system that is relatively stable, but not ossified because it only exists in its constantly recreated strategically motivated instantiations. This is, of course, what Giddens's (1984) concept of structuration is all about.

Systems of Genre

To understand the implications of this picture of legal participation through generic forms for the theory of genre, I would like to introduce the notion of *systems of genre*. These are interrelated genres that interact with each other in specific settings.

Only a limited range of genres may appropriately follow upon another in particular settings, because the success conditions of the actions of each require various states of affairs to exist. That is, a patent may not be issued unless there is an application. An infringement complaint cannot be filed unless there is a valid patent. An affidavit about the events in a laboratory on a certain date will not be sworn unless a challenge to the patent is filed. The intervention of each of the follow-up genres with its attendant macro-speech act, if successful, will have consequences for other genres and speech acts to follow.

In domains structured more loosely than the law, the sequencing and consequences of actions may be harder to discern, nor may the illocutionary force–perlocutionary effect link be compulsive, therefore allowing a wider array of consequent actions. Nonetheless, the nature of activities may be such as to establish a limited set of genres and acts that may appropriately follow in each situation. So handouts in college classes describing written assignments are typically followed by questions and answers about the constraints of assignments, advisable procedures and the appropriateness of various ideas for projected papers. Then if all goes according to plan student papers, following the generic constraints established by the handout, are handed in. Then teacher marginalia is returned, concluding in some evaluation encapsulated in a grade. We usually hope that settles the matter, but students will then turn up at our offices with certain genres of arguments and hard luck stories, some of which we might be susceptible to, but others which we rule as ineligible. Or job ads are followed by letters of application, which are in turn followed by phone calls setting up interviews, and so on.

In each case to achieve our ends we must successfully hold up our ends of the generic exchanges. That is we must successfully identify the generic utterance appropriate for our needs at each point and successfully fulfil the conditions that will constitute the perfected act. If we can't write the job letter, or fill out the necessary forms, or appear intelligent and cooperative at the interview; if we can't make a well-defined assignment, or answer student questions satisfactorily, or produce grades that we can then justify upon challenge, we get into various kinds of trouble.

This notion of systems of genres extends the concept of genre set first presented in Devitt's analysis of tax accountants' work (1991). The genre set represents the full range of kinds of texts tax accountants must produce in the course of their work. These generic texts have highly patterned relationships with the texts of others. Tax accountants produce only a limited number of kinds of documents which are related, but distinct. An opinion letter to a client is distinct from a response letter to a client and distinct from a letter to the taxing authorities, even though they all have the same subject matter and are framed within the tax code and the specifics of the client's tax situation. By extension we may say that for each status that exists in the world – teacher, police officer, hod carrier, philosopher – there are only a limited number of genres in which each needs to perform to carry out the full range of that status.

The genre set represents, however, only the work of one side of a multiple person interaction. That is, the tax accountants' letters usually refer to the tax code, the rulings of the tax department in this case, the client's information and interests, and these references are usually presented in highly anticipatable ways appropriate to the genre of the letter, but the genre set is only the tax accountant's participations, as intertextually linked to the participations of the other parties. The system of genres would be the full set of genres that instantiate the participation of all the parties – that is the full file of letters from and to the client, from and to the government, from and to the accountant. This would be the full interaction, the full event, the set of social relations as it has been enacted. It embodies the full history of speech events as intertextual occurrences, but attending to the way that all the intertext is instantiated in generic form establishing the current act in relation to prior acts.

Generic Rhetoric

By identifying the current text to be produced as a speech act in generic form, and thus requiring the fulfillment of certain attendant felicity conditions or conditions of success, we give a new kind of precision to rhetorical aims and means as we step outside the traditional rhetorical realms of political and forensic oratory. Moreover, in considering generic speech acts in structured relation to prior generic speech acts that have been successfully performed (or that we wish to treat as successful, or the success of which we wish to challenge, or the failure of which we wish to capitalize upon, etc.) we give a new precision to the notion of rhetorical situation. By considering the ways in which generic utterances open up pathways to certain consequent speech acts and close off other pathways, we give a new precision to the concept of *kairos*, or timeliness. By gaining a grasp of how entire discursive systems operate through generic turns, we can locate ourselves, our potential speech acts and the criteria our utterances should seek to meet; we can start to understand what we can achieve rhetorically at any moment, and what we cannot, and how. By identifying how representations realized within speech acts are interactive with and accountable to other representations within the generic system and states of affairs that extend beyond discourse but drawn into the discourse at various junctures in the system of generic activity, we can see how our discursive activity is bound to the symbolic and non-symbolic environment.

Through an understanding of the genres available to us at any time we can understand the roles and relationships open to us. An understanding of generic decorum will let us know whether it is ours to ask or answer, to argue or clarify, to declare or request. We can find system in speech acts without reducing them to a system and without excluding evolution, novelty, and the multiplicity of human life. We can follow Austin's cautions not to believe too much our simplifying, investigatory abstractions and to look to local circumstances for the meaning of acts. We can avoid Searle's attempt to bind the particulars of action to general principles from which the particularities have been abstracted out and in which the acts have been turned to a logical calculus, while still learning from Searle how rigorous systems of action may be realized.

This understanding of the way genres structure social relations could be highly conservative in that decorum would urge repeating only the familiar, reproducing old dramas, prompting only replayings of the old songs at the familiar moments.

It can also give us the understanding to lead old hopes and expectations down familiar-seeming garden paths, but that lead to new places. Only by uncovering the pathways that guide our lives in certain directions can we begin to identify the possibilities for new turns and the consequences of taking those turns. When we are put on the spot, we must act, and in acting we must act generically if others are to understand our act and accept it as valid. Without a shared sense of genre others would not know what kind of thing we were doing. And life is mysterious enough already.

Acknowledgement

I would like to thank all the participants in the Rethinking Genre conference for their discussion of this paper, and particularly John Dixon for his penetrating critique of my use of Searle in an earlier version of this paper. I would also like to thank Charles Goodwin and the students in my fall 1992 Language Theory course for helping me think through the puzzle John handed me.

Notes

1 For outlines of the history and operations of the patent system in Britain and the US see Gomme (1946), Fox (1977), Vaughan (1956), Bugbee (1967), Jones (1971), Davenport (1979), Federico (1982), and MacLeod (1988). See also various articles by Federico in the *Journal of the Patent Office Society*, and the special issue of *Technology and Culture* devoted to patents (**32**(4), October 1991). A comprehensive bibliography on patents appears in Weil and Snapper (1989).

2 A further feature of the patent system at that time, the reissuance of patents to correct defects, created other opportunities to redefine the object being patented and the scope of the claim. Abuse arising from this opportunity to readjust patents on the basis of later knowledge about competition, workability of ideas, further developments of the product and marketplace considerations, led to the removal of the reissue option in the middle of the nineteenth century.

3 These represent the five general kinds of speech acts Searle recognizes (1979: Ch. 1). For discussions of speech acts within the law see Kuzon (1986) and Bowers (1989).

4 One can even suggest that in creating property (as all property is created by legal identification) our legal system serves to create the primary value of our society which allows the continuation of the life of society built on those values. In a Durkheimian sense we can see this as a sacred and sacralizing activity.

References

Austin, J. L. (1962) *How to Do Things with Words*, Oxford: Oxford University Press.

Bazerman, C. (1988) *Shaping Written Knowledge*, Madison, WI: University of Wisconsin Press.

Bowers, F. (1989) *Linguistic Aspects of Legislative Expression*, Vancouver: University of British Columbia Press.

Bugbee, B. (1967) *Genesis of American Patent and Copyright Law*, Washington, DC: Public Affairs Press.

DAVENPORT, N. (1979) *The United Kingdom Patent System*, London: Kenneth Mason.

DEVITT, A. (1991) 'Intertextuality in Tax Accounting', in BAZERMAN, C. and PARADIS, J. (eds) *Textual Dynamics of the Professions*, Madison, WI: University of Wisconsin Press.

FEDERICO, P. J. (1982) 'Bibliography of Patent Law Articles', *Journal of the Patent Office Society*, **64**, January, pp. 9–11.

FOX, H. G. (1947) *Monopolies and Patents*, Toronto: University of Toronto Press.

GIDDENS, A. (1984) *The Constitution of Society*, Berkeley, CA: University of California Press.

GOMME, A. (1946) *Patents of Invention*, London: Longmans Green and Company.

HOLMES, O. W. (1881) *The Common Law*, Boston, MA: Little, Brown, and Company.

JONES, S. (1971) *The Patent Office*, New York: Praeger.

KURZON, D. (1986) *It is Hereby Performed...: Explorations in Legal Speech Acts*, Amsterdam: John Benjamins.

LATOUR, B. (1988) *Science in Action*, Cambridge, MA: Harvard University Press.

MACLEOD, C. (1988) *Inventing the Industrial Revolution: The English Patent System, 1660–1800*, Cambridge: Cambridge University Press.

MILLER, C. (1984) 'Genre as Social Action', *Quarterly Journal of Speech*, **70**, pp. 151–76.

SCIENTIFIC AMERICAN (1881) *Scientific American Reference Book*, New York: Munn and Company.

SEARLE, J. (1969) *Speech Acts*, Cambridge: Cambridge University Press.

SEARLE, J. (1979) *Expression and Meaning*, Cambridge: Cambridge University Press.

SEARLE, J. (1984) *Intentions*, Cambridge: Cambridge University Press.

SEARLE, J., KIEFER, F. and BIERWISCH, M. (eds) (1980) *Speech Act Theory and Pragmatics*, Dordrecht: Reidel.

SWALES, J. (1990) *Genre Analysis*, Cambridge: Cambridge University Press.

VAUGHAN, F. W. (1956) *The United States Patent System*, Norman, OK: University of Oklahoma Press.

WEIL, V. and SNAPPER, J. (1989) *Owning Scientific and Technical Information*, New Brunswick, NJ: Rutgers University Press.

Part III
Research into Public and Professional Genres

Chapter 6

The Lab vs. the Clinic:
Sites of Competing Genres

Catherine F. Schryer

Voices

Dr W (pathologist): Personally I dread it when a clinician dumps a manuscript on my desk for my comments. I know it's going to be badly written.

Dr B (biomedical science); The clinicians are not scientists. They are practitioners. They feel threatened by a mind set that is geared towards research. There are virtually no people in the clinics with advanced degrees. Such purely applied people can only write reviews. They lack the sort of curiosity needed for research.

Dr K (clinician): The traditional way, IMRDS [Introduction, Methods, Results, Discussion, and Summary], can lead to boredom, and it suggests that there is a finite amount of information which can be memorized by rote memory. But we're trying to emphasize problem solving – the ability to dig out data and then transfer towards plans.

G (first year student): On the one side is the faculty and on the other side are the clinicians. The faculty deal with basic science and clinicians with practical information. Both views are important, but the practical is more important. When we graduate we are going to have to trade and barter with information, and we will benefit from the practical experience they provide.

Dr F (biomedical science); The writing in the clinic is different. In the basic sciences we have a different mandate. We're interested in long term proposals and ongoing research problems. It is exactly the opposite in the clinics. They have to solve problems instantly.

The above voices, taken from a study of literacy[1] at a veterinary school (Schryer 1989) were not located in the same time and space. Yet these different voices articulate a conversation that haunts professions such as medicine and engineering that attempt to unite research and practice. As this constructed conversation reveals, researchers and practitioners often have deeply shared prejudices about each other's activities. Schön (1983), a thoughtful observer of professional education, identified a dominant epistemology of practice that he called 'technical rationality' (p. 21) as the source of this division. Technical rationality is the belief that 'professional activity consists in instrumental problem solving made rigorous by the application of scientific theory and technique' (p. 21). In Schön's view, the hierarchy involved in this model, the fact that scientific theory and technique are perceived as more 'rigorous' than 'instrumental problem solving', has led to a serious devaluation of practitioners' skills and abilities. Practitioners' artistry, the ability of some expert practitioners to address complex, 'messy' (p. 42) problems, is being ignored, Schön suggests. Yet an understanding of this artistry is clearly needed to address the complicated problems that such professions as engineering, medicine, social work and teaching actually encounter. Schön calls for a practitioner-oriented model of education that would require practitioners to become more reflective of their own activities. Practitioner artistry is often tacit, Schön (1987) argues. By becoming aware of the strategies and tactics that actually work, practitioners will improve their own performance, pass on their skills to neophyte practitioners, and include their clients or patients in the problem solving process.

Schön's project is humane and liberating, but this chapter contends that his enterprise is more difficult than he might imagine. The worlds of the lab and clinic (research and practice) have been in conflict for several hundred years. This tension is expressed in their genres, their recurrent ways of representing their problem solving and knowledge construction. This chapter will focus on two central genres characteristic of research and practice in a medical, specifically a veterinary medical, context: the experimental article, expressed as Introduction, Methods, Results, Discussion and Summary (IMRDS), and the medical record keeping system, the Problem Oriented Veterinary Medical Record (POVMR). These genres reflect and help to maintain a research–practice division characteristic of disciplines like medicine. Furthermore, these genres exist in a hierarchy in which one genre, IMRDS, is more highly valued than the other. Thus, one of the forces continuing to keep researchers and practitioners apart is their information producing and recording systems, their central genres. In my view, researchers in professional writing and writing instructors associated with professional programs such as applied health, engineering or computer science need to be aware of the complex, competing values associated with different writing practices – especially those related to competing genres.

Methods

Ironically, perhaps, much of the original data for this chapter is derived from a research project, an ethnographic study of literacy at a veterinary school (Schryer 1989). Prior to the study, members of the curriculum committee had called me in as consultant. They wanted to know if they had a problem with literacy among their students. In response, my essential questions to them were

1 what did literacy mean in their professional context;
2 were students being taught these characteristic ways of speaking, writing, reading and listening; and
3 was this literacy appropriate or sufficient for their future professional needs?

The project, reflecting the ethnographic methods of Heath (1983) and Fetterman (1984) and literacy researchers such as Levine (1986) and Street (1984), was conducted between January and June of 1988 and consisted of 80 interviews with students, faculty and practitioners; over 200 hours of participant observation in classrooms, labs and clinics; ten reader protocols of faculty evaluating student papers; extensive document collection; and a review of medical and veterinary literature on education. Data (fieldnotes, interview transcripts and documents) were analysed using Glaser and Strauss's (1967) grounded theory techniques. I located a range of categories that seemed relevant and then moved the data (specific comments and documents, for example) into appropriate categories. It was during this process that I became aware of the tensions existing between researchers and clinicians/practitioners[2] and the relationship of discursive practices to each group.

Theory

In an effort to explain this relationship between groups and their discursive practices I turned to genre theory and developed the following definition (Schryer 1993). The concept of genre can help researchers describe a 'stabilized-for-now or stabilized-enough site of social and ideological action' (p. 200). This definition reflects my agreement with Miller (1984; revised version Chapter 2, this volume) who defines genre as 'recurrent, significant action' (p. 165). Each of these three terms – recurrent, significant and action – reflect key insights. As a recurrent phenomenon, a genre represents a series of texts sharing features at the levels of content, form and style. These discursive practices shape their users while at the same time their users affect the genre. This notion of recurrence also involves the social actors who construct the genre. Only those involved can interpret a situation and any possible responses as recurrent and significant. Consequently, genre researchers must consult the users of discursive practices to see if these practices are both recurrent and significant. Most importantly, Miller, and Bazerman (1988), observe that rhetorical genres are forms of social action. A genre coordinates work – from the simplest action of constructing a shopping list to the complex activity involved in conducting scientific research.

Bakhtin (1981) acknowledges that genres are not only sites of social action – they are also sites of ideological action. As Bakhtin makes clear, these discourse structures are imbued with 'concrete value judgments'. He suggests, 'They knit together with specific objects and with the belief systems of certain genres of expression and points of view peculiar to particular professions' (p. 289). Genres express deeply held values or, to echo Williams (1983), the tacit sets of shared values that constitute common sense for particular groups (p. 38).

Bakhtin's (1986) most important contribution, however, to this reconceptualization of genre is his paradoxical observation that genres are sites of both stability and instability. Speech genres are in Bakhtin's term 'utterances', and the boundaries of an utterance are determined by a *'change of speaking subjects'* (p. 71, original emphasis). Consequently, built into his notion of genre is a sense of 'addressivity' or attitude to the audience. This audience has a rich repertoire of utterances at its disposal. These genres or utterances are in a dialectric with each other and thus constantly influencing and changing each other. Bakhtin pointed out, for example, that both secondary and primary speech genres exist (p. 62). Secondary genres, such as the novel or research paper, are in a constant process of subsuming more primary genres such as letters or lists. From Bakhtin's perspective even the most monologic and thus ideological genres such as scientific articles or medical records are sites of struggle between the centripetal and centrifugal forces within language.

In this chapter, then, genres are viewed as stabilized-for-now or stabilized-enough sites of social and ideological action. This definition builds in a sense of genres as simultaneously diachronic and synchronic. All genres have a complex set of relations with past texts and with other present texts: genres come from somewhere and are transforming into something else. Because they exist before their users, genres shape their users, yet users and their discourse communities constantly remake and reshape them. Most importantly, genres are inherently ideological; they embody the unexamined or tacit way of performing some social action. Hence they can represent the ways that a dominant élite does things. This theoretical perspective allows researchers to ask the following kinds of questions: Where does this genre come from? What are the stabilizing (recurrent conventions and structures) features that characterize these texts? What are the destabilizing features? What are the values and beliefs instantiated within a set of practices? Who can or cannot use this genre? How does this genre affect its users?

History – The Larger Context

There is no doubt that divisions between research and practice extend well beyond the bounds of the college I studied. In *Educating the Reflective Practitioner*, Schön (1987) explores the normative curriculum that governs professions such as medicine which insist that 'instrumental problem solving is grounded in systematic, preferably scientific knowledge' (p. 8). Such a curriculum implies the following hierarchy of knowledge:

> basic science,
> applied science,
> technical skills of day-to-day practice (p. 9).

Within even such minor (according to Schön) professions as social work and education, proximity to research, basic science or the making of theoretical, propositional knowledge brings both prestige and power. Between professions, those disciplines which present themselves as 'rigorous practitioners of a science-based knowledge' (p. 9) generally have a higher status. Schön and others interested in professional education are radically questioning this model of education. They ask whether 'the prevailing concepts of professional education ever yield a curriculum adequate to the complex, unstable, uncertain and conflictual worlds of practice' (p. 12). They point to the gaps existing between the professional schools and the workplace, between research and practice. Schön advocates the development of a 'reflective practicum' (p. 18), a practicum aimed at helping students 'acquire the kinds of artistry essential to competence in the indeterminate zones of practice' (p. 18).

Latour reminds us that disciplines like medicine have been enacting this scene of struggle between research and practice for over a hundred years and that research has not always dominated practice. In *The Pasteurization of France* (1988), Latour recreates the negotiations and transformations which resulted in the recognition of the microbe and in the establishment of the lab as an important site of knowledge production. Hygienists in the late 1800s immediately acknowledged the relevance of Louis Pasteur's laboratory research, but medical practitioners were slow to accept his findings. Pasteurian researchers viewed humankind as under constant attack by virtually invisible entities and advocated mass inoculation plans as well as regimented schemes to clean sewers, waterways, and the lifestyles of all social classes. Practitioners, however, viewed their patients as individual unities, not as collectivities. As Latour suggests, practitioners were 'translators not of public health but of a multitude of doctor–patient relationships' (p. 118). Other social factors also prevented medical doctors from appropriating the new technology. During the 1890s, medical practitioners in France were struggling to carve a 'space where it was possible to treat people for money' (p. 119). The forces opposing them included

> pharmacists who prescribed drugs...the sisters of charity who, out of religious zeal, took the bread from the mouths of young physicians...the health societies which persisted in teaching the public how to bind up wounds...(Latour 1988: 118–9)

The battle between research and practice was fought out in the research and practice journals, the *Revue Scientifique* and the *Concours Médical*. The Pasteurian agenda was clear. Based on the Pasteurian's control of colonized microbes and the subsequent development of vaccines, they wanted to redefine pathology so that disease could be prevented instead of simply cured. They wanted physicians to denounce their contagious patients and to become delegated agents of public health rather than confidants of individual patients. In the end, physicians agreed to this new agenda but only after several internal (to the profession) and external (societal) deals were struck. To satisfy the physicians, the Pasteurians developed serums, particularly for diphtheria, which could be used after a patient had been diagnosed. Thus doctors could retain their control over curing diseases. Also physicians began appropriating those aspects of Pasteurian research which substantiated their own social status. In essence, they agreed to become agents of the state and stamp out parasites as long as the state rid them of the parasites who were sucking their blood: 'the pharmacists, the charlatans, the nuns, and so forth' (p. 126).

The belief structures and ideologies of this elemental battle between research and practice were enacted in a pivotal article written by Dr Jeanne in *Concours Médical* in 1958. He laments that:

> The ardor and skill of the champion of our old clinical methods were wasted, for the adversary advancing against him was not a theoretician, one of those dreamers who create a fashion...but it was a scientist, it was the experimental method, it was progress...
>
> Surgery and hygiene have been conquered: the old medicine is no longer able to fight alone for the terrain. Diagnosis, that primordial element of our art, will soon no longer be able to do without the microscope, bacteriological or chemical analysis...in a word everything that may give our clinical judgments absolutely precise data. (quoted in Latour 1988: 130)

Jeanne advised his contemporaries to return to the lecture halls and laboratories or read the medical journals if they wished to compete with newly trained, more scientific physicians. As Latour makes clear, this translation or rapprochement of research results into practice concerns was tenuous at best and not always in the practitioner's best interests. The language of battle, war and victory that characterized Dr Jeanne's discourse was no accident. Neither is it an accident that a century later Schön questions the common-sense belief or ideology that describes the world of research as 'rigorous' and 'systematic' while practitioners work in a 'complex' 'conflictual' world requiring 'artistry'.

History – The Local Context

The divisive belief structure that both Schön and Latour identify was at work in the college that I studied. It was clearly evident that researchers and clinicians (the group mostly closely associated with practitioners) viewed themselves as distinct groups. Researchers in the biomedical sciences, pathology or immunology had doctorates. To achieve their degrees they worked closely with a senior researcher who supervised both their research and their writing. One researcher who supervised graduate students spoke in detail about her students' papers and the suggestions she provided to make them publishable. As a group, researchers valued doctorates since this research represented their initial contribution to the knowledge or theory development of their disciplines.

This value placed on contributing knowledge to the discipline was echoed in a curious way in an undergraduate ethics course. A panel of speakers representing both researchers and clinicians was addressing the issue of using live animals in experimentation. The one hundred or so undergraduate students in the course were deeply concerned about this issue. In several of their other courses they were learning surgical techniques using live animals, and many found themselves in an ethical dilemma, especially since the previous semester the anaesthetic they had been using in the 'bunny labs' had not worked effectively. The clinicians on the panel understood the concern for a better anaesthetic but not the revulsion at using live animals. Knowing how live animals responded to surgery would prevent future errors in the students' own surgeries, the clinicians argued. The researchers, however, did sympathize. A prominent biomedical researcher told the students 'I am very uneasy about the ethical implications of using animals to add to your own data banks. In research, it is more defensible since you are adding to information banks, not just improving your own expertise.' In other words, it was ethical to 'sacrifice' animals if their deaths led to new knowledge, but not appropriate if their deaths only served to enhance the students' surgical skills.

This belief in the greater value of collective knowledge was also reflected in the teaching strategies of these researchers. They believed strongly that they provided the 'basics', the fundamental knowledge that students needed in order to solve individual clinical problems. These 'basics' included all the fundamental systems of anatomy, biochemistry, physiology, etc. 'Basic' information, of course, was valid, collective knowledge that originally derived from empirical research. Students were expected to memorize these fundamentals. The material itself was often presented through lectures characterized by massive amounts of handouts, overheads and slides. In veterinary medicine in particular this emphasis on the 'basics' is becoming problematic. Veterinary students have traditionally studied every biological entity except humankind. From the students' perspective the effect of this massive inundation of information was 'overwhelmosis'.

The value placed on developing new information was matched by the value placed on the ability to write up and publish such information. It was on this level that many researchers critiqued clinicians and practitioners. One pathologist observed that he would like to see the students more involved in writing, but lamented that students were too influenced by the clinicians, and that clinicians did not research or publish. Another pointed to a clinician-oriented journal and complained that the worst writing appeared in such journals – not only was the writing sloppy, but even worse, the research was derivative. Other commentators were fairer in their assessment. They pointed out that clinicians lacked training in research and writing and more importantly perhaps the time required for such activities.

Of course, the clinicians had a different perspective. Students can memorize 'like stink' the clinician told me, but they are lost in their books, and they cannot solve clinical problems. This individual described herself as a clinician first, then a teacher, then an administrator and finally as a researcher. Her training did not include a dissertation and a doctorate. Rather she had passed a series of board exams for which she had read five years of recent journal articles. She had completed an intense multiple choice exam (five to six hours) and written a series of short reports explaining solutions to medical problems. Her work day was also very different from a researcher's. When she was not teaching, she was in the clinic on call for at least eight to 10 hours and always supervising the actions of a group of four to six students.

Like most clinicians, she lacked the freedom to control her own time. Like other clinicians, she also seemed to prefer ambiguity to certainty. In medical and surgical rounds, students were constantly warned that nothing was black and white and that most rules were only rules of thumb to be adjusted to a specific case. Her teaching techniques were distinct as well. As a third year student described,

> I like her clinical approach. She presents us with cases and says here's a picture of this case. And then she asks us questions. I'm tired of a pure science approach, frustrated with copious scientific material which we have to memorize immediately.

Like many clinicians, however, she may not get her tenure, since she may not publish enough to remain at the college.

This perceived difference between research and practice and the hierarchy at work is nowhere more evident than in a set of definitions found in documents of particular interest to the college. Veterinary colleges across the North American continent are restructuring their programmes in response to recent social and economic changes. While I was at the college, a report on the Purdue plans for reformulating their program was circulated among faculty. Essentially the report advocated educating rather than training new veterinarians. According to the report, '*Education* is the instruction in and cultivation of an understanding of the system of ideas and conviction which are valued by society, including the philosophy and method of science. Education is generalizing, expanding.' On the other hand, '*Training* is the mastery of knowledge and skills by practice and apprenticeship and is aimed at the identification and solution of problems. Training is focused.' The value system at work in these definitions is self-evident. Education means medical research; training means medical practice.

Latour (1987) and Schön's insights as well as events and documents at the college suggest that a set of binary opposition traverses complex professional contexts that attempt to unite research and practice. The list below attempts to summarize these competing interests and values:

Research	*Practice*
Science	Medicine
Information development	Case problem solving
Memorization of facts	Problem or case-oriented teaching
Communalistic	Individualistic
Long term	Short term, immediate
Validity	Ambiguity and complexity
Methods	Skills
Education	Training

It would be simplistic to suggest that all health professions divide simply and easily along these lines. Several faculty members worked in both research and clinical areas. Both researchers and practitioners would also contend that they engage in problem solving, but each group defines problems quite differently. In her study of biomedical researchers, Adams-Smith (1984) quotes her researcher informants as acknowledging that problems are the life-blood of research projects. One of her informants then explained:

> Biomedical research. . . is not a matter of problem-solving. Rather it is the observation of something interesting that does not seem to fit the pattern, followed by the observation of this phenomenon over a period of time, and the recording and explanation of the findings. (pp. 19–20)

In fact, researchers identify and choose to work on particular problems, and they can work towards simplifying and controlling the variables associated with their problem. Practitioners, especially clinicians, must work with the complex, often interrelated problems that a particular case presents. Neither clinicians nor practitioners can choose their problems, and, in fact, the art of practice might exist in actually recognizing the interconnecting problems that characterize a case. This essential difference in task and the socialization process used to prepare students for their careers is deeply embedded within the profession's basic genres.

Competing Genres

The above insights gathered during an ethnographic study of a veterinary college reflect a research–practice division characteristic of many disciplines such as medicine. Commentators such as Donald Schön suggest that some rapprochement is possible to span the growing fault lines between researchers and practitioners. Research gathered during this study, however, indicates that power relations in fields such as veterinary medicine are often expressed through genres related to research or practice. These genres are distinctly polarized in their epistemology, their values, their organizational structure, their purpose and their perceived validity. Depending on key career decisions, students will be deeply socialized into either of these competing traditions located in the lab or the clinic.

A genre choice indicates the nature of the writer's own socialization. In the veterinary college that forms the basis of this study, students training to be practitioners were rarely taught to be producers of research. They were, however, always taught to be consumers of research. On several occasions student-practitioners were referred to as 'data banks' or were directed to file information in their data banks. The only students specifically taught research skills and supervised as to the writing up of their results were graduate students in either the basic sciences or in the clinical areas of the college. However, different research traditions existed for each of these groups – one based on the experimental article (Introduction, Methods, Results, Discussion, Summary or IMRDS) and the other on medical problem solving systems, specifically the Problem Oriented Medical Record (POMR) system. These two systems capture the paradigmatic difference in world view between two traditions, that of the lab and that of the clinic.

Experimental Genre

The IMRDS approach to presenting information is so ubiquitous and pervasive that it is difficult to isolate it and see its history, the social action that it enacts, its inherent values, and epistemology. On the surface IMRDS appears a simple heuristic. The introduction defines the problem (why?); the methods section explains how the problem will be analysed (how?); the results relate what was discovered (what?); the discussion reveals the significance of the results (so what?); and the summary reduces the content found in the above structure into a microcosm again answering why, how, what and so what.

As Bazerman (1988) reminds us, the experimental article has a complex history. From its beginning as narrative accounts of experiments embedded within letters exchanged between experimenters, the research article has evolved into 'a logical and empirical juggernaut, with every step in the reasoning backed up with carefully described experimental experiences precisely related to the formal proposition' (p. 121). In his seminal account of the experimental article Bazerman points out the constructed nature of the rhetorical strategies that provide this sense of inevitable logic and order. For example, he points to Issac Newton's brilliant invention of the second person imperative in the method section (pp. 115–6). As Swales (1990) observes, this tactic turns readers into virtual witnesses (p. 111) compelled to cooperate with the writer in reconstructing the experiment.

Accounts of the purpose or social action that IMRDS enacts exist at various levels. At the college, gradute students in the biomedical sciences were sometimes directed to handbooks such as *A Guide to Scientific Writing* by Lindsay (1984), an animal scientist at the University of Western Australia. From Lindsay's perspective, the article is 'no more and no less than an objective and accurate account of a piece of research' (p. 3). Several research studies (Latour and Woolgar 1979, 1988; Knorr-Cetina 1981; Gilbert and Mulkay 1984) challenge this perspective by documenting the relationship between an article and the research on which it was based. In her study of a large research centre, for example, Knorr-Cetina (1981) observes that the published account was a reversed version of the actual research process. Prelli (1989) agrees that research reports routinely suppress false leads or unsuccessful procedures. He suggests, in fact, that:

> Research articles are thus more persuasive because the articles present an image of determinacy in science and obscure the influences of historical and situational circumstances and possibilities of alternate approaches and judgments. (p. 103)

As Swales recognizes, the research article is in fact a very different genre than the laboratory report (1990: 118). The real task of IMRDS, Swales argues, is to provide 'complexly distanced reconstructions of research activities' (p. 175). Because they are so driven by the need to anticipate audience reactions, these reconstructions are filled with rhetorical strategies at all levels. Bazerman would add that the real task of IMRDS is to provide symbolic representations of the phenomenal world

(1988: 187). These representations are expressions of the need for order and control of the natural world.

This need for order and control is central to the common-sense belief structures or ideologies that pervade much of the empirical research tradition and its genres. In his generative work on scientific ethos, Merton identifies the institutional norms of universalism, communality, disinterestedness, organized scepticism, originality and humility that govern science and facilitate 'the establishment and extension of certified objective knowledge of the physical world' (Prelli 1989: 105). The scientific article with its emphasis on inductive style, a style that Prelli suggests 'implies that claims were found through impartial investigation of phenomena that have independent, objective, and undeniable existence' (p. 103) is the ideological vehicle for such values.

The ideological or common-sense system of beliefs embedded with IMRDS is nowhere more apparent than in its organizational structure, an arrangement which Gross (1990) identifies as epistemological (p. 85). The sequence of introduction, methods, results, and discussion Gross insists is essential to mirror the transition of contingent laboratory events to the necessity of natural processes (p. 89). Introductions work to 'recreate a theoretical world in which the otherwise contingent events of the laboratory will attain their significance as scientific experiments, instantiations of particular natural laws' (p. 90). However, introductions, as Swales observes, must create this theoretical world in relation to other current work and researchers. Introductions, in fact, have to create a research space which accomplishes three tasks or moves:

1 establish the relevance of the research field itself;
2 locate the specific research project in relation to the field; and
3 occupy and defend a particular niche in the field by means of the research project (Swales 1990: 142).

Lindsay also advises neophyte article writers to create space for their research in their introductions. He advises his readers to construct carefully their hypotheses or focal points. Lindsay is clear in his definition of the hypothesis. 'It is not a statement of fact', he announces, 'but a statement which takes us just beyond known facts and anticipates the next logical step in a sequence of facts' (1984: 7). A good hypothesis exists on the cutting edge between the old and the new, past and future fact. It creates new space.

Method sections, because they embody the deeply shared value placed on replication, continue to be obligatory in most scientific disciplines. Yet much research (Knorr-Cetina 1981) suggests that such replication is not really possible. Laboratory skills have become so complex and background knowledge so specialized that methods have become in Swales's terms 'highly abstracted reformulations of final outcomes in which an enormous amount is taken for granted' (1990: 121). In explaining the methods section, Lindsay suggests, the only criterion is that a knowledgeable colleague should be able to repeat procedures. In fact, the art of writing methods sections exists in knowing what one can safely omit. Methods are inherently rhetorical enthymeme structures built on current knowledge and beliefs about procedures. For example, the following methods section taken from a research article in a veterinary journal presumes extensive knowledge of accepted procedures:

> For the clitoral fossa, Culturette swabs (Canlab, Toronto, Ontario) were used; a disposable sterile 'guarded culture instrument' (Kalayjin Industries Inc., Long Beach California) with a protective sheath capped at the tip was used to collect vaginal, cervical, and uterine samples. Swabs were taken by the technique of Higgins *et al.* (p. 11). (Bermudez *et al.* 1987: 520)

Only the initiated would recognize a 'guarded culture instrument' or the Higgins technique.

Deeply enacted in the results section is the attempt to create a 'reader-environment in which the tentative facts can be allowed to "speak for themselves"' (Swales 1990: 121). Lindsay supports this normative position when he advises his reader that only results should appear in the results section. Results must preserve their 'objectivity' and remain aloof from the interpretation found in the discussion section. Of course, as Lindsay admits 'Most data requires some treatment' (1984: 15), and the data of most relevance to the hypothesis and consequently the discussion must be highlighted.

The task of the discussion section is to align the results with the theoretical frame of the introduction and thus create and defend the new research niche. Or as Gross, reflecting Bazerman, notes, 'in the Discussion the data from Results will be transformed into candidate knowledge by adducing in their favor their close correspondence to the report's claim' (1990:90). Gross comments, too, that the data of results and the claims of discussions derive from two different worlds: the world of the lab and the world of nature. The essential task of the discussion is to convince readers that the data are consistent with the already known, constraining 'facts' about nature and that the article is making a valid claim to knowledge production. Appropriately then in his advice regarding discussions, Lindsay is at his most overtly rhetorical. If the writer has planned his or her introduction and results carefully, he suggests, the reader need only be guided gently 'by logical steps to see things from your point of view' (p. 18) and with careful positioning of arguments and evidence and precise management of style 'you can manipulate the reader into ranking the priorities of your arguments in the same way as you have' (p. 22).

Recording Genre

When genres are perceived as stabilized sites of social action, then professional record keeping, the formalized accounts of doctors, social workers, police etc., also assume a special importance. The sociologist Dorothy E. Smith (1984) explored the impact of such practices both on the organizations that construct and use them and on larger social interests. Our lives, she said are 'infused with a process of inscription' (p. 59) or the rendering of an event or object in documentary form (p. 65). Documents such as records are the very fabric of organizations, their fact-making mechanisms. From both the perspective of genre conceived as social action and from Smith's critical account of the function of professional records, it is clear that the social processes which produce records need to be examined as well as their impact on both their producers and the larger community.

The Problem Oriented Veterinary Medical Record (POVMR) is a variant of the Problem Oriented Medical Record system developed in the 1960s for human medicine by Dr Lawrence Weed (1969) in an effort to make medical records more readable, more open to monitoring, evaluation and standardization.[3] Prior to Weed, record keeping had been generally haphazard but basically dominated by the Source-Oriented Record (SOR) system. In the SOR system the practitioner records the presenting complaint, a review of symptoms, and physical exam results. This is followed by 'a statement of the most likely provisional diagnosis, often accompanied by one or more differential diagnoses' (Tugwell and Dok 1985: 148). The investigation and management of the case are then listed together below the diagnosis. Progress notes follow the same format with no standardized approach for recording.

Weed was intensely critical of the SOR system. He believed that the system encouraged physicians to jump to diagnostic conclusions and to ignore the complex problems that could afflict a patient. He saw that medical records, because of their failure to break problems down into manageable units, and their failure to connect those problems to subseqeuent investigation and treatment, were often comprehensible only to their initial writers. This meant that medical records could not be used for either evaluation or research purposes, and were sources of mismanagement when more than one health care provider was involved in a case. Finally, he wanted to redesign records to mirror the medical problem solving process itself. They could become 'audits of action' (introduction). From a rhetorical perspective, we might add that his system offers new physicians a heuristic that reflects the actual problem solving structures that Weed believed many experienced physicians employed.

Figure 6.1 illuminates Weed's project. It is a visual depiction of his system as it is presented to veterinary students at the college I studied. During the early 1980s, younger clinicians converted the animal hospital's record system from the SOR to a variant of Weed's POMR, a variant they call the Problem Oriented Veterinary Medical Record system (POVMR).[4]

For rhetoricians, the recursive nature of the system is particularly interesting. The data is analysed and used to create a hierarchical set of 'problems'. These problems are a clustered set of symptoms, observations or laboratory results. During their training, students are taught to recognize and name provisionally these configurations. At this stage in the process, the experienced practitioner might hazard a diagnosis, but veterinary students are urged to keep their options open and thus prevent premature and often incorrect diagnoses. Instead these related configurations are named as 'problems'.

After an initial plan for the management of the case is drawn up, practitioners put their plans into action and then observe the results of their intervention through progress notes. These notes are central to Weed's contention that records could be audits of thought and action. Instead of a haphazard collection of action, observations and data, the POVMR notes are organized according to the problems identified in

DATA BASE

signalment – age, sex, breed
complaints – symptoms
history (hx)
physical exam (pe) – signs

PROBLEM LIST
(all listed
and numbered)

diagnosis
physiological finding
physical finding
abnormal lab finding

INITIAL PLAN

diagnostic (dx)
therapeutic (rx)
client education (ce)

PROGRESS NOTES (numbered according to problem)

Data – lab results
– pe results
– flow charts
– consult notes

Assessment – diagnostic rule outs
– explanations
– diagnosis
– prognosis

Plans – dx
– rx
– ce

DISCHARGE SUMMARY

Figure 6.1   Problem Oriented Veterinary Medical Record System (POVMR)

the initial assessment of the case. Under each problem, the practitioner lists data, assessment and plans. As the initial intervention is put into action, symptoms should change and laboratory results will arrive. These results become data. As the data changes, the practitioner's assessment or explanation of the disease or metabolic processes at work will also change. The practitioner might even reach a diagnosis. All this interrelation of data and the practitioner's knowledge of physiology and medicine is recorded in the assessment section. Finally, as the practitioners's understanding of a case increases, so will the plans change. These changes in plans, of course, produce more data. Progress notes record this recursive interaction of data, assessment and plans until the problem is resolved.

IMRDS vs. POVMR

A comparison between IMRDS and POVMR as genres reveals some areas of similarity but also some startling differences. Both genres as found in medicine use similar technical language. In fact, one of the main aims of medical education is to teach both researchers and practitioners the precise meanings of technical terms. Both genres are also problem solving heuristics. IMRDS is meant to be a linguistic reconstruction of the research procvess. POVMR is meant to be an audit of action, a representation of the problem-solving techniques used by experienced physicians.

However, their differences outweigh their similarities in terms of purpose, audience and epistemology. IMRDS is essentially a reporting rather than a recording genre. In composing a report, the writer looks back in time towards a set of events. The writer has the opportunity to select and control the kinds of material that go into the report. IMRDS does not reflect the possibly messy, recursive nature of scientific research. Research is essentially an effort of 'bricolage'; yet IMRDS turns it into a work of 'engineering'. In the report, a problem is identified, variables are controlled, and a hypothesis is tested. In fact, the purpose of the experimental article is, as Law notes (1986b), to act as a funnel of interests. Experimental articles begin with as broad a focus as possible and then through a series of interconnecting arguments ('interessements') draw or channel readers into accepting a specific finding. Law explains:

> The mouth of such a funnel is broad in order to suck in as wide an audience as possible, focused on a particular series of points. Interests are thus channelled and flow along a course that is determined by the linked series of interessements. These are deployed by the authors in order to prevent escapes – to ensure that the reader reaches the approved conclusion and then moves with this back to the general once more. (Law 1986b: 77)

The article wants to compel acceptance of its findings and thus is inherently argumentative in its purpose.

POVMR, in contrast, is essentially a recording genre, even though it sometimes appears in article format. Practitioners cannot afford the luxury of looking back on events. As little time as possible must elapse between events and their recording, their translation into identifiable problems. Practitioners have little choice as to the complexity of problem they deal with. They often deal with 'zebra' cases, cases with multiple and rare interacting problems. The work of 'bricolage', the recursive often messy nature of problem solving, is entirely evident. Variables cannot be eliminated; they can only be discovered, identified and managed. In fact, the purpose of records is quite distinct. Records not only document events and cases (animals or people), they are records of intervention. Records order treatments – diagnostic, pharmaceutical or surgical. Records act immediately to change phenomenological events. Finally in today's litigious world, records are acts of justification. Practitioners need to be able to reconstruct their actions in order to defend their interventions.

The two genres differ in their addressivity as well. IMRDS writers are hyperaware of a critical audience both during the research and writing process. Law suggests (1986a), in fact, that particular problems are selected and refined as they are of interest to particular audiences. During the research process, researchers are on the lookout for publishable results – results that will interest their projected audience. Much current research suggests that the experimental article, despite its claims to objectivity, is, as noted earlier, an inherently rhetorical act. Even methods sections, according to Latour and Bastide (1986) are polemical. Methods are filled with passwords (one word descriptions of techniques which those in the know realize must be done if a procedure is to work) and secret recipes (certain procedures are omitted since those in-the-know know that such procedures are always performed). Methods sections are carefully written to prevent objections from critical readers.

Records, on the other hand, have a different sense of audience and audience awareness. Records are written for a narrower audience of those involved in a case and those socialized into reading records. Records themselves are extraordinarily elliptical in their sentence structure and style. In my earlier research (1993), I noted the effect of this elliptical quality on the students and faculty – the deeply shared conventions that make communications rapid but exclusive – only for those in the know (p. 224). These shared conventions also extend to organizational patterns even when records lie behind published articles. The following paragraph, written by two clinicians, appeared in the clinician/practitioner oriented journal produced by the college. This paragraph follows the signalment (information regarding the animal's age, sex and breed), initial data regarding the history and physical exam results, and identification of the main presenting problem, 'a grade III lameness, with a short anterior phase of the stride in the affected left forelimb'. The paragraph reads:

> Radiographs of the left shoulder demonstrated a focal osteolysis restricted to the proximal physis and greater tubercle of the humerus. The cartilaginous space of the scapulohumeral joint was widened and indistinct, a finding that was consistent with a diagnosis of septic arthritis accompanying physeal osteomyelitis.

Those who read records would recognize not only the sections devoted to history and physical exam results and the focus on the presenting problem or problems but would also recognize the interaction between data, assessment and plans echoed above. In the first sentence a plan, a radiographic test, produces data, evidence regarding 'osteolysis'. An assessment emerges from the data – a possible diagnosis of 'septic arthritis accompanying physeal osteomyelitis'. The action of DAPing a case or the interaction of data, assessment and plans is the central problem solving and reading strategy of users of the POVMR. Yet the main moves of this organizational structure are never signalled in these kinds of texts with heading or with any other typographical feature.

In the rest of this journal, basically devoted to research articles, the structure of IMRDS was always visually identified by means of headings. The main moves, the problem identification structures, were always identified, but more importantly perhaps is the narrow range of interests or 'interessements' covered by POVMR articles. This is evident both in their introductions and references. IMRDS articles begin with a large funnel of interests so as to attract as many interested researchers as possible. POVMR articles often begin with a narrowly defined case. This narrowness is nowhere more evident than in the reference section. IMRDS articles normally have extensive bibliographies in order to align the interests of the lab with other researchers and labs. POVMR articles rarely have extensive reference sections.

This pattern of restricting the POVMR to narrow interests and thus limited audience extends to oral presentation as well. During my research at the college I observed graduate students from both the biomedical and clinical areas presenting their research in progress at grand rounds. Those trained in IMRDS's tradition not only used the IMRDS's structure but always connected their research to wider interests in their disciplines. Graduate students in the clinical areas had a harder time. They usually presented in the POVMR format, and rarely connected their cases either to other cases or to wider research interests. As a result they were often critiqued, even by clinicians. Their research was seen as unsubstantial and invalid.

Finally the epistemological assumptions and status assigned to the production of knowledge in each genre differ. At the college, knowledge produced by IMRDS was simply deemed more valid, more 'real' (i.e. scientific), than information produced by POVMR. As a genre, IMRDS allows its users to select and narrow problems, to control variables, to present results as the work of 'engineering' rather than 'bricolage', and to align the interests of a specific lab to the wider research community. These strategies are inherently more persuasive than the strategies available in the POVMR. The strategies embedded within IMRDS allow researchers to instantiate the central ideology of science – the need to order and control the natural world. The strategies involved in the POVMR reflect practitioners' inability to select and simplify problems and their consequent need to respond to problems as they emerge and develop.

In my view, the consequences of this division between research and practice, a division partially held in place by competing genres, are serious for professions like veterinary medicine. Before I left the college, I wrote a report for the Curriculum Committee. The report echoed many of the divisive comments also found in this chapter and explored with college members the possibility that the research–practice split had important implications for the college. In particular, I noted that the students disliked intensely the lecture-driven 'basic' pedagogy characteristic of the first two years and that this pedagogy stood in sharp contrast to the problem-oriented, case-driven pedagogy of later years. The labelling of students as 'data banks' into which information would be poured was also problematic. The metaphor assumed that students were passive and that as practitioners they would never produce valid 'data' themselves or, in other words, contribute to the knowledge basis of the profession. In fact, one of the problems this college faces is that after graduation most of its students do not contribute to the college's development. In my view, the very socializing genres at the college were working to maintain this division. I recommended to the college that they consider two actions. Entry level instructors, mostly researchers in the basic sciences, needed to be aware of the case method as expressed in the POVMR and could develop simple cases to illustrate their points. The assessment section in the POVMR was also a part of the record keeping system that research-oriented faculty could use in their pedagogy because during assessment practitioners test their judgments against known medical knowledge. At the same time, I advised the college that all students should be exposed to both kinds of genres and traditions. A new option is opening up in veterinary medicine – consultancy work in which veterinarians will need both sets of skills. Consultants will not be working on individual cases, but will be hired to identify and prevent problems occurring in large groups of animals. Thus they will need to be able to diagnose from a complex set of problems (the practitioner's skill), gather and test data (the researcher's ability) and develop a plan to prevent future problems. The information consultants produce will be valuable both to researchers asnd practitioners.

The college is slowly moving to implement these suggestions, although not perhaps because I identified this set of problems. Rather the tensions in disciplines that attempt to link research and practice are so high that solutions, even temporary ones, must be found to alleviate the pressure. However, change, in my view, will come very slowly indeed to professions like medicine and engineering. In these professions, their genres, their ways of speaking, writing, reading and listening, deeply enact their ideology. And in professions with research and practice traditions, the genres of research instantiate far more closely the central ideology of science – the belief in order and controlling the natural world.

In conclusion, recent research on genre has suggested that genres conceived as stabilized sites of social action coordinate the work of groups and organizations. The research gathered in this study contributes to this notion by illustrating some of the work that certain genres can and cannot do. IMRDS and POVMR perform different tasks. This study adds to the growing work on genre by illuminating some of the inherent ideological asnd socializing forces at work within genres. These forces can define groups and the work they can do; they can even keep members of apparently the same discourse community separate and apart. Clinicians and practitioners who speak and write only the POVMR will not be able to compete as effectively as those socialized into IMRDS. Research will continue to dictate to practice in disciplines such as medicine and engineering, despite the efforts of reformers such as Donald Schön, as long as groups are socialized into different genres, especially when one genre is more highly valued.

Acknowledgement

I am grateful to the organizers of the Rethinking Genre Conference for comments and suggestions on the original draft of this paper. I extend particular thanks to Carolyn Miller who provided useful comments on the final version.

Notes

1 The college and all participants in this study remain anonymous.
2 I saw three separate groups at the college: researchers, clinicians and practitioners. Researchers are those faculty, usually associated with the biomedical sciences, who engage in original research activities. They teach academic and laboratory courses. Clinicians are faculty who work in the clinics on difficult cases referred to the college hospital. They oversee students working in the hospital and often are teaching as they are working. Most clinicians are also involved in research projects on their cases. Practitioners refer to veterinarians who have their own practices outside of the college. Most students were training

to be practitioners. Overlap existed between these groups. Some practitioners did clinical work on a part-time basis; some clinicians were former practitioners and intended to return to practice; a few researchers were also clinicians, but only if they were associated with the Clinical Studies unit of the college.

3 An extended version of this account of medical record keeping appears in Schryer (1993).

4 The main difference between the POMR and POVMR lies in the structure of the progress notes. Medical doctors 'SOAP' a case. They collect Subjective and Objective data, Assess the data, and arrive at a Plan. Subjective data is what the patient tells the doctor. Objective data is what the physician actually sees. Veterinarians, on the other hand, 'DAP' a case. They cannot collect subjective data because animals cannot talk. So they only collect data. The actions of assessment and planning remain the same in both systems.

References

ADAMS-SMITH, D. E. (1984) 'Medical Discourse: Aspects of Author's Comment', *The ESP Journal*, **3**, pp. 25–36.

BAKHTIN, M. M. (1981) 'Discourse in the Novel', *The Dialogic Imagination: Four Essays*, (trans. C. Emerson and M. Holquist, ed. M. Holquist) Austin, TX: University of Texas Press, pp. 259–422.

BAKHTIN, M. M. (1986) 'The Problem of Speech Genres', *Speech Genres and Other Late Essays*, (trans. V. W. McGee, ed. C. Emerson and M. Holquist) Austin, TX: University of Texas Press, pp. 60–102.

BAZERMAN, C. (1988) *Shaping Written Knowledge: The Genre and Activity of the Experimental Article in Science*, Madison, WI: University of Wisconsin Press.

BERMUDEZ, V., MILLER, R., JOHNSON, W., ROSENDAL, S. and RUHNKE, L. (1987) 'Recovery of Mycoplasma spp. from the Reproductive Track of the Mare During the Estrous Cycle', *Canadian Veterinary Journal*, **28**, pp. 519–22.

FETTERMAN, D. (1984) *Ethnography in Educational Evaluation*, Beverly Hills, CA: Sage.

GILBERT, G. N. and MULKAY, M (1984) *Opening Pandora's Box: A Sociological Analysis of Scientists' Discourse*, Cambridge: Cambridge University Press.

GLASER, B. and STRAUSS, A. L. (1967) *The Discovery of Grounded Theory: Strategies for Qualitative Research*, Chicago, IL: Aldine.

GROSS, A. (1990) *The Rhetoric of Science*, Cambridge, MA: Harvard University Press.

HEATH, S. (1983) *Ways With Words: Language, Life and Work in Communities and Classrooms*, Cambridge: Cambridge University Press.

KNORR-CETINA, K. D. (1981) *The Manufacture of Knowledge*, Oxford: Pergamon.

LATOUR, B. (1987) *Science in Action: How to Follow Scientists and Engineers Through Society*, Milton Keynes, Bucks: Open University Press.

LATOUR, B. (1988) *The Pasteurization of France*, (trans. A. Sheridan and J. Law) Cambridge, MA: Harvard University Press.

LATOUR, B. and BASTIDE, F. (1986) 'Writing Science – Fact and Fiction: The Analysis of the Process of Reality Construction Through the Application of Socio-Semiotic Methods to Scientific Texts' in CALLON, M., LAW, J. and RIP, A. (eds) *Mapping the Dynamics of Science and Technology*, London: Macmillan, pp. 51–66,

LATOUR, B. and WOOLGAR, S. (1979) *Laboratory Life: The Social Construction of Scientific Facts*, Beverly Hills, CA: Sage.

LAW, J. (1986a) 'Laboratories and Texts', in CALLON, M., LAW, J. and RIP, A. (eds) *Science and Technology*, London: Macmillan, pp. 35–55.

LAW, J. (1986b) 'The Heterogeneity of Texts', in CALLON, M., LAW, J. and RIP, A. (eds) *Mapping the Dynamics of Science and Technology*, London: Macmillan, pp. 67–83.

LEVINE, K. (1986) *The Social Context of Literacy*, London: Routledge and Kegan Paul.

LINDSAY, D. (1984) *A Guide to Scientific Writing: Manual for Students and Research Workers*, Melbourne: Longman Cheshire.

LYNCH, M. and WOOLGAR, S. (1988) 'Introduction: Sociological Orientations to Representational Practice in Science', *Human Studies*, **11**, pp. 99–116.

MILLER, C. R. (1984) 'Genre as Social Action', *Quarterly Journal of Speech*, **70**, pp. 151–67.

PRELLI, L. J. (1989) *A Rhetoric of Science: Inventing Scientific Discourse*, Columbia, SC: University of South Carolina Press.

SCHÖN, D. A. (1983) *The Reflective Practitioner: How Professionals Think in Action*, New York: Basic Books.

SCHÖN, D. A. (1987) *Educating the Reflective Practitioner*, San Francisco, CA: Jossey-Bass.

SCHRYER, C. F. (1989) 'An Ethnographic Study of Literacy at a Veterinary College: A Consultancy Model of Research', doctoral dissertation, University of Louisville, KY (Dissertation Abstracts International, 51, 9026449).

SCHRYER, C. F. (1993) 'Records as Genre', *Written Communication*, **10**, pp. 200–34.

SMITH, D. E. (1984) 'Textually Mediated Social Organization', *International Social Science Journal*, **36**, pp. 59–75.

STREET, B. (1984) *Literacy in Theory and Practice*, Cambridge: Cambridge University Press.

SWALES, J. M. (1990) *Genre Analysis: English in Academic and Research Settings*, Cambridge: Cambridge University Press.

TUGWELL, P. and DOK, C.(1985) in NEUFELD, V. R. and NORMAN, G. A. (eds) *Assessing Clinical Competence*, New York: Springer, pp. 142–82.

WEED, L. L. (1969) *Medical Records, Medical Education and Patient Care: The Problem-Oriented Record as a Basic Tool*, Chicago, IL: Year Book Medical Publisher.

WILLIAMS, R. (1983) *Keywords: A Vocabulary of Culture and Society*, New York: Oxford University Press.

Chapter 7

On Definition and Rhetorical Genre

Eugenia N. Zimmerman

If genre theory is a type of categorization,[1] I think it only fitting for a set of papers devoted to matters of genre to return to that source in antiquity from which rules for categorization historically derive: the logico-rhetorical tradition engendered in Greece, systematized by Aristotle, then extended by Cicero and Quintilian in Roman times (cf. Kennedy 1980: Chs 1–5).

Now, although I only realized this after the fact, the expression 'engendered' is not an ornamental metaphor; it is, rather, an argument and as such, focuses our attention on the scope of the conceptual object under inquiry and raises questions about how it may reasonably be named.

If, for example, I were given permission to call upon the analogical power inherent in discourse linked to the computer, that 'electronic Aristotle'[2] of late twentieth-century technology, then I could say that I first go to a 'menu bar' definable as 'categorization in natural languages', from that menu bar I then select the 'pull-down menu' called 'English', and, by so doing, I gain access to the following set of options:

1 'genre' for literary and artistic categorization;
2 'genus' for biological and logical categorization;
3 'gender Old Style' for grammatical categorization;
4 'gender New Style' for sexual/ideological categorization.[3]

If, however, I were to choose a different pull-down menu, the one called 'French', I would have access to a much more restricted set containing only one option, for the term 'genre' would here have to do triple duty for categories 1, 2 and 3, and as far as category 4 is concerned, I would have no option – no single term – at all. So since the linguistic resources at my disposal, by limiting or extending what I have the means to say, control how I then think or 'rethink' what is meant by 'genre', there might be times when the categories accessible through French would be constraining while the categories accessible through English were enabling – and, of course, given that the term 'genre' even when used in English, is still recognizably French, there might be times when the contrary was the case.

For example, if I wished to find a 'path' back to the 'engendering' directory not only for the terms just mentioned but also for allied terms such as 'general' or 'generate', French, by its phonetic capabilities, more quickly shows us the kinship.

Then, too, when I search for the origins of 'genre' in the *Oxford English Dictionary*, I am told I must first of all 'see gender', (*Compact Edition* 1971, I: 1130); however, if I access 'genre' in the *Dictionnaire alphabétique et analogique de la langue française*, I am immediately referred to the Latin *genus* (Robert 1977: 861) and thus, by implication, to the Greek *genos*, which is to say, 'race', 'kind', 'sort', 'class' (*Compact Edition* I: 1126). Now, the ideological reverberations of this 'root' definition are tremendous, but a comprehensive study at this time would lead us too far afield.[4]

So if in a preliminary analysis, we use the term 'genre' synecdochically – one type of categorization for categorization as a whole – then the divisions into which classical rhetoric is organized may reasonably be described as a network of 'genres': *genera* and *species*, parts and wholes.[5]

There are, first of all, the five great rhetorical categories of: invention, disposition, style, memory, delivery. Focusing on the subdivisions of invention yields the two types of proof: inartificial proof (evidence) and artificial proof. Artificial proof is then divisible into the three proofs of *logos*, the appeal to reason, *pathos*, the appeal to the passions or the emotions and *ethos*, the appeal to the character and authority of the speaker.

Logos then not only subdivides into deductive and inductive reasoning, it also generates the category of the topics: special topics and common topics. These 'topics' for their part, expand and contract in number according to whose authority is being invoked: 28 valid topics and 10 fallacies for Aristotle, 16 topics for Cicero, etc.

If we now pass to 'arrangement' (Lanham 1969: 112), we get the seven parts of the oration: entrance, narration, exposition, proposition, confirmation, confutation, conclusion.

If we contemplate 'style',– and, once again, depending on whose authority is being invoked – we get either three or four types of style and either three or four types of 'virtue'.

However, there is also another major logico-rhetorical category and one to which, along with Aristotle, we can in good conscience apply the term which defines the scope of this collection. I am, of course, referring to the three 'genres' of deliberative, judicial and epideictic rhetoric (*Rhet.* 1.3.3.).[6]

Deliberative rhetoric, 'to exhort or persuade' is concerned with 'deliberation about the future action in the best interests of a state'.

Judicial or forensic rhetoric, 'to accuse or defend', encompasses 'speeches of prosecution or defense in a court of law seeking to determine the just resolution of actions alleged to have been taken in the past'.

Epideictic or demonstrative rhetoric, to 'blame or to commemorate', designates 'speeches that do not call for any immediate action by the audience but that characteristically praise or blame some person or thing, often on a ceremonial occasion such as a public funeral or holiday' (Lanham 1969: 106; Kennedy in Aristotle 1991: 7).

Historically, the ancient genre of forensic rhetoric has occupied a central place in the logico-rhetorical tradition and its basic categories are clearly discernible in the modern world. Indeed, if arguing from probable rather than necessary premises is what distinguishes the genre of rhetoric as a theory of argumentation from its allied genre of logic (*Rhet.* 1.1.1; *Topics* 1.1–3 quoted in Aristotle 1991: 289–92), then the subgenre of forensic rhetoric, persuasion by means of proofs and probabilities (Kennedy 1980: 20–21) encapsulates the properties of rhetoric as a whole.

Were the shades of the founding rhetoricians to find themselves in North American courtrooms, they might well have problems with specific aspects of Common Law or Civil Code legal systems. The Greek rhetors, in particular, might look askance at the importance placed on evidence or inartificial proof (Kennedy 1980: 21) but neither Greek nor Roman would have any difficulty recognizing variants of the artificial proofs they all, in one way or another, helped to establish or extend.

Logos, the appeal to premises and probable inferences based upon cultural presuppositions or *endoxa* is clearly represented by the following argumentation:

> a Jan 21, 1992 report prepared for the Ministry of the Attorney General by investigator Diane Desjardins says that while there is no direct proof of sexual harassment, 'in view of the balance of probabilities demonstrated in the analysis, it is reasonable to conclude that the respondent has committed acts of verbal sexual harassment which were offensive to the complainant and are known, or should reasonably be known, to be unwelcome'. (Rusnell 1992: A1)

Furthermore, the capacity to 'identify the kernel issue in the decision', standard subject matter for first year students at Harvard Law School, along with the 'typical law-school test...usually referred to as an "issue spotter"' (Turow 1988: 76, 170) can both be reconciled with *stasis* theory, a construction of Hellenistic rhetoric.

Ethos, the appeal to the authority of the speaker acquires modern garb in the notion of the 'expert witness', this century's version of Aristotle's 'wise man'.

Both *ethos* and *pathos*, redefined in the Roman tradition as, respectively, the weak and strong form of the appeal to the emotions is discernible in the following *exemplum* from a classic American 'technical handbook', *The Art of Cross-Examination*; here, beginning advocates are instructed in the art of *captatio benevolentiae*.

> The counsel who has a pleasant personality; who speaks with apparent frankness; who appears to be an earnest searcher after truth; who is courteous to those who testify against him (sic)...he it is who creates an atmosphere in favor of the side which he represents...On the other hand, the lawyer...who is constantly losing his temper and showing his teeth to the witnesses; who wears a sour, anxious expression, who possesses a monotonous, rasping, penetrating voice...soon prejudices a jury against himself and the client he represents, entirely irrespective of the sworn evidence in the case. (Wellman 1986: 14–15)

Ethos in its peculiarly modern guise as the fundamental notion of 'credibility', also appears in the comments of F. Lee Bailey, a 'wise man' of the American juridical world who echoes the words of the earlier text. When asked to comment on the then ongoing William Kennedy Smith rape trial, he opined that there was always a danger attached to putting a defendant in the witness box. It would not matter what the evidence showed, it would not matter what the rules said concerning burden of proof, if the jury did not believe the defendant, they would find him guilty as charged.[7]

As a genre, forensic rhetoric is amazingly robust. No less eminent a commentator than Aristotle tried to reduce its hegemony (*Rhet.* 1.1.3) and there are some modern commentators who follow Aristotle's lead. Henry W. Johnstone, Jr, for example, when reviewing Nicholas Rescher's *Dialectics: A Controversy-Oriented Approach to the Theory of Knowledge*, minimizes this study's legal bent (Johnstone 1979: 271–3).[8] However, when I went to the text itself, I found out that not only had Rescher based his own model on that of the medieval dispute but that the medieval dispute itself was constructed in terms of an analogy with forensic rhetoric (Rescher 1977: Chs 1–2).

I should now like to turn to deliberative rhetoric. Here, it is not so much that the basic definition constituting the genre has been changed; it is, rather, that who may take part in deliberation, who must be persuaded to future action rather than merely coerced – as would have been the case in other centuries – what they must be persuaded of, etc. have all been considerably expanded, at least in countries with democratic, parliamentary-like institutions.

There is, of course, the general domain of political oratory, as recognizable now as it was in ancient times. And, indeed, Aristotle's standard topics of 'finances, war and peace, national defense, imports and exports, and the framing of laws' (*Rhet.* 1.4.7) clearly belong to the realm of what modern electoral campaigns call 'the issues'. However, we have also added as permissible for debating in an open forum 'issues' such as abortion and euthanasia[9] that would have probably given Aristotle a considerable number of sleepless nights. If we allow an even wider definition of this particular category, then practically any time we try to persuade anyone to do anything, we are practising the genre of deliberative rhetoric.

Epideictic rhetoric, the last rhetorical genre to be considered, is at once completely recognizable and completely transformed.[10] It is completely recognizable because the ancient function of commemoration or blame on ritual occasions is still being practised in the modern world. Any reader of the obituaries appearing regularly in *The New York Times* has constant access to typical examples of epideictic rhetoric.

It is radically transformed because somehow during the long and convoluted history of rhetoric in the West, the epideictic somehow turned into literature. This literary 'turn' has been extensively chronicled and is of particular interest to those modern rhetoricians who when carving out a privileged domain from the five great rhetorical divisions, tend to foreground and value *elocutio* (see Kibédi-Varga 1970; Harwood 1977; Kennedy 1980; Vickers 1989a, 1989b).

We are now at a point in the analysis where the characteristics of all three rhetorical genres have been briefly described and the distinctions between them seem reasonably clear. Would this still be the case, however, if we were to re-examine them not as separate entities but rather in terms of the boundaries they share?

In a different set of arguments, constructed for a different purpose, Sister Miriam Joseph observed that although the artificial proofs of *ethos*, *pathos* and *logos* may well be analysed separately, in actual practice they are 'closely interrelated' (1947: 393–4). So, for my set of arguments and for my particular purposes at the present time, I should like to extend Joseph's observation by suggesting that what is mostly the case for the three rhetorical proofs is at least sometimes the case for the three rhetorical genres.

What, after all, was that rhetorical circus of 1991, the Clarence Thomas–Anita Hill affair, if not a joint production of forensic and deliberative rhetoric? The US Senate, a legislative body, was asked to decide whether a particular individual, Judge Clarence Thomas, had sufficient *ethos* to be appointed to a judicial body, the Supreme Court. This involved determining the past, the domain of forensic rhetoric. Did Clarence Thomas do or did he not do what Anita Hill said he did? It also involved determining the future, the domain of deliberative rhetoric. Was it or was it not in the best interests of the state that Clarence Thomas be appointed to the Supreme Court?[11] As always, the fundamental question was that which dominates epideictic rhetoric and indeed which dominates discourse as a whole, the question of *ethos*: Who is lying? Who is telling the truth? Who has credibility? Whom, in the final analysis, shall we believe?

For another illustration of generic intermingling, I turn to the *exemplum* which constituted introduction to Shakespeare for my generation during our high school years: Mark Antony's funeral oration in *Julius Caesar* (3.2). By means of this oration, the initial judgment of the Citizens that 'This Caesar was a tyrant. . .[and] We are blessed that Rome is rid of him' was turned into the injunction to 'Go, fetch fire. Pluck down benches. Pluck down forms, windows, anything'. And Antony was led to comment: 'Now let it work: mischief, thou art afoot. Take thou what course thou wilt' (Shakespeare n.d.: 733–4).

If this funeral oration is defined strictly in terms of the generic rule of praise or blame on ritual occasions, then it obviously belongs to the genre of epideictic rhetoric. But the epideictic, strictly speaking, does not call for any future action on the part of the hearers. Yet, here, as a direct result of the oration and of the oration only, the temper of the audience is so radically changed that they are prepared to perform the most violent of future actions. So is this an instance of the epideictic, of the deliberative, or of both?

We appear to have a paradoxical instance, governed by two conflicting definitions. The apparent definition, arguing according to the topic of what (general) type of speech on what (general) type of occasion, assigns it to the domain of epideictic or ceremonial oratory. However, the hidden definition, which may be argued either or both according to the topic of what intentions on the part of the speaker and what reactions on the part of the hearers, assigns it to the domain of deliberative or political oratory.

Is it possible to draw inferences from a major premise that there are times when the rhetorical genres are governed by hidden definitions? I believe that at least a partial answer lies in an interpretive strategy I have not until now had reason to expound. I am referring to the work of Chaïm Perelman and Lucie Olbrechts-Tyteca and to the theory of argumentation they called 'New Rhetoric'. Here, *logos* occupies a privileged place, the categories foregrounded are those of *inventio* and *dispositio* and a figure perceived as a figure is a failed argument (Perelman and Olbrechts-Tyteca 1960: 169). In this tradition, the epideictic is defined not in terms of its conversion into literature but rather in terms of its persuasive force: it is that which 'strengthens the disposition toward action by increasing adherence to the values it lauds' (Perelman and Olbrechts-Tyteca 1960: 50; Kennedy in Aristotle 1991: 7).

In a certain sense, there is nothing new here and the modern definition merely renders explicit what was already present in the classical one: that the function of epideictic rhetoric is to praise or to blame. However, by making it explicit, it lays manifest what might otherwise have remained less clear: that 'praising or blaming' implies value judgments and therefore if there is, indeed, a 'specific difference' distinguishing the epideictic from the other two genres, it is its role, indirectly confirmed by Aristotle in *Rhetoric* 1.9 and 2.1, as the official *organon* of ideology.[12]

Some years ago I heard a well-known specialist from Germany address his audience on how to teach and how not to teach a second language. That was in my pre-rhetorical days so it was only with hindsight that I came to appreciate this speaker's grasp of rhetoric. He informed us that there were three things he had never much liked about France: Jeanne d'Arc, de Gaulle and the audio-visual method. I, myself, was neutral on the first, shared his position on the second and, having recently come in contact with that now defunct piece of technology known as the Betamax, was more than ready to be convinced by his analysis of the third.

The thesis of his oration, as I remember it, was that too much stress was placed on methodology and that the claims made for one or another particular methodology were unrealistically high. Teach as you can, he told us, don't expect too much, be happy you get any results at all. Although I later learned that some members of the audience who espoused the benefits of specific methodologies took umbrage, I for my part, left that room thoroughly convinced – but convinced by what? By a brilliant set of arguments that caused me to re-examine my position on the topic debated or by my own desire to have what I either believed or hoped to be the case confirmed by someone whose *ethos*, presumably, was beyond reproach?

I was persuaded because I had already been. . . persuaded and so this apparently straight-forward example of deliberative rhetoric became, at least as far as this member of the audience was concerned, a rather less straight-forward example of epideictic rhetoric. It reinforced my disposition toward a certain type of action and my lack of disposition toward a contrary type of action in terms of values that, respectively, it either praised or blamed (for a related discussion, see Gumbrecht 1979: 363–84).

Since I am a passionate rhetorician but only a moderate reader-response critic, it is with a certain amount of misgiving and for purposes of inquiry only, that I will allow myself some possibly dubious generalizations based on this admittedly peculiar instance.

Limited generalization: If we view epideictic not in terms of the type of occasion nor yet in terms of the aims of the speaker but only in terms of the responses of the hearer, then there are certain circumstances under which any rhetorical instance, if we value it primarily because it confirms what we already believe, can be defined as essentially epideictic.

Extended generalization: If we decide to view definition as ultimately pragmatic according to a rule that 'genre is as genre does', then how we assign an instance to a genre may depend less on intentions than on results.

Notes

1 Cf. 'A unique contribution of the Greeks...was their interest in describing [rhetoric], dividing it into categories, and giving names to the various techniques observed so that they could be taught to others. This conceptualization of rhetoric is parallel to the conceptualization of philosophy, political theory, grammar, and other subjects in Greece' (Kennedy in Aristotle 1991: 8).

2 This expression is reconstructed from memory as approximating an expression used in the first segment of *Bits and Bytes*, a series on computers presented by TVOntario in the early 1980s.

3 Cf. 'Copps probably knows what she's doing, though "Her lack of *genderizing* could give her power as an individual" in the male-dominated world of national politics' (MacDougall 1991: H2; emphasis mine).

4 I have examined the relationship between 'genus' and ideology in a recently completed book-length manuscript, 'Coercion, Demonstration, Persuasion: On the Margins of Rhetoric'.

5 These categories and divisions are taken from Lanham (1969: 106–16).

6 All references to Aristotle's *Rhetoric* will be from the translation by George A. Kennedy (1991).

7 Paraphrased from an interview on the NBC television program, *Today* (9 December 1991, 7:20 a.m.).

8 'Like Perelman, Rescher construes rationality on a disputational model. But he moves beyond Perelman in two directions. While for Perelman the paradigm of all disputation is legal disputation, Rescher sees in addition to the "conventional" dialectics of legal disputation...the "natural" dialectics of rational controversy. And unlike Perelman, Rescher bases his analysis upon an explicitly stated philosphical view' (Johnstone 1979: 272).

9 Cf. '*euthanasia*: the right to die, or the right to kill?' arguments by passionate advocates in the current issue of *Canadian Speeches: Issues of the Day* (Bookcase 1992: S13).

10 Cf. 'Epideictic, in particular, needs to be looked at in a variety of ways not recognized by Aristotle' (Kennedy in Aristotle 1991: 311).

11 Cf. 'Even before the nomination of Clarence Thomas to the US Supreme Court, American historians had begun to debate the relationship between character and high office. At its simplest, the question is "Can a bad character achieve public good?" ' (Bennett 1991: 4).

12 For a comprehensive discussion of the many ways *ethos* has been defined by modern commentators, see Sullivan (1993: 114–18).

References

ARISTOTLE (1991) *On Rhetoric: A Theory of Civic Discourse*, (trans. G. A. Kennedy) New York: Oxford University Press.

BENNETT, D. (1991) 'LBJ's Career Provides Fodder for Historians', *The Ottawa Citizen*, 18 January, p. F4.

BOOKCASE (1992) *The Financial Post*, 20 January, p. S13.

The Compact Edition of the Oxford English Dictionary (1971) Vol. 1, Oxford: Oxford University Press.

GUMBRECHT, H. U. (1979) 'Persuader ceux qui pensent comme vous', *Poetique*, **39**, pp. 363–84.

HARWOOD, S. (1977) *Rhetoric in the Tragedies of Corneille*, New Orleans, LA: Tulane Studies in Romance Languages and Literatures.

JOHNSTONE, H. W., Jr (1979) 'Review. N. Rescher, *A Controversy-Oriented Approach to the Theory of Knowledge*', *Philosophy and Rhetoric*, 12, pp. 271–3.

JOSEPH, M. (1947) *Shakespeare's Use of the Arts of Language*, New York: Columbia University Press.

KENNEDY, G. A. (1980) *Classical Rhetoric and its Christian and Secular Tradition from Ancient to Modern Times*, Chapel Hill, NC: University of North Carolina Press.

KIBÉDI-VARGA, A. (1970) *Rhétorique et littérature: études de structures classiques*, Paris: Didier.

LANHAM, R. A. (1969) *A Handlist of Rhetorical Terms*, Berkeley, CA: University of California Press.

MACDOUGALL, D. (1991) 'Mr Blackwell looks north', *The Ottawa Citizen*, 28 November, p. H2.

PERELMAN, C. and OLBRECHTS-TYTECA, L. (1960) *The New Rhetoric: A Treatise on Argumentation*, (trans. J. Wilkinson and P. Weaver) Notre Dame, IN: Notre Dame University Press. [Originally published in 1958 as *La Nouvelle rhétorique: traité de l'argumentation*, Paris: Presses Universitaires de France.]

RESCHER, N. (1977) *Dialectics: A Controversy-Oriented Approach to the Theory of Knowledge*, Albany, NY: State University of New York Press.

ROBERT, P. (1977) *Dictionnaire alphabétique et analogique de la langue française (Petit Robert 1)*, (rev. A. Rey and J. Rey-Debove) Paris: Société du Nouveau livre.

RUSNELL, C. (1992) 'Official accused of harassment', *The Ottawa Citizen*, 28 February, pp. A1–A2.

SHAKESPEARE, W. (n.d.) *The Complete Works*, Cleveland, OH: World.

SULLIVAN, D. (1993) 'The Ethics of Epideictic Encounter', *Philosophy and Rhetoric*, **26**, pp. 113–33.

TUROW, S. (1988) *One-L*, New York: Warner.

VICKERS, B. (1989a) *Classical Rhetoric in English Poetry*, Carbondale, IL: Southern Illinois University Press.

VICKERS, B. (1989b) *In Defence of Rhetoric*, Oxford: Clarendon.

WELLMAN, F. L. (1986) *The Art of Cross-Examination*, New York: Dorset Press.

Chapter 8

A Genre Map of R&D Knowledge Production for the US Department of Defense

A.D. Van Nostrand

Overview

The subject area of this study is knowledge production within a large social system. It concerns the patterns of interaction by which such knowledge is generated. The system is the US government's sponsorship of military research and development (R&D). The Department of Defense (DoD) spends about 40 billion dollars annually on R&D, which is nearly 60 per cent of the federal government's total R&D budget. This volume of purchase has a decided effect on knowledge production, but even more noteworthy in this regard is the way in which DoD buys research and development. In DoD the process of procurement is itself a means of producing knowledge.

The public documents that record this process also enable it to occur. They are initiated by the DoD agencies that purchase R&D and by the laboratories that perform it. Although numerous, these documents form only a partial record of the procurement process, which also entails electronic transmissions and unrecorded conversations. Moreover, many of the records are private and proprietary and, therefore, inaccessible. Like the glyphs on Mayan architecture, however, these documents constitute the public record of a culture; they are what we have to work with.

Used repeatedly in the procurement process, the documents represent coded and keyed events in a discourse exchange system; they are conspicuously genres. The more they can be analysed and tracked, the more they will reveal about knowledge production. If genre analysis is to become a reliable tool for this purpose, however, it can usefully sustain some rethinking, some refinement.

Swales has examined the literature of genres and constructed a broad theory of their characteristics, their relationships and their behaviour. His thorough and precise study, *Genre Analysis* (1990), is the primary reference I have used to help classify and analyse the documents I am about to describe. It has especially guided me in focusing on the social context of their authorship. In the course of framing his study, Swales cites Fowler's emphasis (1982: 31) on the value of genre to the writer, in that it provides a matrix, a set of formal ideas, by which to order one's experience during composition, thereby guiding the writer in combining various textual constituents. Building on this relationship between writer and genre, Swales formulates a genre theory based on three interactive elements: the writer's *task*, the concept of *genre*, and the concept of *discourse community*, a socio-rhetorical community formed for the achievement of certain common goals.

For the sake of useful argument, Swales proposes that these elements interlock. Since members of a discourse community know and use the genres that help to achieve such common goals, he says, 'genres are the properties of discourse communities; that is to say, genres belong to discourse communities, not to individuals, other kinds of grouping or to wider speech communities' (Swales 1990: 9). This proposition about the close ownership of genres presents an intriguing puzzle over the genres that enable the military R&D procurement system to function. Although their various rhetorical purposes are readily evident, their relationship to discourse communities is not. This anomaly is what I chiefly address.

The complexities of the system appear to obscure boundaries that might delineate discourse communities, so they present an opportunity to test this genre theory at its core. If analysis should reveal a functional relationship between genre and discourse community in this procurement system, then the theory that Swales proposes can be seen to explain certain problematic border conditions that pertain to knowledge production.

I have framed the anomaly as a problem, contextualizing it in four stages. After first noting the systemic elements of the R&D procurement process, I explain how the documents function in this discourse system and then point out their genre characteristics. Thereafter, I analyse the relationships between these genres and their possible discourse communities. I hope my remarks will raise a larger, informing question about how genre analysis can explain knowledge production in this and comparable social systems.

Systemic Elements in R&D Procurement

That portion of DoD's annual R&D budget which is set aside for research is awarded largely to extramural R&D organizations, primarily university laboratories and other non-profit entities. Their research activities contribute knowledge to a kind of escrow account called the DoD technology base, parts of which may support the possible development of subsequent weapon systems.[1]

These budgeted funds maintain a complex procurement system that entails many recursive cycles of knowledge production in various stages of implementation at any one time. Within this system, the chief institutional actors are either customers or vendors. The customers are the several dozen agencies within DoD that fund research; the vendors are several hundred university laboratories and other non-profit entities that perform the research. In their respective roles, these organizations engage each other in progressive stages of project development.

The customer and the vendor are two systemic elements in the procurement process, and a third is the research project which they mutually address. The project is the basic unit of R&D effort. Each project is a related set of activities undertaken to meet certain limited objectives within a specified budget and a designated period of time. The activities in a project tend to be multidisciplinary, typically involving related subdisciplines of physics, engineering and information technology. Each project is a limited and pragmatic response to a stated need for some specified kind of knowledge.

The interaction of customer and vendor is marked by both pressure and tension, to use those terms in an engineering sense. On the one hand, each party needs the other; they seek each other out. On the other hand, federal regulations work to keep them apart. In addition to these procedural regulations, moreover, customer and vendor have differing interests. Each party has its own range of objectives, which are disparate and not always mutually consistent.

The customer, for example, is both a consumer and a patron. These roles are not always compatible, and they may cause conflicting priorities in contracting. For its part, the vendor typically engages in a broad range of research activities, some of which accommodate the consumer, some of which serve the patron, but none of which are instantly compatible with the customer's needs for a given knowledge product. In this situation, the interaction of customer and vendor is animated by the strategy of marketing: by the definition of needs, and by the accommodation of commodities to those needs.

Although all R&D activity is project-oriented, myriad projects are ongoing at any one time. In a laboratory's current agenda, a given project might be one of a cluster of related projects under the sponsorship of different military agencies. Within the broad field of radar research, for instance, one project might entail experiments in millimeter wave technology, which might serve the later development of high altitude surveillance capabilities. A concurrent project might entail low frequency transmissions for close, underwater surveillance. A third research project might consist of testing semiconductor materials for their optical properties. A comparable spectrum of activity typically holds for any sponsoring agency, which is probably funding an array of projects in various stages to support its own appointed mission.

Rhetorically, the R&D project culminates a history of negotiation that has proceeded in stages by means of a discourse exchange system. The documents exchanged by customer and vendor refine the objectives, budget and duration of the project by iterating the activities that will comprise it. These iterations progressively shape the project and define the deliverable knowledge products that the project is intended to generate. On some occasions, documents that have helped formulate other, related projects are invoked and drawn into the cumulative record – the intertext – of the project at hand.

The deliverables of a research project are typically reports of empirical research, describing the outcome of some phenomenon or the behaviour of some system or structure under certain conditions: an assessment, perhaps, or a validation design or a set of critical measurements or test results. The deliverables are quantifiable and certifiable; they are what the customer is actually purchasing. Much of this deliverable knowledge has already been developed by contract time, however.

A distinguishing feature of the DoD contract system, compared to research projects funded by grants, is the degree to which the procurement process itself generates knowledge. Figure 8.1 shows this comparison, highly generalized, in terms of epistemic activity. In this model, such activity occurs at an earlier stage and at a higher level of effort in contract funding than it does in grant funding. The model also shows that post-contract activity tails off at a lower level, since it is devoted largely to confirming or modifying the knowledge specifications already known as a result of pre-contract activity.

Although the comparison is not readily measurable, this activity model is familiar to research managers. It fits the distinctive conditions of contract funding. Because the customer and the vendor are so mutually engaged in project definition, and because their negotiations occur over such long periods of time, lasting many months and sometimes several years, most specifications of the knowledge product that a project should yield have already been made prior to the project's formal beginning.

Interpreting epistemic activity in terms of knowledge products is arguable. Narrowly speaking, a project's intended knowledge product does not yet exist when the contract is signed; the exact quantification of values remains to be discovered.

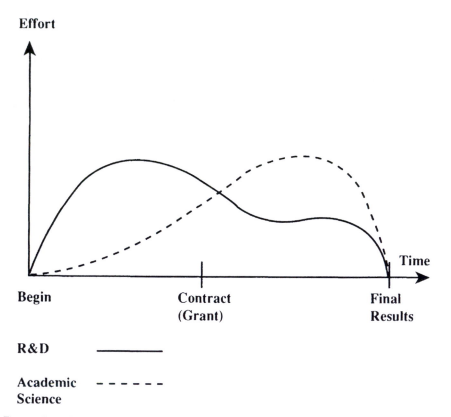

Figure 8.1 Distribution of epistemic activity in Project Cycle

But many components of a knowledge structure have already been established before a contract has been signed. Such components include the values to be quantified (by curves or numbers), the conditions of the tests that will yield those quantitative values, the rationale for such tests and the means of assessing them, and even the parameters of expected results. These components of a knowledge structure will have normally been established before the project formally begins.

The Documents

The formidable terrain of the R&D marketplace is defined by the Federal Acquisition Regulations (FAR) and its various supplements, sets of encyclopedic rules that mandate elaborate procedures to insure free and open competition and to provide gateways for new vendors to enter. The project directors for the various vendors and their counterparts, the technical monitors who represent the various customers, are presumed to know these rules.

A genre map of this terrain consists of pathways, sequences of document exchange between customer and vendor, that might lead from the inception of an idea to the contract for a project. The documents themselves are coded markers along these pathways. Figure 8.2 displays six kinds of formal transactional documents prior to the contract in the R&D procurement system, three initiated by the customer and three initiated by the vendor. Repeated in the procurement process from one project to another, these documents constitute genres. Contract documents comprise a seventh genre. In the aggregate these seven genres are referential and cumulative.

The most comprehensive genre is the contract, which delineates the project and legally binds the agency and the laboratory to its terms. The contract specifies the project's scope and objectives; the work to be done, with measurements of its quantity and quality, and its deliverable outcomes; the price and payment terms; and the duration of these related activities. In the intensely competitive environment of the procurement process, most initiatives do not arrive at a contract, but whether or not a proposed project is funded, all the documents that pertain to its formulation, issued by either party, anticipate a presumed contract. This genre is the force that powers the system.

Initiated by Customer:
    Sources Sought Announcement   (SSA)
    Request for Proposal   (RFP)
    Broad Agency Announcement   (BAA)
        or
    Program Research Development Announcement   (PRDA)

Initiated by Vendor
    Sources Sought Response   (SSR)
    White Paper   (WP)
    Proposal   (Prop)

Figure 8.2   Pre-contract documents in R&D procurement process

Although each contract specifies the terms of a unique agreement, its textual structure and most of its content are standard. Four parts contain up to thirteen sections of descriptive material:

1 the schedule of conditions that delineate this particular project;
2 pertinent contract clauses excerpted from the FAR, the regulations governing all federal contracts;
3 appropriate attachments from printed or published material that contextualize the work to be undertaken; and
4 various certifications of intent and status to which the performer agrees.

Most of this material is boilerplate, extending from possibly twenty pages to several hundred, depending on the variable length of Parts 2 and 3, the regulatory clauses and the attachments.

The one section of the contract that makes it unique is Section C of Part 1, known as the statement of work (SOW), which specifies the tasks to be undertaken, the deliverable outcomes that they are intended to yield, and the form in which the outcomes are to be delivered. The SOW is that part of the contract agreement that defines the project. In addition to whatever else it might specify, the SOW also incorporates into the contract the terms offered by the vendor, simply by referring to the vendor's proposal. This incorporation by reference converts the two documents, the final proposal and the contract, into a macrotext.

As for the six transactional genres that occur prior to any presumed contract, three are initiated by the customer and three by the vendor. Figure 8.3 displays their

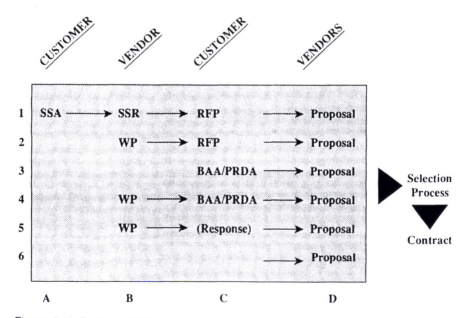

Figure 8.3 Paths to R&D project contract

various relationships to one another, and it also illustrates the possible pathways to a final contract.

The customer's initiatives describe certain needs, that is, certain new knowledge products to support the agency's mission. There are two substantive initiatives. One is the BAA, or broad agency announcement (sometimes called a 'proposed research and development activity', or PRDA). This document describes an extensive field of possible research that would serve the agency's mission, and it invites vendors to propose limited projects within that activity field. The other customer initiative, the RFP (request for proposals), is limited to a project already defined; the RFP includes a SOW, that has already been specified.

The RFP and the BAA serve different purposes; they are independent of each other; they initiate different responsive procedures, different pathways to a possible contract; and they are likely to occur at different times in an agency's funding cycle. The broad announcement (BAA), occurs early in a longer funding cycle, perhaps one to three years long, and it signals the possibility of several different projects as yet undefined; the RFP occurs later, in a shorter time cycle, after a specific project has been conceived. Both documents are statements of need, however.

The vendor's formal initiatives are the white paper and the proposal. These two instruments also serve a common purpose but at different stages in the development of a proposed project. The white paper is a preliminary technical proposal; it addresses a presumed need or problem of the customer and describes some means of meeting that need. Later, as modified and developed after responses from the customer, the white paper becomes a section in the full proposal, which is the vendor's other formal transactional instrument. The proposal is a comprehensive claim statement; it contains a complete technical section, which is the bulk of the document, and it includes appropriate sections on research management and cost.

The vendor writes many more white papers than proposals, sometimes as initiatives and sometimes in response to queries by a customer. The white paper offers the great advantage of not requiring a formal response by the prospective customer. It avoids the need for expensive protocol which federal regulations demand in the treatment of proposals. Its relative informality enables a white paper to be recycled many times in somewhat different forms for different customers. Like the proposal, however, the white paper is essentially a claim.

Two other documents complete the transactional genres. These documents are paired: there is a 'sources sought' announcement by the customer, and the 'sources sought' response by the vendor. 'Sources sought' is a brief description of a pending project; it appears in the pages of the *Commerce Business Daily*. Federal regulations mandate its publication prior to an RFP, and usually it appears some weeks prior to the issue of the RFP.[2] It briefly describes a pending project and invites vendors to state their interest in bidding on it and to describe their credentials for doing so. The purpose of this announcement is to limit the number of bids to be considered in the selection process, and this purpose serves all parties. As a regulatory procedure the announcement provides an entry for new vendors into the procurement system; for the customer it is an efficient screening device.

The important document in this exchange is the vendor's sources-sought response. It is a capability statement; its purpose is to validate a right to bid on the pending project. Invited by the customer, it is candidly a set of claims, wherein the vending organization can describe its research capabilities in terms of the knowledge product that a pending project is intended to yield. To all intents, the sources-sought response is an invited white paper.

These are the principal pre-contract genres: the customer's BAA or RFP, the vendor's white paper and proposal, and the 'sources sought' exchange. They all reveal signs of positioning, of juxtaposing the customer's mission requirements and the vendor's research capabilities, as appropriate to either perspective. In addition to these six transactional genres, customer and vendor both use one other instrument to contextualize their ideas: the formal conference paper, presented at joint meetings for specialists representing both customer and vendor within given fields of research. Such technical papers help to clarify a customer's interests or to inform prospective customers of a vendor's capabilities.

Genre Characteristics

Reviewing genre scholarship in several fields, Swales finds five criterial features of genres (Swales 1990: 45–58). The genres in this R&D procurement system reflect all five. Two of the features are already obvious: they are classes of communicative events, and each class bears a functional name (or acronym). The relevance of these genres to the three other criterial features merits some elaboration. One feature pertains to the rationale of each genre and its constraining effect on textual form, positioning and content. In the R&D genres this feature is striking. All the transactional genres prior to contract between customer and vendor share a remarkable formal resemblance: they variously formulate one prevailing rhetorical mode, the pattern of problem–solution.

The vendors' white papers and proposals are explicit problem formulations, and the customers' needs statements are at least implicitly so. A few other rhetorical modes occasionally serve in individual texts: description, explanation and analysis are appropriately supportive. Narrative almost never appears; there is little or no story sense in these texts. Needs and claims are their substance: needs, formulated by the customer in various problem statements, and claims, contextualized by the vendor within various problem–solution formats. Moreover, these transactional genres all formulate problems whose solutions are assumed to be achievable, given enough time and the right capability. In the idiom of R&D literature, they are fundable problems.

The basic structural similarity of these genres, however, does not preclude other differences among them. These differences illustrate a fourth generic feature, namely, that there are variations in prototypicality. These genres vary widely, for example, in their rhetorical complexity: from the customer's simple 'sources sought' announcement to a vendor's highly complex proposal. They also vary widely in their sense of the reader. In this connection, Swales qualifies Flower's contention (1979) that the immature writer produces 'writer-based prose' and the mature writer produces 'reader-based prose'. He observes, 'it would seem equally clear that in certain genres mature writers also produce "writer-based prose" ' (Swales 1990: 65, citing Flower). These transactional documents bear him out. There is a startling difference in register between the vendor's proposal, which is categorically responsive to the reader's expectations, and the customer's RFP, which has all the sensitivity of a landlord's contract.

The principal criterial feature of genres, according to Swales, is their shared communicative purpose. These R&D documents literally embody this feature. The communicative purpose of each class of documents is insistently explicit, but it is so explicit that it raises a large question about the relationship between genre and discourse community. This is the anomaly that I addressed at the beginning of my remarks.

Genres and Discourse Communities

Derived from the genre features that Swales describes, three interlocking relationships prevail: each genre represents some common communicative purpose; each genre is the property of a discourse community; and commonality of purpose is what links each genre to its discourse community. In his definition of genre, Swales summarizes this tight conceptual relationship:

> The communicative purposes of a genre are recognized by the expert members of the discourse community, and thereby constitute the rationale of the genre. This rationale shapes the schematic structure of the discourse and influences and constrains choice of content and style. (1990: 58)

The elegance of this formulation is its radical economy, its tight linkage of genre and discourse community through their shared rhetorical purpose.

This linkage offers the tempting possibility of explaining how discourse community shapes genre properties, and therefore knowledge production, in the R&D procurement system, but it is precisely the linkage of these three elements that becomes problematic in this system. There is some kind of discrepancy; the nature of the shared purpose that might link the two other elements is not wholly clear. Genre, the first of these elements is already fixed; it is a given. The second element, discourse community, could be causing the discrepancy because it is so narrowly defined by Swales, but this narrowness is also a given. Aware of the possibility of broadening the concept of a discourse community, Swales has already considered and rejected Herzberg's idea (1986) that the notion of a discourse community might better be suggestive than definitive. Swales finds such tentativeness unacceptable if, as he says, we are to make practical use of genre analysis (1990: 22, citing Herzberg).

So the next task on the agenda is to analyse the shared purpose that presumably links the genres in this document exchange system. If such analysis reveals a viable commonality of purpose, then the tight linkage that Swales proposes might be generalized to other complex genre systems that display similar boundary conditions. It is worth a try.

In this discourse exchange system, shared rhetorical purpose functions at different operational levels. At the lowest level, customers and vendors use the genres to serve their separate, individual purposes. At a more abstracted level, customers convey their needs through one subset of genres, and vendors use another subset to claim their capabilities. At the most abstracted level of operation, all customers and vendors mutually participate in the same genre system. What does each level of operation reveal about the linkage between genre and discourse community?

We can readily discard the first possibility. At the lowest operational level, where individual customers support their separate missions and individual vendors attempt to secure individual contracts, rhetorical purpose is clear and evident. We are left in each case, however, with a discourse community of only one party – a trivial concept. At the next higher operational level, there is some justification for grouping all customers together and all vendors together. The code of federal acquisition regulations (FAR) does recognize these virtual categories, but they are not discourse communities, since neither one designates any shared communicative purpose. Customers and vendors alike use the genres to support their own individual objectives.

The remaining possibility is a single discourse community of all customers and vendors together. Do they share a common communicative purpose? Yes, they do, but not in any conspicuous way. It might be argued, for example, that they jointly support the development of a sound technology base for national defence, but this commonality is chiefly the purpose of policy makers who, after all, do not directly participate in this discourse exchange system. Since rhetorical participation is a necessary condition for any discourse community, we might better look at the nature of such participation.

These customers and vendors all subscribe to the R&D procurement system and make it function, despite several conditions that might seem to separate them. What binds them into a single discourse community is the *manner* in which they make the system function. One limiting condition that blurs their common purpose is the FAR, the code of regulations intended to promote fair competition by keeping all vendors equally distant from prospective customers. Yet customers and vendors need each other in this marketplace; customers deliberately search for vendors and, often in the role of patron, nurture them. So the constraining protocols, on the one hand, and the market economy, on the other, engender a delicate balance of competition and collaboration.

In this situation, the notion of exchange is basic. The exchange of transactional documents in the development of a possible research project – one that may or may not come to contract – entails a reciprocity between customer and vendor. Starting from two distinctly different rhetorical perspectives, they successively reify some technological idea. In their respective positioning with reference to this idea, defining a viable research project becomes a fixed, shared purpose. Their rhetorical exchanges form a dialectic. Surely, such reciprocity reflects commonality of purpose.

Yet another condition that blurs this sense of common purpose is the changing rhetorical role of both customer and vendor from one research project to another. So far it has been convenient to observe the dynamics of discourse exchange between one customer and one vendor, but expanding this universe to include even two customers and two vendors reveals an exponential complexity of rhetorical relationships.

A population of merely two customers and two vendors, for example, engenders six possible dyadic relationships. It enables three dyads in each of two distinctly different rhetorical situations. The three dyads are customer-with-vendor, customer-with-customer and vendor-with-vendor. Within each dyad the two possible situations relate both parties operationally as being either segregated or affiliated. So customers and vendors in this system do actually exchange their roles.

Figure 8.4 helps to illustrate this rhetorical complexity. It describes instances of these six rhetorical situations (that is, two parties engaged in any one of three relationships) and displays a linear diagram for each one. By combining the diagrams in various ways, we can infer the multiple purposes inherent in different situations.

As this figure indicates, research projects in the aggregate entail rhetorical purposes that range from collaboration to competition. Each of the dyads can generate

Three dyads   *Symbols*
   customer 1 and vendor 1:   C1 and V1
   customer 1 and customer 2:   C1 and C2
   vendor 1 and vendor 2:   V1 and V2

Two rhetorical relationships
   affiliated, operating jointly: <———>
   segregated, competing: ——> <——

Six possible situations
  1 A customer retains a vendor, as a consultant, to help
    prepare an RFP.   C1 <———> V1
  2 A second vendor responds to this RFP with a proposal.   C1 ——> <——V2

  3 One customer initiates a project but assigns to another
    customer the process of selecting a vendor.   C1 <———> C2
  4 Two customers have similar missions in the same military
    service. Located in different Congressional districts, they
    compete for funds. Each issues a BAA, causing overlap
    in research projects.   C1 ——> <——C2

5 Two vendors team up to offer a proposal.   V1 <———> V2
6 These same two vendors separately respond to a different
  RFP.   V1 ——> <——V2

Figure 8.4   Various rhetorical relationships among customers and vendors

both extremes. The same two vendors might collaborate in one project, for example, yet they might also compete for another. Less obvious but more volatile is the combination of rhetorical purposes that any one project might entail. R&D projects frequently engage three parties from two dyads, thereby involving one of the parties in two polar relationships. For example, one customer might compete with another customer while affiliating with a vendor. Or, conversely, one customer might affiliate with another customer while bargaining with a vendor.

Such is the rhetorical nature of this document exchange system. Like other genre systems, it is social as well as linguistic; it is comprised of actions and reactions. Unlike many other genre systems, however, it accommodates so broad a spectrum of rhetorical situations and such complex interactions that relationships between communicative purpose and discourse community tend to blur. Although each genre serves some finite purpose recognized by the participants, affiliations among these participants frequently shift. And, as they shift, rhetorical purpose becomes a dependent variable from one research project to another.

To accommodate current genre theory to this particular genre system, therefore, some redefinition is in order. It is feasible to conceive of common communicative purpose from two different perspectives, synchronic and diachronic. These perspectives are compatible; they do not exclude each other. In a synchronic sense, communicative purpose consists of a primary commitment to the formation of any given R&D project, wherein the genres variously serve this ruling purpose. Yet this commitment also entails different temporary roles among the participants who use these genres from one project to another, so the notion of communicative purpose can also be seen in a diachronic sense. This latter perspective depends upon separating the notion of audience from the notion of discourse community. Considered over a period of time, the discourse community is a construct of separate audiences that form and dissolve and form again in different alignments to serve the governing purpose of forming an R&D project.

Understanding communicative purpose in this dual sense preserves the linkage of genre and discourse community through the agency of shared purpose, and it also enables such linkage to explain this particular discourse exchange system. Conceiving of purpose from both static and temporal perspectives loosens up the constraining notion of a discourse community, freeing it from being seen as some kind of homogenizing entity. Moreover, this bifocal view of common purpose can also explain other complex genre systems with boundary conditions.

Chief among these conditions is the rhetorical shifting of participants from one alignment to another. The legislative body, for example, is one such discourse community. Its members not only represent different political parties but also engage in temporary, informal alliances that cut across party lines. All of the participants are initiates, and the genres they use enable some kind of ruling communicative purpose to evolve through systemic abrasion. Even more adversarial is the judicial discourse community. Bound by common rules of procedure, all of the participants utter typically generic statements. Moreover, some of these participants regularly change their roles from one litigation to another.

To arrive at this bifocal view of common purpose, as I have mentioned, it is first necessary to separate the concept of discourse community from the concept of audience. This separation enables us to conceive of a discourse community as a set of shifting authors and shifting audiences variously serving one communicative purpose.

So much for this agenda. New business might entail the testing of this analytical tool by using it to describe other rhetorical communities with similar boundary conditions. There are many of them. How well, for example, would it explain other formal genre systems, such as the interactions of investors and analysts in the stock market or in a commodities exchange? Or, for that matter, how well would this analytical tool explain the community that participates in an electronic bulletin board?

Notes

1 The DoD technology base is one component of a much broader category of capability that is referred to as the defense technology base. This broader category encompasses national resources for R&D in both the public and private sectors. See US Congress (1988).
2 *Commerce Business Daily* (*CBD*) is a daily list of US Government procurement invitations, contracting awards, subcontracting leads, sales of surplus property and foreign business opportunities.

References

Commerce Business Daily. Superintendent of Documents, Government Printing Office.
FLOWER, L. (1979) 'Writer-Based Prose: A Cognitive Basis for Problems in Writing, *College English*, **41**, pp. 19–37.
FOWLER, A. (1982) *Kinds of Literature*, Oxford: Oxford University Press.
HERZBERG, B. (1986) 'The Politics of Discourse Communities', paper presented at the CCCC convention, New Orleans, March.
SWALES, J. (1990) *Genre Analysis: English in Academic and Research Settings*, Cambridge: Cambridge University Press.
US CONGRESS, OFFICE OF TECHNOLOGY ASSESSMENT (1988) *The Defense Technology Base: Introduction and Overview – A Special Report*, March, OTA-ISC-374.

Chapter 9

Observing Genres in Action: Towards a Research Methodology

Anthony Paré and Graham Smart

Until recently the study of written genres focused on textual patterns. When researchers wanted to examine a particular genre, they looked across multiple texts for regularities of form and effect. Over the last decade, scholars in composition studies have been reinterpreting genre as social action: a complex pattern of repeated social activity and rhetorical performance arising in response to a recurrent situation. This reinterpretation presents a dilemma for the researcher who wishes to *observe* a particular genre in a specific setting. When conceived as social action, what, in addition to texts, are the observable constituent elements of a genre? And what are the relationships among the elements?

In this chapter, we wish to propose a definition of genre that can serve as a lens for naturalistic research into the use and influence of genres in workplace settings. Our view of genre follows from a social constructionist perspective. From that perspective, a written genre can be seen as a broad rhetorical strategy enacted within a community in order to regularize writer/reader transactions in ways that allow for the creation of particular knowledge. Research in workplace settings has begun to show how professional organizations develop the range of genres they need for constructing the specialized knowledge required to conduct their business (e.g. Miller and Selzer 1985; Winsor 1989; Barabas 1990; Cross 1993; Paré 1993; Smart 1993). This research suggests that when an organization has a stable mandate and a well-defined structure, recurrent problems or exigencies arise, each of which calls for a different type of discourse and knowledge.

Bazerman (1988) suggests that a genre is associated with a pattern of regularity that includes not only repeated features in multiple texts, but also regularities in the production and interpretation of those texts and in the social relations of writers and readers. According to Bazerman, 'These regularities encompass when and how one would approach a test tube or a colleague, how one would go about reading a text, as well as how one would draw a diagram or frame an argument' (1988: 314). Bazerman suggests that the regularities associated with a genre provide a community with the rhetorical stability needed to construct a particular type of knowledge effectively. Thus, genre can be seen as a way to ensure the production of what could be called 'community-based' discourse, a discourse whose meaning is created by and for the collective or group.

Building on the work of Bazerman and others, we propose to define genre as a distinctive profile of regularities across four dimensions: a set of texts, the composing processes involved in creating these texts, the reading practices used to interpret them, and the social roles performed by writers and readers.

To illustrate what the definition allows a researcher to see and describe, we will apply it to genres in two different settings: we will look at a genre known as the *predisposition report* in a Montreal social service agency and at a genre known as the *automation proposal* in the Ottawa head office of a large Canadian bank. Both these organizations have a relatively stable mandate and a well-defined, hierarchical structure.[1]

The predisposition report is written by a social worker as an advisory report to a judge on the sentencing of an adolescent found guilty of a criminal offence. The report describes the events leading to the offence, assesses the youth and his or her family situation, and recommends an appropriate sentence, usually consisting of probation, community service, and/or financial restitution. The report is entered as evidence at a sentencing hearing, and is read by the judge, the defence and prosecuting lawyers, the adolescent and his or her family, and other professionals within the social service network. The genre produces the specialized knowledge that the social service agency and legal system need for what they feel is the fair and appropriate treatment of adolescent offenders.

The bank's automation proposal presents an argument for developing or purchasing a computer system for processing data in some area of the institution. The proposal is produced jointly by employees from the computer department and employees from what is known as 'the user area', that part of the institution that would use the computer system. The user area might be, for example, a group of economists, financial analysts, auditors or personnel specialists. The genre provides the senior management of the bank with the knowledge they need to make a decision about whether to proceed with the project and, if so, how to proceed.

Below we elaborate on the four dimensions of our definition and look at how they apply to the two genres we have studied.

Regularities in Textual Features

Repeated patterns in the structure, rhetorical moves and style of texts are the most readily observable aspects of genre (for exemplary analyses of this dimension of genre, see Freedman 1987, condensed version Chapter 12, this volume; Bazerman 1988: 153–86). Thus, for example, one can identify individual components of a generic text, their usual sequence, and their common function or purpose. Covering letters or memos, title pages, tables of content, abstracts, introductions, problem statements, summaries, analyses of options, recommendations, conclusions and so on perform the same function, in the same order, again and again.

Likewise, texts within a genre employ particular rhetorical moves. As others have noted, modes of argument vary from community to community and, within communities, from one type of discourse to another (Toulmin 1958; Toulmin *et al.*

1979; Willard 1982). The provision of evidence, appeals to authority, citation practices, patterns in causation and comparison, exemplification, definition, and other rhetorical moves recur with definite regularity. Moreover, the acceptable use of these moves is often governed by community conventions. So, for example, some types of evidence or claims for causation are acceptable, while others are not.

Finally, a common style is often discernible in generic texts. Sentence and paragraph length, use of active and passive voice, references to self or to readers, specialized terminology, set phrases and tone, for example, remain relatively constant across multiple texts within a genre. Some organizations attempt to ensure the standardization of certain textual features by codifying structure, rhetorical moves, and/or style in in-house guidelines or manuals. In other organizations, these features are often conventionalized by tacit agreement – the lore of the tribe, as it were.

The predisposition report, for example, is structured according to printed guidelines that provide a broad schema for the report – that is, the titles of the individual report sections and their appropriate sequence. The section titles identify their function: 'Summary of Offences', 'Assessment of Adolescent', 'Family Assessment', and so on. Under each title is a brief description of what the section should contain. For example, for 'Assessment of Adolescent', the guidelines recommend the following:

> (i) Describe the adolescent according to age, maturity, character, and personality. (ii) Evaluate the adolescent's degree of motivation and his (*sic*) capacity to curb his delinquent behaviour. (iii) Assess any plans put forward by the adolescent to change his conduct or to participate in activities or undertake measures to improve himself.

As can be seen, the guidelines do more than prescribe the sequence and function of the report sections. They also provide a set of rhetorical moves: describe, evaluate, assess. In addition, although not recorded in the guidelines, there are generic restrictions on the types of evidence social workers can employ. Hearsay and self-reported delinquencies, for instance, are inadmissible.

Also not present in the guidelines, but nonetheless codified by tacit agreement, are regularities in style. For example, writers avoid the use of first person pronouns, which leads to the passive voice in such phrases as 'it is believed' and 'it is assessed', or to formulations like 'the undersigned' and 'this worker' to refer to the self.

Although no printed institutional guidelines exist for the automation proposal, and although no standard headings are used, by convention the document is typically divided into six parts, each performing a particular function: the first part provides an overview of the argument presented in the proposal; the second part describes the business activities of the area under study, its current method of processing data, the limitations of this method, and the consequent risks; the third part stipulates requirements such as system performance, compatibility with existing systems, security, cost constraints, and timeliness that any acceptable computerized data-processing system must meet; the fourth part assesses the advantages and disadvantages of the feasible automation alternatives; the fifth part recommends, and justifies, one of these alternatives; and the last part outlines an implementation plan that includes resource requirements, work activities and a schedule.

Overall, this discourse structure embodies an extended argument situated in a world of perceived problems, risks and solutions. In each part of the proposal, particular rhetorical moves are deployed. For example, the fourth part typically assesses the feasible automation alternatives by comparing them on the basis of such factors as performance, security and cost. This analysis then becomes the underpinning for the recommendation and justification in the next part of the document.

Stylistically, texts within the genre exhibit a high degree of similarity. For example, sentences tend to be relatively short, specialized computer terminology is translated into plain English, unnecessary adjectives and adverbs are stripped away, imperatives such as 'must' and 'should' are avoided, and English spelling conventions are usually followed rather than American.

Regularities in Social Roles

Writers and readers play various roles in organizations and in the creation and use of texts. These roles are described, in part, by organizational charts and job descriptions; however, a full appreciation of the part that roles play in the production and use of generic texts can only be gained by observing an organization's drama of interaction, the interpersonal dynamics that surround and support certain texts.

Individuals may play a variety of different roles within a collective, with certain roles being specific to a given type of document. Moreover, a single genre may involve the individual in a variety of different relationships with other people implicated by the discourse. Roles and the networks of relationship that connect them are often generic – they serve to regularize the social interaction, as well as the writing and reading, involved in the production of knowledge.

The roles related to a given genre are defined within certain parameters, such as responsibilities, levels of relative power and influence, division of labour, channels of and access to information, and the obligation and freedom to report. These generic characteristics of role and relationship determine what can and cannot be done and said by particular individuals, as well as when, how, where and to whom.

Thus, for example, in her role as adviser to the court, the writer of a predisposition report *must* make recommendations to the judge on the sentencing of an adolescent, while looking ahead to her role as probation officer. At the same time, in her role as witness to the court, she typically has an adversarial relationship with the defence lawyer, who is seeking leniency for the adolescent, and a collegial relationship with the prosecuting lawyer, who is seeking legal consequences for the offence. And so on. As one predisposition report writer put it, 'I write with one pen and twenty hats.' Within this complex network of relationships, the social worker follows rules governing her provision of information. She cannot, for instance, mention other charges pending against the adolescent or report previous offences mentioned in interviews.

149

The genre of the automation proposal also includes well-defined roles and a network of social relationships. To organize the research and analysis, the resolution of issues and the decision-making required in a major automation project, the bank employs a methodology known as the 'Information System Delivery Series'. For the duration of the project, this methodology establishes a microcosm of roles and relationships within the larger environment of the institution.

Specifically, six roles are defined: the project team, which includes one or more employees from the user area and one or more from the computer department, carries out the basic research and analysis; the business system manager, a mid-level employee in the user area, ensures that the automated system will provide the necessary functionality for the area's data-processing operations; the project manager, a mid-level employee from the computer department, deals with technical concerns related to hardware and software; the system owner, a senior employee in the user area with overall responsibility for the data-processing operations to be automated, helps resolve business and political issues as they arise; the project steering committee, which includes the system owner and other senior people from both the user area and the computer department, provides a periodic forum for decision-making; and the bank's Automation Committee, a standing committee of five executives, makes the final decision on whether a proposed automation initiative is justified and, if so, how it should proceed. As defined formally by the methodology and informally by convention, each of the six roles carries with it a structure of relationships with other individuals involved in the project as well as specific, generic responsibilities for the writing and reading involved in the production and use of an automation proposal.

As part of an organization's 'repeated strategy' (Bazerman 1988), generic roles ensure the consistent and effective production of discourse and knowledge required by the organization's mandate, despite the idiosyncrasies of the various individuals who fill the roles. As a result, no matter who acts as social worker, judge, project manager or system owner, the genre is enacted in much the same way from one instance to another.

Regularities in Composing Processes

In our definition, the notion of composing processes includes a broad range of activities. We use the term to refer to the following:

1 an initiating event;
2 information gathering (such as interviewing people, participating in meetings, observing work activities and reading documentation);
3 analysis of information (such as identifying significant patterns, defining problems, forming opinions);
4 individual writing and rewriting;
5 collaborative activities (such as brainstorming, cocomposing, sharing of drafts among peers, reviewing, evaluating); and
6 the technology of production (e.g. typing, word-processing, electronic mail).

The predisposition report is initiated when a social worker receives a young offender's file and a judge's request for a report. The file contains a police report and a formal statement of the charge on which the adolescent was found guilty.

In an attempt to explain the offence and place it in the context of the adolescent's life, the social worker gathers information by conducting telephone and face-to-face interviews with the adolescent, parents, the school, employers and others. In addition, she or he reviews files on the adolescent, if there are any, and talks to other social workers who have worked with the youth or family.

During her or his investigation, the social worker keeps 'progress notes', in which she or he records contacts and comments on the information she or he is collecting. In the first stage of composing the actual report, the worker creates a handwritten draft by arranging the information under the various report headings listed in the guidelines that were mentioned earlier. At this point, she or he may decide to discuss the draft with one or more of her or his colleagues. As well, in a serious or difficult case, the worker's supervisor reviews the draft before submission. The final draft is typed by a secretary and reproduced by photocopier.

The composing processes involved in producing an automation proposal are also predictable. A major automation project is usually initiated when the computer department and a user area collaborate in conducting an 'opportunity evaluation' that results in a written recommendation to study the advantages and costs of computerizing some part of the area's data-processing operations.

Next, during what is known as the 'preliminary analysis' phase of the project, a project team is assembled to gather detailed information about the business activities of the user area and to research the feasible automation options. As the members of the project team proceed through the preliminary analysis phase, they collaborate in producing a sequence of documents called 'deliverables', which are intended both to orient the work of the team and to demonstrate to the business system manager and the project manager that the project is on track. At the end of the preliminary analysis phase, if the business system manager and the project manager agree that a convincing case can be made for computerizing the data-processing operations under study, they prepare an automation proposal intended for the Automation Committee, drawing on the project team's deliverables. Successive drafts of the proposal, composed on a microcomputer, are reviewed by the system owner and the other members of the project steering committee, who will frequently ask for revisions. When finally approved by the project steering committee, the proposal is sent to the Automation Committee for a decision.

With both the predisposition report and the automation proposal, generic composing processes allow for consistency in the making of knowledge. For example, in both cases, regularized composing processes ensure that the perspectives and expertise of different people are incorporated into the evolving text at the appropriate times.

Regularities in Reading Practices

In our definition, reading practices are also viewed rather broadly. We use the term *to refer to:*

1 the way a reader approaches a text (where, when and why it is read; along with what other documents);
2 how the reader negotiates his or her way through the text (e.g. previewing the text, deciding what parts to read carefully and what parts to skim);
3 how the reader constructs knowledge from the text (the questions asked, the interpretive frameworks applied); and
4 how the reader uses the resulting knowledge (e.g. to perform an action, to make a decision or participate with others in decision-making, or to produce a piece of writing).

Regularities in the reading practices associated with the predisposition report are shaped in large part by the legal context within which the report operates. The judge, defence lawyer and prosecutor receive the report before the sentencing hearing. The judge is concerned primarily with the recommendations for sentencing. The defence lawyer, as advocate for the adolescent, looks for inadmissible evidence, unfounded assumptions, overly harsh recommendations and other opportunities to discredit the report. The prosecutor, who works closely with the social worker and tends to support her or his perspective, looks for the key points that justify the recommended sentence. The adolescent and family are the subjects of the report; they read to discover its implications for them. Later, if the adolescent is placed in custody, other social workers will read the report as a basis for a treatment plan.

Generic reading practices are also associated with the bank's automation proposal. In producing the proposal, the business system manager and the project manager draw upon deliverables produced by the project team. When reviewing this material, the business system manager is concerned with how accurately it depicts the user area's business activities and data-processing operations, while the project manager focuses on how the computer hardware and software are represented. When drafts of the proposal are forwarded to the system owner and the other members of the project steering committee for review, they too read it from a particular stance. For example, they read in anticipation of questions they assume the executives on the Automation Committee will ask. These questions include the following:

- Which of the bank's business activities and data-processing operations are involved?
- What is the problem inherent in the status quo?
- What is the risk if something isn't done, and why is it important to act now, rather than later?
- Why is a computer system the best way to go?
- What automation alternatives have been considered, and what are the advantages and disadvantages of each?
- Which alternative is recommended and why?
- How will the recommended hardware and software fit into the institution's larger network of computer systems?

Recurrent reading practices allow an organization to replicate the activity of interpretation. They ensure that readers will take the appropriate stance, ask the right questions, draw the relevant implications, and thus make informed decisions. To a significant degree, they conventionalize the highly idiosyncratic act of reading.

Conclusion

As we mentioned at the outset, our purpose has been to propose a definition of genre for researchers examining writing in workplace settings. We believe the definition can help researchers explore the full range of social action that constitutes an organization's repeated rhetorical strategies, or genres.

Moreover, we believe that the definition provides a lens through which researchers can examine the influence and acquisition of genres. In other words, as a research tool, the definition allows us to consider some of the questions posed in this volume.

If we wish to know more about how a genre both constrains and enables writers and readers, we can examine textual features, writing processes, reading practices and social roles to see how they act as positive or negative heuristics. How do these dimensions of genre enable or prevent ways of seeing and knowing? What kind of thinking or problem-solving does the genre facilitate? And how much leeway do individuals have within any one dimension of the genre? Can textual features be altered without jeopardy? How far can writers and readers stray from the roles they conventionally perform within a genre before the collective is threatened?

Likewise, the definition can help us understand the process of learning genres, of becoming initiated into a community. Are initiates introduced to generic features of texts by way of guidelines or manuals, or must they learn tacitly held conventions governing structure, rhetorical moves and style by trial and error? How do writers learn to participate in the community's repeated composing processes and how do they come to understand and anticipate the generic reading practices of the people who receive their texts? Finally, how can we use an increased understanding of how a genre is typically learned to inform our teaching? For example, what aspects of a genre can be taught explicitly and what aspects must a writer learn on his or her own through active participation in a community?[2]

We wish to sound two notes of caution. First, the very term 'genre', and the definition we propose, imply stable social activities and rhetorical performances and, indeed, that patterns of similarity are a defining characteristic of genres. However, a workplace genre is an extremely complex interaction. Though similar, no two occurrences of the genre are ever identical, and genres are in a constant state of evolution. They change as the nature of the exigencies to which they respond change. They may also change in response to dissatisfaction with one or more of the dimensions of genre we have described.

Another caution: whenever we create categories for analysis, we 'trade a loss of reality for a gain in control' (Moffett 1968: 23). Genres are complex social actions, and the dimensions we describe are not discrete or mutually exclusive; they are reciprocal and interactive. In a sense, our definition extends Miller's (1984: 159; revised version Chapter 2, this volume) definition of genres as 'typified rhetorical actions based in recurrent situations'. We suggest that genres are typified rhetorical actions *and* recurrent situations. Our definition should help researchers examine the parts in this dynamic whole.

Notes

1 With their well-defined hierarachy and stable mandate, the social service agency and bank examined in this chapter differ both from emerging organizations and from mature organizations with shifting mandates. In such organizations, writing and knowledge production may be less regularized because the organizations do not, to the same degree, exhibit the recurrent situations and exigencies that evoke the development of distinct genres.
2 See articles (pp. 222–82) in *Research in the Teaching of English*, **27**, 3 (October 1993) for an extended discussion of this issue.

References

BARABAS, C. (1990) *Technical Writing in A Corporate Culture: A Study of the Nature of Information*, Norwood, NJ: Ablex.

BAZERMAN, C. (1988) *Shaping Written Knowledge: The Genre and Activity of the Experimental Article in Science*, Madison, WI: University of Wisconsin Press.

CROSS, G. A. (1993) 'The Interrelation of Genre, Context, and Process in the Collaborative Writing of Two Corporate Documents', in SPILKA, R. (ed.) *Writing in the Workplace: New Research Perspectives*, Carbondale, IL: Southern Illinois University Press, pp. 141–52.

FREEDMAN, A. (1987) 'Learning to Write Again: Discipline-Specific Writing at University', *Carleton Papers in Applied Language Studies*, 4, pp. 95–115.

MILLER, C. R. (1984) 'Genre as Social Action', *Quarterly Journal of Speech*, **70**, pp. 151–67.

MILLER, C. R. and SELZER, J. (1985) 'Special Topics of Argument in Engineering Reports', in ODELL, L. and GOSWAMI, D. (eds) *Writing in Nonacademic Settings*, New York: Guilford, pp. 309–41.

MOFFETT, J. (1968) *Teaching the Universe of Discourse*, Boston, MA: Houghton Mifflin.

PARÉ, A. (1993) 'Discourse Regulations and the Production of Knowledge', in SPILKA, R. (ed.) *Writing in the Workplace: New Research Perspectives*, Carbondale, IL: Southern Illinois University Press, pp. 111–23.

SMART, G. (1993) 'Genre as Community Invention: A Central Bank's Response to Its Executives' Expectations as Readers', in SPILKA, R. (ed.) *Writing in the Workplace: New Research Perspectives*, Carbondale, IL: Southern Illinois University Press, pp. 124–40.

TOULMIN, S. (1958) *The Uses of Argument*, New York: Cambridge University Press.

TOULMIN, S., RIEKE, R. and JANIK, A. (1979) *An Introduction to Reasoning*, New York: Macmillan.

WILLARD, C. A. (1982) 'Argument Fields', in COX, J. R. and WILLARD, C. A. (eds) *Advances in Argumentation Theory and Research*, Carbondale, IL: Southern Illinois University Press, pp. 24–77.

WINSOR, D. (1989) 'An Engineer's Writing and the Corporate Construction of Knowledge', *Written Communication*, **6**, pp. 270–85.

Chapter 10

Genre and the Pragmatic Concept of Background Knowledge

Janet Giltrow

The pragmatic concept of Background Knowledge[1] identifies propositions unstated by a text but necessary for its interpretation. So Background Knowledge can explain what is called conversational implicature – the message arising from an utterance which, on the surface, appears to be irrelevant in the context, but which a listener can interpret as relevant by consulting certain unexpressed propositions. Background Knowledge is thus a factor in a text's *coherence*, capable of providing the basis for understanding why the speaker chose to continue with one sentence rather than another.

Background Knowledge is a resource shared by the producers and receivers of utterances. In her or his design of the utterance, the producer assumes the availability of certain Background Knowledge to the receiver, and the receiver assumes that the producer does indeed make that assumption, and interprets the message accordingly. By identifying this shared resource, the concept of Background Knowledge takes account of the fact that not everything is spelled out. If a community of language users is very practised in a situation, it may develop ways of leaving things unsaid, these unsaid things marking a condition of mutual understanding. In fact, to actually say what is usually assumed may sound mistaken.

There are some signs that ways of assuming Background Knowledge (BK) are relevant to the study of genre. Prince's study (1981) of the linguistic evidence of 'assumed familiarity' in a conversational narrative and a scholarly article revealed very different patterns of assumptions about BK, suggesting that, in the article at least, ways of constructing the reader's prior knowledge of the world were distinctive. A study of BK assumptions in a technical manual (Giltrow 1992) revealed a pattern which changed as the document converted itself from procedural manual to reference manual. This change appeared to be generically characteristic. A small study (Giltrow and Valiquette 1991) of the response of academic readers to student papers in psychology and criminology revealed that readers made some of their judgments about the appropriateness of claims by referring to their sense of what should be explicitly stated and what should be left unsaid and assumed as BK. And, at a more general level, Bakhtin's 'The Problem of Speech Genres' (1986: 96) claims that speakers select genre on the basis of their estimate of the addressee's 'apperceptive background' – that is, that genre is a portrait of 'the scope of [the reader's] specialized knowledge'.

Closer to genre study itself, however, are the inquiries which Swales cites and conducts in speculating on distinguishing features of the method section of the research article. Swales cites two studies (Bruce 1983; Weissberg 1984) that discovered in method sections conditions which called on readers to bring to bear their 'shared knowledge' (from Bruce, cited by Swales) to construct coherence or to perform 'inferential bridging' (from Weissberg, cited by Swales) – that is, the passages '[relied] on readers' background knowledge or experience . . . for coherence' (Swales 1990: 168). Speculating on readers' performance at these gaps, Swales goes on to propose that

> Method sections, like other condensed texts such as abstracts and telexes, evince in Hallidayan terms coherence but little cohesion . . . In many methods paragraphs the sentences are like islands in a string, islands which only those with specialist knowledge and experience can easily jump across from one to the next. (p. 168)

Island-jumping, then, may be both a distinguishing feature of certain genres, and a site of crucial affinity among users of the genres.

Background Knowledge operates at two levels in the life of a genre. The first level is well known in genre study, although not necessarily identified as a matter of Background Knowledge: users of a genre share knowledge of the genre's conventions. Readers of, for example, real-estate advertisements in the classified sections of newspapers know how to use expressions of sizes, cost and age to construct the intent of these texts about human shelter. Writers assume this BK of their readers, and readers assume that writers have made these assumptions. At the second level of operation, writers assume on behalf of the reader some knowledge of the world which the reader can consult in order to interpret the utterance.[2] This chapter asks whether these assumptions occur with regularity that can be linked to genre formations.

1 Does a particular genre provide for the assumption of particular kinds of knowledge?
2 Is the assumed Background Knowledge 'low' enough to qualify as belonging to the domain of genre? (For example, assumed knowledge of the decline associated with ageing, or of the coldness of winter and the heat of summer, or the intentions of doctors to heal rather than harm may belong to domains – human experience or culture – too high to be captured by genre.)

Method

I investigated a collection of texts from an intuitively recognizable genre: from three months (November to December 1990, January 1991) of a Canadian metropolitan daily, all instances (13) of reports of sentencing for violent crime.[3] The collection was analysed along lines common in genre study: that is, a readerly familiarity with the genre (acquired as part of life experience and by reading the collection) alerted the researcher to distinguishing features. An example of this readerly research style is the abiding interest in citation practices in the scholarly genres; readers notice that citation is a prominent feature, and, as researchers, they investigate this eye-catching phenomenon – or the role of present tenses, or the distribution of claims across the partitions of the research article's parts. In the report-of-sentencing genre, I noticed and analysed three features:

1 mentions of types of events;
2 the use of reported direct and indirect speech;
3 the forms of expression used to refer to the offender.

The same analysis was carried out on all instances (8) of reports of sentencing for violent crime in the same newspaper November to December 1950.

I then analysed the samples for configurations of Background Knowledge by estimating the *relevance* of propositions to their neighbours. Analysis of relevance gets to the heart of Background Knowledge, but this is an occluded heart, and difficult to diagnose. Although BK is available as a concept to discourse analysis, it is not exactly a discourse feature, because it is, after all, what is left unstated by the text. Nevertheless, guided by the work of theorists and investigators in this area (principally Sperber and Wilson 1986; Siklaki 1988), I tried to evaluate the grounds on which propositions' appearance was justified by cotext. Where I found a gap – that is, where an unstated assumption had to be consulted to grasp the relevance of a proposition to its cotext – I estimated the Background Knowledge which the writer assumed the reader would bring to the text. Generally speaking, these gaps were associated with a diminishment in cohesive ties.[4]

To demonstrate how I detected Background Knowledge assumptions, I will here present first an instance in which BK is *not* assumed but spelled out as information, and then an instance of information retracted to Background Knowledge. The first instance is from a report (1992) of an inquest into the deaths of 15 children in a home for the severely handicapped:

(8) The 15 deaths at the home were all morphine-related, and occurred from 1986 to 1990. (9) All the children faced shortened life spans.

(10) Dr Sliwowicz testified that morphine was the best drug available to alleviate the children's suffering, even though many of the children had respiratory ailments. (11) He acknowledged that morphine represses the 'respiratory drive', but at the same time it makes the child less apprehensive, he said.

(12) A dose of between 1.5 and three milligrams is the general guideline for a child, but Dr Sliwowicz often prescribed five milligrams.

(13) He said he only rarely relied on X-rays to detect pneumonia. (14) The home did not have an X-ray unit.

(15) [X-rays and blood tests are the standard tools to diagnose viral or bacterial pneumonia.]

(16) Dr Sliwowicz said he also avoided blood tests, partly because they would cause discomfort. (17) He added he thought they were unreliable in detecting bacterial diseases.[5]

Sentence 9 (S9) is relevant to S8 via BK that 15 child deaths in four years is a lot; S9's presence is a sign of that BK being assumed, for it addresses questions which immediately arise as to this mortality rate. The independent clause of S10 ties via 'morphine' to 'morphine-related' in S8. But the dependent clause of S10 introduces 'respiratory ailments' as an untied item – a potentially irrelevant mention. The writer evidently constructs the reader as *not* having access to Background Knowledge which explains the relevance of 'respiratory ailments' to morphine prescriptions, for, with S11, he provides the information which demonstrates its relevance: 'morphine represses the "respiratory drive".' Similarly, the first clause of S12 provides the grounds for the interpretation of 'Dr Sliwowicz often prescribed five milligrams'; the writer assumes that the amount of the 'general guideline' dose is not in the reader's store of Background Knowledge. With S13 and S14, a new item is introduced – 'X-ray' – untied to previous items except through medical collocations. Once again, the writer constructs the reader as not having the BK to interpret this item's relevance. S15 explicitly provides the ground for interpretation – and, at the same time, provides a cohesive anchor for S15's 'blood tests' and grounds for the interpretation of the relevance of S15 and S16.

When this information is retracted to Background Knowledge, the passage reads like this:

The 15 deaths at the home were all morphine-related, and occurred from 1986 to 1990. All the children faced shortened life spans.

Dr Sliwowicz testified that morphine was the best drug available to alleviate the children's suffering, even though many of the children had respiratory ailments. It makes the child less apprehensive, he said.

Dr Sliwowicz often prescribed five milligrams of morphine.

He said he only rarely relied on X-rays to detect pneumonia. The home did not have an X-ray unit.

Dr Sliwowicz said he also avoided blood tests, partly because they would cause discomfort. He added he thought they were unreliable in detecting bacterial diseases.

At the same time as it leaves certain items stranded – 'respiratory ailments', 'five milligrams', 'X-rays', 'blood tests' – this version constructs the reader as having access to BK which explains the grounds for determining the relevance of respiratory ailments, dosage, X-ray, and blood tests to evaluating the doctor's behaviour. The witness's and/or the reporter's explanations are seen as unnecessary and possibly redundant – as they would no doubt be for certain specialist audiences.

In the next example, taken from the collection of analysed texts, some BK *is* assumed – Background Knowledge that might be considered, in some sense, specialist. This comes from the report of sentencing of a 'child molester' convicted of 'repeatedly stabbing a woman, after they watched a movie that ended with the main character being butchered in her bed' (S1):

(4) The judge agreed with prosecutor Wendy Sabean that Blakemore, 31, of Georgetown 'poses a real threat to the safety of others'.

(5) The judge was told that Blakemore has confessed to sexually assaulting at least 17 boys and girls ranging in age from 6 to 10.

(6) Blakemore wants his mother, father and Sunday school teacher charged for abusing him when he was a child, court was told.

(7) Lyon [the judge] recommended that Blakemore receive psychiatric treatment while in custody but pointed out that the prognosis is poor.

(8) A jury found Blakemore guilty of attempting to murder the 31-year-old victim in her downtown apartment on 23 October 1989.

(9) The jury was not told the name of the movie but Sabean identified it after the trial as *Gorillas in the Mist*.[6]

Leaving aside the problem that, while 'abuse' ties with 'assault', the damage done in S6 is to the offender, not to his own victims, as in S5, here isolated items are 'psychiatric treatment' and 'mother, father and Sunday school teacher'. BK is necessary to 'jump' these 'islands' – BK which, if spelled out, and converted to information like that in the inquest passage, might look something like this:

(4) The judge agreed with prosecutor Wendy Sabean that Blakemore, 31, of Georgetown 'poses a real threat to the safety of others'.

(5) The judge was told that Blakemore has confessed to sexually assaulting at least 17 boys and girls ranging in age from 6 to 10.

(6) Blakemore wants his mother, father and Sunday school teacher charged for abusing him when he was a child, court was told. A widely observed cause of adult violence is childhood experience of abuse by family members and/or respected members of the community.

(7) Lyon [the judge] recommended that Blakemore receive psychiatric treatment while in custody but pointed out that the prognosis is poor. A standard response to violence is institutional intervention in the form of therapeutic strategies targeting early-life psychological trauma.

(8) A jury found Blakemore guilty of attempting to murder the 31-year-old victim in her downtown apartment on 23 October 1989.

Just as a specialist audience would not need the explanation of X-rays and so on, this audience doesn't need explanations of psychiatric treatment and mother, father and Sunday school teacher. Readers of reports of sentencing are perhaps specialized in their own way. If this specialization shows any regularity, it may be associated with genre.

A Brief Portrait of the Genre in 1990

Discussing the development of the experimental report, Charles Bazerman (1989: 62) poses a question that powerfully compresses the matter of genre: 'How does the world of events get reduced to the virtual world of words?' In reports of sentencing, the number and variety of represented events is very large – and the techniques for their reduction into words therefore all the more remarkable.

Centrally, there is the crime to be reckoned with: the action of stabbing, shooting, punching, hitting, surrounded by the immediate events that led up to the violent act – the preliminary confrontation or intrusion, the escalation of hostility – and the events which comprise the immediate aftermath – injury, hospitalization, the actions of police. More events stretch beyond the crime: arrest, charges, custody, recuperation from injury. Other events arise in the deeper past – episodes from the life history of the offender, and, less frequently, the victim. And then there are the courtroom events to be accounted for: pleading, testimony (often conflicting), legal arguments and rulings, jury deliberations, and, finally, the sentencing – itself accompanied by interpretations, by the offender's reactions, and by the prosecuting and defending lawyers' commentaries.

To further complicate matters, many of these events have already been 'reduced to...words' – as police reports, charges, testimony, presentencing reports and sentencing. Each of these reductions is itself no doubt a genre, and the conventions of these prior genres leave vestigial traces in the report-of-sentencing genre.

Types of Mention: What Kinds of Things Can Be Said

All articles from 1990 began the same way: a single sentence reported both the crime and punishment. For example:

A Mississauga carpenter has been sentenced to six months in reformatory for punching his neighbor three times while demanding payment of a $200 debt.

A former Jamaican police officer has been sent to prison for 21 years for disabling two women and shooting a third in the Etobicoke factory where they worked in December, 1989.

After this highly regular syntactic fusion of *crime + sentence*, the reports continue by developing several or all of the following categories, here ordered roughly from greater to less frequency:

- *interpretation of sentence* (commentary on the relative severity or leniency of the sentence): e.g. ' "This was an offence involving stark horror", Mr Justice William Lyon said yesterday in the Ontario Court, general division, in Toronto.'
- *events of the crime*: e.g. 'The officer hit the dirt when he saw the .357 magnum being pointed at him, Manarin said.'
- *effects on victim*: e.g. 'Eberhardt, 26, who works out of Metro's Central Traffic unit, received stitches to his right shoulder.'
- *legal events* (charging, pleading, jury deliberation, staying of charges, appealing, etc.): e.g. 'The girl, who can't be identified, has also been charged with first-degree murder in Sepp's death and has been ordered to stand trial in adult court.'
- *sentence provisions*: e.g. 'He prohibited Melo from associating with anyone with a criminal record or other persons deemed "disreputable" by his probation officer and he directed Melo to find and keep a job.'
- *pre-crime history* (usually of the offender but sometimes of the victim as well): e.g. 'Harrison was the principal of Northern Agincourt Junior Public School and had lived with Hollyhock since 1969 when they both taught music in Ottawa.'
- *offender's reaction* to sentence: e.g. 'He showed no emotion yesterday at his sentence.'

The preferred order of these categories appears to follow the opening *crime + sentence* with *interpretation*, then *events* and *effects*, other categories appearing in less predictable order (see Table 10.1).

The genre's stability permits just these categories (only a handful of propositions were unclassifiable) and loosely predisposes their order. At the same time, this stability also permits the texts' producers to select and interpose some of the rarer categories according to their perception of the situation, and to move abruptly from one category to another without disrupting the reader's expectation. For example, the narrative of the events of the crime can appear suddenly after an account of the jury's gender composition and its hours of deliberation.

Reported Speech: Who is Entitled to Say

Like a grid overlaying a map, another system settles over the sequence of categories: a system of reported direct and indirect speech. Bell (1991: 41, 52–55) has observed that news reporting is as much a matter of compiling the words of others as it is a matter of actually writing words of one's own. In the 1990 report of sentencing, compiling techniques are a stylization of the courtroom itself.

Table 10.1 Order and categories of utterance 1990

s	1	2	3	4	5	6	7	8	9	10	11	12	13
1	sentence and crime	sentence and crime	sentence and crime	sentence and crime	sentence and crime	sentence and crime	sentence and crime	sentence and crime	sentence and crime	sentence and crime	sentence and crime	sentence and crime	sentence and crime
2	sentence	events	interpret.	effects	interpret.	interpret. and effects	interpret.	off.'s react., int. and effects	interpret.	interpret.	legal and crime	interpret.	legal and crime
3	legal	interpret.	interpret.	effects	interpret.	legal and effects	interpret.	legal and crime	interpret.	interpret.	legal and interpret.	interpret.	interpret.
4	legal	events	effects	?	interpret.	effects	interpret.	legal and crime	legal	interpret.	interpret.	interpret.	interpret.
5	crime	events	events and effects	effects	interpret.	interpret.	legal and crime	victims' reactions	legal and crime	interpret.	off.'s reaction and legal	interpret.	offender's reactions
6	crime		cause	events	interpret.	crime and effects	sentence and effects	events	legal	interpret.	events	history and legal	offender's reaction
7	events		cause	events	legal and crime	effects	events	events	legal and crime	interpret.	events	sentence	events
8	events			events	events	legal	events	effects	legal	events	history	legal and crime	events
9					events	legal	events	events	effects	interpret.	history	legal and events	history
10					events	interpret.	events and effects	events	history	events	history	events	legal and crime
11					events	legal		effects	effects	sentence	events	events and effect	legal
12					sentence			effects	effects	sentence	events and arrest	effects	legal
13					sentence			effects	events		history	effects	history
14								sentence	events		events	effects	history
15									events		sentence	effects	history
16												effects	history
17												effects	history
18												events	offender's reaction
19												arrest	offender's reaction
20												events	legal and sentence
21												history	interpret.
22												history	legal
23													legal

In the 13 articles, words attributed to others (through either direct or indirect report) range from 10 per cent of total words in the shortest article to 79 per cent (see Table 10.2). In seven of the articles, reported speech comprises more than 50 per cent of total words. Overwhelmingly, judges are the most voluminous speakers, and victims the least. Prosecutors and defenders have their say as well, and in three cases, so do offenders. Offenders are principally entitled to give their account of the crime, however, and these accounts not only contradict the judicial version but also tend to be postponed to the end of the article.

The grid of reported speech further partitions a genre already partitioned by the stability of categories. Just as the narrative of crime events can follow reports of jury deliberations, or report of intended appeal can follow the narrative of crime events, one speaker can abruptly fall silent and another can begin – as long as they both belong to groups to which the genre assigns speaking roles.[7] This continuation is not simply a replica of speech in the courtroom – prosecutors and offenders do not interrupt judges delivering sentences – but a technique of the genre's reduction of events into words.

Referring Expressions: Who These People Are

Officers of the court are uniformly identified in restrictive appositives by their courtroom role: e.g. 'Mr Justice Victor Paisley', '[d]efence lawyer Brian Greenspan', '[p]rosecutor Ann Morgan'. The limitations on expressions referring to officers of the court are apparent when these expressions are compared to those which refer to offenders.

Offenders are identified in the first sentence – which invariably reports crime + sentence. In all but three cases

- James Tobin;
- Former metro boxer Eddie Melo, 30;
- North Bay's leading pediatrician;

offenders first appear in noun phrases with indefinite determiners:

- a Mississaugua carpenter;
- a 31-year-old cocktail waitress;
- an 18-year-old man who pointed a powerful handgun at a Metro police officer after a high-speed car chase;
- a man who repeatedly stabbed a Metro police officer with an industrial screw;
- a 28-year-old Peterborough man of borderline intelligence and abused as a child;
- a carpenter who smashed a woman in the face with a tree during a driving dispute;
- a high school teacher who had sex with 17 of his female students and photographed the sexual encounters;

Table 10.2 Reported direct and indirect speech 1990

		Judge	Prosecutor	Defence	Offender	Victim	Agentless	total	Total Words
1	Dir			10—				—	
	Ind			10% } 10%				10% } 10%	111
2	Dir	—						—	
	Ind	32% } 32%						32% } 32%	130
3	Dir	12%	5%	3%				19%	
	Ind	18% } 30%	9% } 14%	23% } 25%		— 9% } 9%		60% } 79%	197
4	Dir		—					—	
	Ind		72% } 72%					72% } 72%	203
5	Dir	25%						25%	
	Ind	15% } 40%						15% } 40%	255
6	Dir	24%						24%	
	Ind	43% } 67%						4367	260
7	Dir	—	—					—	
	Ind	50% } 50%	16% } 16%					66% } 66%	269
8	Dir	9%		—		—	—	9%	
	Ind	10% } 19%		4% } 4%		4% } 4%	10% } 10%	28% } 37%	289
9	Dir	10%			—			10%	
	Ind	— 10%			21% } 21%			21% } 31%	321
10	Dir	35%		—				35%	
	Ind	21% } 56%		9% } 9%				3065	351
11	Dir			7%	5%			12%	
	Ind			— 7%	9% } 14%			9% } 21%	376
12	Dir	14%	—				—	14%	
	Ind	11% } 25%	35% } 35%				10% } 10%	56% } 69%	457
13	Dir	17%		—	6%			23%	
	Ind	22% } 39%		7% } 7%	3% } 9%			32% } 55%	512

- a former Jamaican police officer;
- a 72-year-old man with failing health, eyesight and hearing;
- a child molester.

Relative clauses in these indefinite expressions are always derived from the crime; nominal heads, premodifiers and non-clausal postmodifiers never are. Still these other elements of the Noun Phrase are quite richly endowed – with materials from age, address, occupation and elsewhere.

In 1990, the connections between the non-clausal elements of the identifying expression and the subsequent discussion range from no connection at all to strong, sustained connection. '[C]arpenter' – the designation of two of the 1990 offenders – has no ties to what follows. '[L]eading pediatrician', 'former boxer', and 'high school teacher', on the other hand, are all extremely relevant, and Background Knowledge of these occupations combines productively with many stages of the subsequent discussion. Premodifier '72-year-old' is also very relevant, tying to many subsequent items and contributing to the interpretation of both the crime and the sentence.

But what about 'a 31-year-old cocktail waitress'? Her occupation is not mentioned again, although her own lawyer attributes her violence to alcohol. And her age is a premodifier like that of the 72-year-old man; perhaps readers will use Background Knowledge of norms for the relative age of sexual partners to provide grounds for interpreting her jealous attack on her former boyfriend – a '27-year-old man'.

Background Knowledge in 1990

Each occasion for the conceptual operation of Background Knowledge is an occasion for the construction of the genre's audience. Just as resort to Background Knowledge in method sections of research articles constructed the shared experience of the research community (and full explanations would defy the community's solidarity), here the resort to Background Knowledge also constructs the shared experience of a community. In both cases, the shared knowledge contributes to the definition of group members' affinity. In the research article, BK density occurs at just the point where the momentum of the empirical project is at stake; as Bazerman has shown, techniques for reporting empirical procedure enabled the experimental genre to develop the characteristic and practical dispositions of science. We might speculate, then, that the occasions for the operation of Background Knowledge in the report-of-sentencing are also sites of crucial community understanding.

If this is so, we should anticipate patterns in BK content that are captured by the genre. First, however, we should eliminate those BK assumptions that do not belong to the domain of genre but to higher levels – to cultural, or, even more generally, human experience. For example, BK of sexual jealousy explains the relevance to the violent act of expressions like 'a former girlfriend', 'former boyfriend', 'in bed with another woman'. Background Knowledge of sexual intimacy may explain the otherwise irrelevant details presented in S7 and S8 in the passage below:

(5) Hollyhock stared directly ahead and said nothing when the verdict was delivered by the seven women and five men on the jury.

(6) The bodies of Harrison and Ripsher were found on the kitchen floor of the condominium with shotgun wounds to their heads.

(7) They had been sharing drinks and hors d'oeuvres on 27 May 1989. (8) There were roses on the table and steaks in the fridge when Hollyhock arrived and was surprised to find Harrison at home, evidence showed.

(9) Harrison was the principal of Northern Agincourt Junior Public School and had lived with Hollyhock since 1969 when they both taught music in Ottawa.

'[R]oses' is an unanchored item, and, while 'fridge' and possibly 'drinks', 'hors d'oeuvres', and 'steak' are collocative with 'kitchen' (S6), they nevertheless achieve relevance only when the reader consults a Background Knowledge entry we might call 'romantic get-together'. They then become coherent with their surroundings by offering evidence of the intimacy shared by the victims – an intimacy which aroused the sexual jealousy of the offender. The interpretation of roses, hors d'oeuvres and steaks is no doubt culturally and historically contingent, but it seems to me to belong to broader planes of understanding than that which shapes the genre. Other forms of Background Knowledge seem to be closer to the domain of this genre and its typifications of violence.

To be admitted to the domain of genre, the forms of Background Knowledge called upon should show some regularity, some pattern of assumptions related to the community practice in question – here the judicial interpretation of violence and its situating *vis-à-vis* other practices, ideas and institutions. From this small collection, a slight pattern does emerge. A larger sample may confirm or erase this pattern, but in the meantime I will describe one detectable regularity: a scheme of related assumptions that occur more often than others do and which seem conjoined to the genre's work of reporting judicial interpretations of instances of violence.

The most frequently occurring BK assumptions have to do with therapeutic responses to violence. We have already seen an example of this kind of assumption in the report of a judge recommending that an offender convicted of attempted murder receive 'psychiatric treatment while in custody'. Here is another instance, the conclusion of the report of sentencing of a teacher convicted of 'sex attacks' on 17 female students:

(12) The crimes had 'effects on normal relationships, relations with [the victims'] spouses – some find it difficult to trust men', the judge said.

(13) At least four have attempted suicide, court was told.

(14) Sheppard [the offender] intends to seek psychological counselling while in prison, his lawyer said.[8]

While the interpretation of S12–S13 depends on Background Knowledge of psychological models of female sexuality, the relevance of S14 depends on Background Knowledge of the role of therapeutic intervention as a response to violence; this Background Knowledge would satisfy the surface contradiction in the victims being the damaged ones and the offender being the object of 'counselling'.

As the above example might suggest, Background Knowledge of the therapeutic responses to violence explains not only certain offender-related mentions but also certain victim-related mentions. In the following example, the need for therapeutic intervention is relevant as an index to the severity of effects of the crime on the victim of violence:

> (15) While the unprovoked attack was taking place, the victim's 11-year-old daughter could hear her mother's screams, Sabean said. (16) The girl later had to undergo psychiatric counselling and still has nightmares about what happened.

In another place, at another time, readers might question mention of counselling as a relevant continuation of a description of this girl's experience.

Associated with assumptions of the reader's ability to connect mention of therapeutic items with violence are assumptions about the reader's ability to make connections between violence and mentions of family life – principally by consulting Background Knowledge of the family's capacity to cultivate conditions that lead eventually to the violent acts of its grown-up male children. We have seen one instance already, which reported the violent offender's desire to have his own parents charged with abusing him as a child. Similar resort to Background Knowledge of the sources of sexual deviance is necessary to understanding the conceptual relevance of a judge's reported speech in an account of the sentencing of a man who raped his stepdaughter and abused her brother.

> (6) It was proved beyond a reasonable doubt that the man also sexually abused the boy in their Brampton home over a five-month period in 1988, 'which virtually destroyed the boy', Langdon [the judge] said.

> (7) More probably than not the boy will come to court some day charged as a sex abuser or sex attacker, he said.

In another case, a judge reports the childhood history of a 20-year-old man convicted of murder:

> (13) Tobias said Tobin had been leading a troubled but non-violent life until he developed 'an unnatural obsession for a very disturbed young woman [his accomplice] and he completely surrendered himself to his girlfriend's lifestyle of drugs, alcohol and sex'.

> (14) He said Tobin 'devoted himself to satisfying his appetites and lived a life of pleasure seeking'.

(15) The judge noted a pre-sentence report said Tobin felt he couldn't earn the approval of his stern father, who favoured his younger brother.

(16) Tobias said he believed that two occasions when Tobin's parents separated discouraged his progress in school. (17) He quit in Grade 9, was drinking heavily by age 14 and bought liquor with money earned as a drug pusher.

(18) His mother, father, an aunt and uncle were in court every day during the trial, but Tobin never looked at them. (19) He showed no emotion yesterday at his sentence.

Readers of this report are constructed as possessing Background Knowledge which can explain the connection between, on the one hand, schooling, sibling rivalry and parental sternness, and, on the other hand, violence.

Ideas about childhood, which are compatible partners for ideas of therapeutic responses, explain the relevance or coherence of a number of passages otherwise stranded. In another example (below) we can witness a striking instance of the historical contingency of this kind of Background Knowledge. In a report of the sentencing of 'North Bay's leading pediatrician. . . for sexually assaulting four female patients' (S1), cohesive ties leave a strange gap:

(7) Mohan was found guilty of carrying out vaginal examinations when they were not required. (8) He also hugged and kissed one of the girls and rubbed another young patient's breasts.

Some items ('Mohan', 'he') tie with other expressions referring to the offender; other items ('the girls', 'young patient') tie with expressions referring to the victims; and 'found guilty' ties collocatively with the report's abundance of legal items (e.g. 'convicted', 'appeal', 'bond', 'defence lawyer', etc.). '[V]aginal', 'hugged and kissed', and 'breasts' tie collocatively with 'sexually', and 'examination' with 'pediatrics' and 'hospital' (S2). Yet none of these items ties with 'assaulting'. In fact, 'hugged and kissed' and 'rubbed' seem, on the surface, to defy relevance to 'assaulting'. But, of course, the surface is not the only common ground shared by the producer of the text and the audience. The writer can assume that, from recent definitions of female sexuality and childhood sexuality, readers will have stored Background Knowledge which they can consult in determining the relevance of mention of seemingly gentle actions to an account of sentencing for assault. No explanation is required for this community of readers, historically situated and experienced in the typifications that support the career of this genre.

The Genre in 1950

Features

Forty years earlier, in the same newspaper, reports of sentencing were comprised of the same types of mentions. Table 10.3 shows that these categories are disposed in roughly similar ways. Some differences are detectable in report of pre-crime

Table 10.3 Order and categories of utterance 1950

S	1	2	3	4	5	6	7	8
1	sentence and crime	sentence	sentence and crime	sentence	events and crime	sentence and crime	sentence and crime	effects and interpretation
2	sentence	legal and crime	events	legal and crime	events	interpretation	legal	interpretation and sentence
3	events	events	sentence	sentence	events	interpretation	history	? and effects
4	events	interpretation	events	interpretation	sentence	sentence and interpretation	legal and events	events
5	events	interpretation	events	interpretation	interpretation	sentence	legal	events
6	legal	interpretation	events	interpretation	events	sentence	history	events
7		interpretation	events	interpretation	events	sentence	history	events
8			legal and history	events	events	interpretation	legal	events
9				interpretation	events	events	legal	events
10				legal	events	events	legal	events
11				history	events	legal and events	legal	events
12				legal	events		legal	events
13				legal	events			events
14					events			events
15								events
16								events
17								events
18								events
19								events
20								events
21								events
22								events
23								events

history, which is somewhat rarer, in report of the effects on the victim, which is much rarer, and in report of events of the crime, which can be much more voluminous than in any instance from the 1990 collection. More evident, however, are differences in the assignment of speaking roles and the expressions referring to the offender.

The proportion of total words devoted to reported direct or indirect speech ranges from 21 per cent to 86 per cent. As Table 10.4 shows, judges then as now have a substantial say, but in 1950 they share the floor with a greater variety of other speakers – including victims (34, 43 and 17 per cent in the reports which include their speech), police, and in one case a witness – a taxi driver – who provides 42 per cent of the report's wording.

In the 1950 collection the technique of identifying the offender by means of an indefinite expression is not in use (with the exception of one instance which reports the sentencing of three offenders at once); offenders are introduced by proper nouns postmodified in all but one case by age. In only two reports are modifications used to contribute the kind of materials that comprise offender noun phrases in 1990:

- James Walter Clarke, 25, Point Edward war veteran;
- William Thomas McGill, 36, a successful Oakville manufacturer;
- Father of a two-year-old boy, McGill.

In both instances, the appositive materials combine with the reports' continuation to provide contexts for the interpretation of the crime. In the 'manufacturer's' case, his business and family status appear to encourage an interpretation of his crime as surprising; armed robbery is not provided for in readers' Background Knowledge of the attributes of successful manufacturers. In the case of the Point Edward man, his military experience becomes an element to be reckoned in understanding the judge's interpretation of the sentence, as we shall see below.

In this small collection, it appears that discretionary materials for identifying the offender are always conceptually relevant and explicitly supported by ties to subsequent claims. This is not the case in the 1990 collection, where the relevance of elements of the identifying noun phrase varies widely.

Background Knowledge in 1950

The Background Knowledge assumed of sexual jealousy and of alcohol and their respective roles in violence resembles that assumed in 1990 – and it seems then as now to occupy a domain beyond genre.[9]

Except for one perplexing passage, no Background Knowledge of therapeutic intervention as a response to violence is necessary to understanding these reports. Lurking in the perplexing passage, however, there may be a precursor of this kind of knowledge, so it is worth looking at the gap that appears in this report of the sentencing of a man '[a]lready serving three concurrent six-year terms for armed robbery' (S1):

Table 10.4 Reported direct and indirect speech 1950

#		Judge	Prosecutor	Defence	Offender	Victim	Police	Witness	Court Officials	Total	Total Words
1	Dir									21%	107
	Ind									— } 21%	
2	Dir		32%							33%	147
	Ind		— } 32%							12% } 45%	
3	Dir					9%	—			9%	170
	Ind					25% } 34%	28% } 28%			53% } 62%	
4	Dir		25%	19%						44%	172
	Ind		— } 25%	— } 19%						— } 44%	
5	Dir	4%	7%		31%	39%				81%	178
	Ind	— } 4%	— } 7%		— } 31%	4% } 43%				4% } 85%	
6	Dir		37%							37%	185
	Ind		— } 37%							— } 37%	
7	Dir				—	—			—	—	268
	Ind				12% } 12%		8% } 8%		16% } 16%	36% } 36%	
8	Dir	3%	17%			5%		34%		59%	341
	Ind	— } 3%	— } 17%			12% } 17%		8% } 42%		20% } 79%	

171

(4) Before passing sentence Judge Forsyth said, 'You have one of the worst records I have seen. (5) You have seven convictions. (6) You should be treated as an habitual criminal and sent to the penitentiary for life. (7) A man like you should be out of circulation.'

(8) Counsel for Phelan [the offender], W.C. Rose, said the robbery was 'one of four robberies in a series within 24 hours. (9) He is an ill man. (10) His only defence was a plea of not guilty.'

(11) Mr Rose then read parts of a letter, written by the head doctor at Kingston penitentiary, which said Phelan was in poor health and would prove a rehabilitation problem.

(12) William Murray was also charged with the offence but the same jury which found Phelan guilty, found Murray not guilty.

The relevance of S9 to its neighbours is difficult to determine. And, while S11 does provide a cohesive tie, 'poor health', with 'ill' (S9), it assumes some Background Knowledge of rehabilitation which can explain its connection with what I take to be physical rather than psychological affliction. Yet, confounding as this sequence is, I dimly recognize some assumption connecting treatment to violence – perhaps an early form of taken-for-granted knowledge of therapeutic responses in 1990.

Assumptions of Background Knowledge of family life appear once in the 1950 collection. But, whereas in 1990 such knowledge defined the family as a corrupting influence, in 1950 the family is a source of rectitude, nourishing compliance rather than deviance:

(6) John Emanuel Cleveland, 18, no home, was sentenced to two years less one day definite and one year indeterminate, concurrent with a one-year sentence Cleveland must also serve for auto theft. (7) He, and Charles McColley, 17, who was sentenced to two years less a day, will go to the Ontario Reformatory.

(8) 'You made the mistake of leaving a good home, good parents, and brothers and sisters who cared about you', the magistrate told McColley.

(9) The boys held up the store, using a home-made pistol with a hair trigger.

In S8's report of pre-crime history, family members enter as unanchored items whose relevance is secured by Background Knowledge of the home's capacity to ward off violent action and keep its children out of jail. Assumed knowledge of family life and violence has reversed itself in 1990, but I think that readers at the end of the century might still have access to the mid-century notion of family – even though current reports of sentencing do not call on it.

Less available is the knowledge which would enable readers to connect mentions of military experience with violent acts. The report of sentencing of the Oakville manufacturer stretches cohesive ties very thin to include mention of military experience.

> (4) He made a statement to police admitting his part in the crime, stating he had provided the guns but had removed the clips from them after getting them from his Oakville home. (5) He had sold his business to make restitution.

> (6) McGill was arrested by Det. Herbert Thurston, who was stationed at a British Columbia air training field during the war. (7) McGill was commanding officer of the field at that time.

> (8) Mrs Ellen Rippy and Thomas Erwin who jointly put up $5,000 property bond for the release of Muir [who was also charged but failed to appear] will each have to mortgage their homes for that amount and pay it over to the clerk of the peace, court officials said today.[10]

Although S6's 'McGill' ties referentially with preceding text and 'arrest' collocatively, the military items in S6 and S7 have no ties except to one another. On a general level, S6–S7 may be relevant through ideas about the unlikelihood of a violent act being committed by a figure the writer assumes readers will recognize as high status – 'successful. . .manufacturer', 'commanding officer'. Perhaps the unexpectedness of the man's behaviour is enriched by the irony of his being arrested by a former subordinate, but there may be more to military mentions than this.

In the sentencing of a man – 'James Walter Clarke, 25, Point Edward war veteran' (S1) – who murdered his fiancée in a 'shotgun killing' (S3), the judge is reported as offering this interpretation of the five-year sentence:

> (4) Mr Justice Treleaven pointed out that normally he would not have thought of anything less than 10 years. (5) 'I do not think you are naturally criminally-minded', he said. (6) 'I respect and will try to give effect as far as possible to the recommendation of the jury for leniency and also for your war record and disability. (7) You are also quite young but society must be given protection.'

S6's 'disability' is unanchored, mentioned nowhere else. For readers in 1990, such reticence is perhaps a surprising condition, but for readers in 1950, in the aftermath of the Second World War and in the midst of the Korean War, perhaps not so surprising. '[W]ar record' ties with S1's 'war veteran' – showing that the postmodifying materials of the referring expression are conceptually relevant. But what is the concept? So compelling is the relevance of 'war record', 'disability' and '[youth]' that the judge appears to apologize for imposing any sentence at all for this murder. Yet now, at the end of the century, Background Knowledge of military experience holds few or no ideas that explain its relevance to this interpretation of violence. In fact, in both these reports mentioning military experience, a late-twentieth-century reader might be just as likely to follow the cohesive tie from 'guns' to 'war' in the report of the manufacturer's sentencing, and from 'shotgun' to 'war' in this report, and perform some unintended interpretation – for example, that military experience had inclined these men to dangerous behaviour.

Genres and Knowledge

Comparative analysis of these two collections revealed the gaps I anticipated: gaps marking sites of community knowledge so assured as not to permit expression, and related to the genre's business of situating the violent act amongst current institutions and ideologies. Over time, these situations change, and so do Background Knowledge assumptions. Evidence of change not only in the way of speaking and but also in the way of not speaking confirms the richness of genre as an archive of cultural imprints – a richness Miller (1984; revised version Chapter 2, this volume) suggested, and Swales and Bazerman have demonstrated.

These conceptual gaps were not the only ones I discovered, however. By the rough measure that analysis of cohesion provides, I also found many other 'islands in a string', and the reader's travel across these islands does not appear to be routed through conceptual Background Knowledge. Here is an example:

> (3) 'The sentence I pass cannot undo the damage you have done', Mr Justice
> H. Ward Allen told Roy Anthony Ergus yesterday. (4) 'I do not seek to
> destroy you or wreak vengeance upon you.'

> (5) A jury of six men and six women deliberated more than 11 hours before
> returning guilty verdicts against Ergus in November.

What is the conceptual connection between S3–4 and S5? Does the length of deliberation or the gender composition of the jury have anything to contribute to our interpretation of the judge's remarks? No concept seems to be available to connect these two paragraphs, so why is this said next? Part of the answer is that both paragraphs are conventional categories in the report of sentencing (interpretation in judge's reported speech + legal), and their ordering here is conventional. So, consulting Background Knowledge of the genre, the reader accepts S5 as a valid continuation. But what prevents readers from attempting a conceptual bridging like the kind that links family, military and therapy to violence? How do readers know how to avoid fruitless Background Knowledge searches for conceptual relevance?

These texts bring only part of the story to the page – wording is a process of reduction, as Bazerman notes. The reduction leaves gaps; the writer provides for readers to bridge these gaps with knowledge they bring to the text. The findings of this study suggest that the design of the gaps is genre-specific: the report-of-sentencing genre routinely and systematically presupposes certain concepts – about therapeutic response, about family life – in its process of reduction. Not all gaps are bridgeable by conceptual materials, however. Many, like the example just cited, defy conceptual bridging, and appear on the surface to defy principles of coherence. In these cases, it is the expressive conventions of the genre itself – its regular features of style – that sustain coherence. At these points, the genre's features reduce knowledge of the world to stylized representations of knowledge. The relations of juries to judges, judges to penal institutions, offending to charging are withdrawn from the surface of the text and replaced by reduced forms; the relations are no longer events but conventional wordings, wordings that are like the fossil imprint of the full organic structure of social behaviours, interests and intentions.

With this in mind, we can look again at the problem of gaps which the knowing reader will not attempt to bridge conceptually. We could speculate that, for the knowing, well-placed reader, the stylization of knowledge of the world must be powerful enough to override conceptual strategies for bridging; that is, the convention must be a *meaningful* formation, not just a rule. At these points where convention alone holds the surface of the text together, gaps are bridgeable not by concepts but by a sense of the world, a sense of the flow of authority, the position of individuals and institutions *vis-à-vis* authority, and the qualities of their contribution to the situation. This sense is not expressible, in so many words, and perhaps that's why it is stylized.

As the change in the assignment of speaking roles suggests, this sense is also historical. In light of 1950, 1990 seems to map a flow of authority towards the court and away from others: a flow of official, expert speech on behalf of individuals. In 1950 the assignment of speaking roles imprints a different community, where people are more likely to speak for themselves, perhaps – but which people and what do they say? What principles delegate the taxi driver? Although we can discover conventions, we may struggle to infer the sense of the world that they have reduced and stylized.

For indigenous users of the genre, conventions will not be only rules and regularities but representations of qualities of a world they know. Thus, when we, as late-twentieth-century readers in a Canadian city, encounter a gap like that between the judge's interpretation of the crime and the statement of the gender-composition of the jury, we choose the bridge that our sense of the world provides (and the conventional ordering represents) as more efficient than any conceptual Background Knowledge. If she or he is ignorant of the conventions, a non-indigenous reader might attempt a conceptual bridge; she might try to figure out if there is some intended connection between 'stark horror' and the proportion of men and women on the jury. Of, if she has 'learned' the conventions as I have learned the conventions of the 1950 report of sentencing, she may recognize the operation of a rule – but not more.

This inquiry was inspired by the apparent relevance of theories of BK to genre study. From experience with students who said too much, who wrote as if their readers didn't know things which they in fact did know very well and didn't want to be told, I speculated that learning the reticence appropriate to a genre can be hard. I still think this is so, and, at the same time, I think that, despite its quantitative limitations, this investigation demonstrates the utility of genre study in cultural inquiry.

Theories of Background Knowledge do appear capable of adding to our understanding of genres; a genre may systematically suppress certain concepts, these concepts forming a common ground shared by its users. But this inquiry has also shown me that the study of genre adds to what we know about the phenomenon of Background Knowledge. Background Knowledge is not always conceptual but sometimes other; sometimes a sense of the world's contingent orderings of relationships, sequences and priorities, routes of power and permission. Perhaps genres like the report of sentencing, or the resumé, or the report of empirical research, whose conventional partitions leave many gaps, are especially dependent on this non-conceptual Background Knowledge.

In addition, I am intrigued by the disposition of changes in the conventions which stylize a sense of the world. It seems that in 1950 the conventions directing the assignment of speaking roles is highly coded – a complex stylization of a sense of the world, a sense now withered, leaving only this husk. In 1990 the assignment of speaking roles has simplified, and the site of coded complexity seems to have shifted to the conventions surrounding the expressions referring to the offender. Now these expressions are deeply cultivated, seeded with diverse materials bearing a variety of conceptual relations to violence (some even a null relation). The sense of the world represented by these expressions shadows the explicit judgment of the crime, proposing but never bringing to light shared ideas about the kind of people who do violent things. On the surface, there's a non-aligned, non-commital digest of information; below, underground, there are the roots of stereotypical inference. I think this 'undergrounding' is itself semiotic – a meaningful system of representing contemporary ways of withholding public recriminations but storing the materials of recrimination just out of sight.

Notes

1 In this chapter, I use a formulation of Background Knowledge (also appearing in the literature as Mutual Knowledge, Common Ground, Assumed Familiarity) developed from Grice's original proposals in 'Logic and Conversation' ([1967] 1989) and from the applications of those proposals by other pragmaticists. I rely in particular on Clark and Marshall (1981), Prince (1981), Sperber and Wilson (1986) and Siklaki (1988).

2 These two levels are parallel to what van Dijk and Kintsch (1983) distinguish as superstructure – the formal development of a text – and macrostructure – the conceptual or semantic development of a text. Readers recognize the first and work to construct the second.

3 The sample was trimmed by eliminating two outliers. These departed from observable trends of the genre: one focused on a victim of the offender; the other conformed until it embarked on a lengthy recapitulation of the offender's crime 'spree' – a 'reign of terror' widely reported at the time. Both these instances appeared on the front page, and they were the only ones to do so.

4 These ties were measured with the instruments provided by Halliday and Hasan (1976),

including the distinction between referential ties and collocative ties (those based on words' tendency to appear together, for example, 'sentence' and 'jury').

5 Square-bracketed material in the original; sentences are numbered according to their appearance in the original.

6 Square-bracketed material added.

7 Although news reports may tend generally to be compilations of the speech of others, not all reports assign speaking roles on the basis of generic regularities. The following passage, from an article about a 550 million dollar order from Argentina to Ford Motor Company, selects speakers on a conceptual rather than generic basis (square-bracketed material added):

(7) The initial Argentine order of 65,000 vehicles would represent about 25 per cent of the Oakville plant's annual production.

(8) The missing link in the complicated deal is financing, Mr Hartford [already identified as 'a spokesman for Ford Canada'] indicated. But Phoenix Plus, Inc., a Toronto-based company working as a liaison between an association of Argentine taxi owners and Ford's US fleet services, says financing is only days away.

(10) Phoenix Plus president Howard Wolle said yesterday his company is close to an agreement with the Argentine government in securing guarantees from the country's national bank.

'Phoenix Plus' and 'Howard Wolle' are selected as speakers on the basis of the conceptual tie to 'financing'; they have things to say about 'financing' and bank 'guarantees' (S10). Presumably, had the report developed other topics (e.g. safety, pollution controls, tariffs), other speakers would have been selected.

8 Square-bracketed material not in original.

9 While assumed knowledge of sexual jealousy appears to be fairly constant, one case is so obscure to this late-twentieth-century reader as to suggest the assumption of some BK of female sexuality that is now obsolete and inaccessible:

(3) Mrs Smith admitted attacking Ann McDonald of Connaught Ave., blackening both her eyes, because 'she's been running around with my husband and she's trying to break up our home'.

(4) His worship suspended sentence. (5) 'Too bad she pleaded guilty', he said.

(6) The complainant said she was telephoning at home Nov. 16 when Mrs Smith came downstairs. (7) 'She grabbed the telephone and threw it down. (8) Then she said "You've been out with my husband. (9) I'm going to kill you".'

S5 is an interpretation of the sentence, but what explains its conceptual relevance? Does the writer assume that readers will have easy access to some BK which defines the attacker's motivations as innocent and the victim as responsible for the crime?

10 Square-bracketed material not in original.

References

BAKHTIN, M. M. (1986) 'The Problem of Speech Genres', in EMERSON, C. and HOLQUIST, M. (eds) *Speech Genres and Other Late Essays*, (trans. V. McGee) Austin, TX: University of Texas Press, pp. 60–102.

BAZERMAN, C. (1989) *Shaping Written Knowledge*, Madison, WI: University of Wisconsin Press.

BELL, A. (1991) *The Language of News Media*, Oxford: Blackwell.

BRUCE, N. J. (1983) 'Rhetorical Constraints on Information Structure in Medical Research Report Writing', paper p?resented at the ESP in the Arab World Conference, University of Aston, UK.

CLARK, H. and MARSHALL, C. (1981) 'Definite Reference and Mutual Knowledge', in JOSHI, A., WEBBER, B. and SAG, I. (eds) *Elements of Discourse Understanding*, Cambridge: Cambridge University Press.

GILTROW, J. (1992) 'Using the Pragmatic Concept of Background Knowledge to Analyse the Technical Audience', *Technostyle*, **10**, Spring, pp. 23–57.

GILTROW, J. and VALIQUETTE, M. (1991) 'The Outsider Is Called In: Audience in the Disciplines', *Inkshed*, **10**(2), pp. 5–11.

GRICE, P. ([1967] 1989) 'Logic and Conversation', *Studies in the Way of Words*, Cambridge, MA: Harvard University Press, pp. 22–40.

HALLIDAY, M. A. K. and HASAN, R. (1976) *Cohesion in English*, London: Longman.

MILLER, C. (1984) 'Genre as Social Action', *Quarterly Journal of Speech*, **70**, pp. 151–67.

PRINCE, E. (1981) 'Toward a Taxonomy of Given-New Information', in COLE, P. (ed.) *Radical Pragmatics*, New York: Academic Press, pp. 223–55.

SIKLAKI, I. (1988) 'Delicate Balance: Coherence and Mutual Knowledge in A Short Story', *Poetics*, **17**, pp. 439–60.

SPERBER, D. and WILSON, D. (1986) *Relevance*, Cambridge, MA: Harvard University Press.

SWALES, J. (1990) *Genre Analysis*, Cambridge: Cambridge University Press.

WEISSBERG, R. (1984) 'Given and New: Paragraph Development Models for Scientific English', *TESOL Quarterly*, **18**, pp. 485–500.

VAN DIJK, T. and KINTSCH, W. (1983) *Strategies of Discourse Comprehension*, New York: Academic Press.

Part IV
Applications in Education

Chapter 11

'An Arousing and Fulfilment of Desires': The Rhetoric of Genre in the Process Era – and Beyond

Richard M. Coe

Form...is an arousing and fulfilment of desires. A work has form in so far as one part of it leads a reader to anticipate another part, to be gratified by the sequence.

Kenneth Burke ([1931] 1968: 124)

Desire is the presence of an Absence.

Alexandre Kojève (1969: 134)

Translated into terms of the composition class, 'form' becomes 'organization' and brings with it...the most dismal stuff that students and teachers must deal with. And yet, the concept of form is utterly fascinating, for it concerns the way in which the mind perceives infinitely complex relationships. The way, indeed, in which the mind constructs discourse.

W. Ross Winterowd (1975: 163)

When composition studies were revolutionized under the banner of 'Process', everything that smacked of its contrary, the F-word 'Form' (as in 'formalist') became suspect. While indubitably valuable, the emphasis on process was accompanied by an excessive underating of formal motives. So terrible was the sterile traditional formalism that we rejected rather than transcending it. There is, however, (and was all along) an alternative, based in the New Rhetoric and an understanding of writing as social process, that can take us beyond the repressive false dichotomy between form and process.

When Aristotle defined rhetoric as 'the faculty of observing in any given case the available means of persuasion' (1954: 24), he was clearly thinking of explicit argumentation. But New Rhetoricians note how much verbal persuasion is implicit, structured into our words and ways with words. 'Aristotle's Rhetoric centers in the speaker's explicit designs with regard to the confronting of an audience,' writes Kenneth Burke. 'But there are also ways in which we *spontaneously, intuitively*, even *unconsciously* persuade ourselves' (1966: 301). The New Rhetoric sublates classical rhetoric largely by comprehending the manifold ways we human wordlings are shaped and moved by words. 'The human animal, as we know it, *emerges into personality* by first mastering whatever tribal speech happens to be its particular symbolic environment, (Burke 1966: 53).[1] Learning generic, socially preferred discourse structures is a crucial aspect of that entry into discourse community.

If rhetoric is the study of verbal persuasion, then the rhetoric of genre is the study of how generic structures influence (i.e. 'persuade') both writers and readers. In Aristotle's terms, generic discourse forms count among the 'available means of persuasion' we apply in particular situations. The social availability and efficacy of particular forms influence writers and speakers – in effect persuade them, as they articulate their intuitions and shape their materials – to make particular selections, create particular emphases, generate particular substance, adopt particular personae. Similarly, an auditor's or reader's recognition of a particular utterance or text as belonging to a particular genre influences her or his strategies of comprehension and response. The rhetoric of genre studies both the formal tyranny of standard structures and the heuristic processes through which generic form guides the creation and comprehension of substance.

Traditionally, form is understood in terms of a form/content dichotomy. In the Neoclassical version of this understanding, form is the container that holds content and conveys it through social space from one mind to another; in this view, good form is socially important – content should be appropriately dressed before being presented publicly – but content is quite independent of form, can be dressed and re-dressed in various forms, poured out of one generic container into another as the occasion demands, without being substantively changed. In the contrasting Romantic version, form grows organically from substance, is determined by content; from this perspective, form matters – substance re-formed is substance trans-formed – but form is a derivative, dependent factor in creative or cognitive processes because form follows from content. Though contraries, these perspectives are both grounded in the form/content dichotomy. Most literary criticism and most literacy education are shaped by one – or even more often (albeit somewhat illogically) by both – of these perspectives.

In Aristotle's opinion, however, substance comes into being only when matter is formed. For substance, Aristotle emphasized (in his *Physics*), is formed matter. From an Aristotelian perspective, form without 'content' is an abstraction; matter without form is barely imaginable but not actually known to human beings. Similarly, I. A. Richards, in *The Philosophy of Rhetoric* (1936; a key text in the development of both modern understandings of metaphor and the New Rhetoric), exposes and criticizes the container metaphor that underlies the form/content dichotomy, arguing that it distorts our understanding of the forming process (pp. 12–13).

The rhetoric of genre can be understood by analogy to the rhetoric of metaphor. Richards's explanation of metaphor is that the juxtaposition of the two aspects of a metaphor initiates a mental process wherein people try to make sense of a proposition that is linguistically self-contradictory if taken literally (as my true love's lips are not literally roses). Modern theorists, including Barthes (1972, 1977), Burke, Derrida, Lakoff and Johnson (1980), Perelman, and Ricoeur (1973), understand metaphor as a *literally* contradictory juxtaposition. The metaphor becomes meaning-full in symbolic action when someone is moved to resolve the contradiction, when the commonplaces associated with the metaphorical term direct a person's attention to particular features of the principal subject (cf. Coe forthcoming). Metaphors are not merely decorative or emotionally suasive, but heuristic and conceptually suasive as they direct (and deflect) our attention. Thus tropes, as first the New Rhetoricians and later the poststructuralists have emphasized, are substantive, ideological, shapers of discourse, not merely a matter of style.

In the New Rhetorical conception, genres (and other forms) function similarly. The juxtaposition of genre with utterance, text, (subject) matter, or rhetorical situation directs attention. Burke emphasizes the psychology of form in the reading process when he defines form as 'an arousing. . .of desires', including 'categorical expectations' evoked by a conventional genre ([1931] 1968: 124, 139). Categorical expectations translate into genre-specific reading strategies (and thus when a genre is misidentified – or evolving – into misreadings).

We must emphasize also the other major aspect of this juxtaposition (and thus of the metaphor of genre): how generic structures influence a rhetor's creative process, for good and ill stimulating and constraining discursive practice. Having accepted, chosen, discovered or invented appropriate forms, speakers and writers are then guided int their selection, arrangement and emphasis by the structure of those forms. The resolution of contradictions between the abstract shape of the form and the concrete particulars of the subject matter yields substance. Generic forms are factors in the creative processes of speaking and writing. Genres serve as 'rhetorical means for mediating private intentions with public exigence; [they motivate] by connecting the private with the public, the singular with the recurrent' (Miller 1984: 163; revised version Chapter 2, this volume). A consistent process approach must take into account how speakers' and writers' individual creative processes are influenced and socialized by their awareness of genres both as available strategies and as reader expectations (cf. Devitt 1993: esp. pp. 583–4).

Generic structures are *pre-pared* ways of responding, frozen in synchronicity. They embody our social memory of standard strategies for responding to types of situations we encounter repeatedly. Like an attitude, a genre may be understood as an incipient action, i.e. a potential action waiting for an activating situation. When we see past the uniqueness of a particular situation and recognize it as familiar, we activate (at least provisionally) a structure we have previously decided is generally appropriate to that type of situation. New and radically different types of situations call for new strategies, which may be embodied in new structures (cf. Coe 1974, 1975, 1992).

Genres are both structures and social processes (Christie 1985; Halliday and Hasan 1985; Reid 1987; Devitt 1993). What Burke says about individual works, that we should understand them as embodying strategies for responding to situations, applies equally to genres: 'These strategies size up the situations. . .in a way that contains an attitude towards them' ([1941] 1957: 3). Just as an individual 'symbolic act is the *dancing of an attitude*' (p. 9), so too genres embody attitudes. Since these attitudes are built into the generic structures, they are sometimes danced without conscious awareness or intent on the part of the individual using the genre.

Although usually identified initially as structural/textual regularities, genres are social processes that correspond to (and also construct) recurring situations. Genres also invoke (and thus tend to construct) particular types of auditors/readers (cf. Ede and Lunsford 1984). Genres are motivated symbolic actions that should be understood in terms of what they *do*, not how they are shaped.[2] Genres are, moreover, important factors in the social construction of orientations, paradigms, ideologies, worldviews and cultural perspectives.

Though the reduction of strategies to generic structures is convenient and facilitates social transmission, it creates an ahistorical abstractness that masks the genre's connection to what Malinowski (1923) called 'context of situation'. It also interrupts the logical flow that should take us from consideration of strategies to consideration of the ends those strategies serve – and hence from rhetoric to ethics. Those who forget the rhetorical situations and contexts of situation in which generic structures arose 'devote themselves mainly to the accumulated internalities of tactics, picking up a special. . .jargon. . .simply as insignia of membership in a lodge' (Burke [1941] 1957: 87, fn. 2). To understand and explain rhetorical structures we should remember the types of rhetorical situations to which they correspond, the strategies they embody, and the ends they are structured to serve – as well as the contexts of situation in which those strategies are viable and those ends desirable.[3]

> When the great executive has finished his murder thriller, and relaxed into a well-earned sleep after having gone, by a certain disciplinary route, from the killing of the victim to the killing of the mystery, our vigil has but begun. We must ask: 'What does the victim equal?. . .What does the killer equal?. . .What are the stages of this journey?' etc.
>
> And we do this, not just to learn something about the given work, but ultimately in the hope of learning something about the ways in which the 'personality' of the work relates to the 'personality' of a social order; and then. . .the malaise of a given property structure. . . (Burke 1955: 275)

In terms somewhat parallel to Michel Foucault's, this leads to an archaeology of form, an analysis of genres as fossilized rhetorical processes. Thus should we exploit the etymological connection between our word *tactics* and the Greek name for the department of rhetoric concerned with selection and arrangement, *taxis*.

Generic structures are abstract; we can consider form *qua* form only by abstracting from the concrete substance of particular instances. As Burke reminds us, 'principles reside in the *genre* only by residing in individuals that compose the *genre*' (1946: 276); any socially standard (i.e. generic) form has been abstracted from specific strategic or tactical responses to specific situations. In terms of information theory, then, form is code (cf. Derrida 1974: 30–32); genres function to code (i.e. to guide and organize) our reading of reality (including utterances and textual realities), hence both our speaking and writing and our responses to speech and writing.

'Clearly the structure of anything limits the uses to which it may be put' (Kinneavy 1979: 1). 'Once committed. . .to a particular genre', however, 'the author finds that the act [of writing] not only makes demands of its own, but has certain built-in resources of its own which beg to be exploited' (Rueckert 1963: 80). Frank D'Angelo summarizes the concept this way:

> Following Aristotle's system I take form to be closely related to the formal principle, i.e., one of the causes of a mode of being which produces discourses. . . . Patterns of development. . . are. . . organizational processes, symbolic manifestations of underlying mental processes, and not merely conventional static patterns. (1975: 56–57)

In this conception, form is both constraining and generative – or, better said, generative because constraining. Form is abstract, but this abstractness has shape. The rhetoric of genre works suasively in part because human beings feel the abstractness of form as an emptiness, which creates a full desire to fill. This formal desire to fill such 'emptinesses' (to give substance to such abstractions) is one of Burke's implications when he wryly defines us as 'rotten with perfection' (1966: 16 ff.). Form in this sense is heuristic, generative as well as constraining.

LeFevre (1986) argues that to understand rhetorical invention we must consider it as a social process. Rhetorical form is equally if not more social. Indeed, one way in which invention becomes social is when an individual's act of creation is mediated by conventional forms preferred or prescribed by a discourse community. One way discourse communities preserve their boundaries, their integrity, is by restricting the communications of those who have not learned the standard forms. The rhetoric of genre is, therefore, especially applicable to studies of social hierarchy, literacy and education.

Foucault, the poststructuralist who most closely approaches the rhetoric of genre, asserts that

> what was altered in the seventeenth century. . . was the way in which one wrote down what one observed. . . Natural history. . . above all [became] a set of rules of arranging statements in series, an obligatory set of schemata of dependence, of order, and of successions, in which the recurrent elements that may have value as concepts were distributed. (1972: 57)

In arguing that discourse should be understood as relationships between statements and what he calls enunciative modalities, Foucault is asserting a relationship between sets of 'rules for arranging statements' (i.e. *taxis*) and social contexts and processes (i.e. situations and strategies).

Foucault's 'first question' is: 'Who is speaking? Who. . . is accorded the right', who is 'qualified' to 'use this sort of language [*langage*]?' (p. 50). In terms of a rhetoric of genre, this question becomes one about the relationship between formal structures 'in' the text and 'enunciative' situations and contexts, about a relationship between genre and power. To what extent, for instance, does the ability to use certain conventional forms 'accord the right' to make certain types of statements? To what extent does restricting knowledge of appropriate forms, if only by leaving it tacit, silence people?[4] To what extent does generic form – even of antecedent genres –

influence or even engender substance (cf. Ohmann's 1976 analysis of English essays and the Pentagon papers), attitude, persona? To what extent do the 'available means of persuasion' persuade the rhetor?

In his discussions of language, rhetoric and poetics, Burke asserts that the practices by which poets make poems implicitly involve precepts (of which the poet *qua* poet may be largely, somewhat or not at all conscious). The critic, says Burke, 'in matching the poetry with a poetics, seeks to make these implicit principles explicit' (1966: 33). Thus Poe, as writer, created a genre, the detective story, but it was Poe as critic who described the genre, articulating principles that create its characteristic effects. The New Rhetoricians' questions focus attention on these effects and the strategies that create them in order to explain the implications for both writers and readers.

Aristotle, generally identified as the first extant genre critic, defined tragedy in terms of its effect – a catharsis of pity and fear – and explained generic structures of plot, character, language, thought, music, and spectacle as means of achieving that effect (1954: 230ff.). Burke amplified Aristotle's discussion of tragic effects by locating them in context of situation, identifying particular social tensions cosmologized (i.e. put under erasure) by the mythologized plots of classical and traditional tragedies (cf. for example, 1966: 81–97, 125–8). Aristotle explained tragedy tactically in relation to what we now call rhetorical situation (i.e. purpose, audience and occasion); Burke extended Aristotle's explanation by explicating it strategically in relation to its function in the social context of that rhetorical situation.

The New Rhetoric explicates generic structures as social processes, discussive strategies for responding to rhetorical situations and adapting to contexts of situation. It directs our attention past the reified structural descriptions and taxonomies[5] of traditional genre studies, moves us to explicate what traditional genre studies put (or at least left) under erasure. Its approach is both archaeological and ecological. Genres are understood as evolving rhetorically in contexts of situation. To persevere, they must somehow 'work', must serve rhetorical purposes, achieve desired effects, be 'ecologically' functional.

The New Rhetoric provides a basis for a critical perspective on genre. What sorts of communication does the genre encourage, what sorts does it constrain against? Does it empower some people while silencing others? Are its effects dysfunctional beyond their immediate context (for example, bureaucratese)? What are the political and ethical implications of the rhetorical situation constructed, persona embodied, audience invoked and context of situation assumed by a particular genre? What does the genre signify (about its discourse community)?

The New Rhetorical perspective on genre as symbolic action and social process also directs our attention in ways that are immediately useful in our reading, writing, teaching and researching. Practitioners – both readers and writers and teachers of reading and writing – can and should investigate and analyse the genres they read and write and teach, should strive to comprehend the interrelation of structure, strategy, situation and context of situation that constitutes each genre. I do it, my students do it – and we are empowered by our increased control of each genre, by our increased ability to master unfamiliar genres, and by our increased understanding of how we can sublate the constraints of genre. To answer the New Rhetorical questions about genre fully and properly is a theoretical and empirical megaproject, but any reader, writer or teacher of reading or writing can – and should – nonetheless ask them, specifically, about the genres that matter to her or him. For thus can the tyranny of genre be overthrown[6] and the 'utterly dismal' study of organization become the utterly fascinating, liberating, and empowering rhetoric of form and genre.

Notes

1 The act of naming is itself rhetorical (and each human child's acquisition of a vocabulary should be understood as a form of unconscious social suasion). Even when we confine ourselves to the most concrete terms, human perceptions are always mediated by a linguistic dialectic of abstraction. When we name we identify what we name *as* of a certain sort, we *sort* it, we *class*-ify it, we direct our attention to salient characteristics (and thus deflect it from other characteristics). For a discussion of this New Rhetorical concept and its implications for teaching, see Coe (1993).

2 Miller's 'Genre as Social Action' (1984; revised version Chapter 2, this volume), which has become a touchstone article, applies to genre the new Rhetoric's first principle: discourse is best understood first and foremost as symbolic action (and only secondarily, albeit very importantly, as representation or symbolic meaning). Perelman asserts that we often misunderstand how discourse works because 'problems of action' are often 'reduced to problems of knowledge' (1982: 7). Richards uses the analogy of 'the physicist's ultimate particles and rays', which are known only by what they do, and argues that we should focus our study on 'how words *work* in discourse' (1936: 5, emphasis added). Burke repeatedly insists his entire method turns on the shift of perspective encapsulated by the phrase 'language as symbolic action' (cf. for example, 1966: 44–45; 1968: 445).

   Most people who have thought a bit about language and discourse find the phrase 'symbolic action' fairly comfortable – at least until we spin its implications, ask what other perspectives it displaces (or demotes). Burke and Perelman set language as *action* in opposition to language as *knowledge*, i.e. in opposition to language as first and foremost symbolic meaning, representation. Understanding discourse as re-presentation, that is, utterance as verbal *copy* (be it of reality or of thought), leads to the questions, what does it mean? is it true? Understanding discourse as symbolic action leads to the same questions we ask about other actions: What does it do? What motivated it? What are its consequences? (Language as action also contrasts with perspectives based on the metaphor of conversation, at least if one assumes that the purpose of conversation is to communicate or negotiate meanings.)

3 Somewhat surprisingly, recent discussions of genre often seem to treat as virtual synonyms *rhetorical situation* and *context of situation* (perhaps because both refer not to texts or utterances, but to situating contexts). This is unfortunate, I think, because the way a genre is situated should be explicated on several levels. Rhetorical situation can be operationally equated with the classical rhetorical formulation – *purpose*, *audience* and *occasion* (itself the narrowest of our situating terms) – which defines a speaking or writing task. Context of situation refers to the context of *that* situation; Malinowski originally coined the phrase to refer to the social context of certain fishermen who were telling their fishing stories. Fortunately, we have already in play three terms that refer to three levels on which genres may be situated: *occasion*, *rehetorical situation* and *context of situation*. (It is also important

to note that there is on the level of context of situation something comparable to rhetorical *purpose* for which we need another term, and the word most commonly used seems to be *function*.)

4 Traditionally, both genre knowledge and the learning/teaching of genres have typically been tacit (cf. Freedman 1993; this volume). There is no question that genres can be – and typically are – acquired without explicit articulation of the sort produced by genre analysts (nor is there any doubt that harm can be done when explicit teaching of genres is based on inadequate or false descriptions). We must also ask, however, to what extent the social processes of tacit genre acquisition serve to limit genre knowledge and thus to limit access to power (in part by justifying meritocracy), thereby reinforcing and even recreating existing social hierarchies. Perhaps tacit genre acquisition serves even to assure that only people whose very natures have been reshaped by those tacit processes acquire certain kinds of power – as Eagleton (1983) suggests about a related sort of tacit process when he asserts that English literature courses were first introduced in British universities in order to instill élite values in middle-class students who would, after graduation, administer the Empire (pp. 17ff.). We should ask to what extent and under what circumstances adopting the persona appropriate to a genre may lead speakers or writers to embody that persona not only in the particular utterance but as an aspect of their personalities – for is this not an aspect of how immersing students in, say, lawyerly discourse helps them evolve into lawyers, people who view events from a lawyerly perspective, have lawyerly attitudes, act like lawyers? Should this not concern us when, to help them gain power and opportunities, we immerse young women in patriarchal discourses, teach them genres that dance patriarchal attitudes and embody patriarchal personae?

(We should also remember to ask whether teachers with explicit genre knowledge might help students acquire genres, explicitly or tacitly, more successfully – just as coaches now do for all sorts of athletic skills.)

5 Too often genre analysts – even those who emphasize genre as social process – speak and write as if a particular text or utterance belongs to one and only one genre. As Anne Freadman reminds us, however, a particular utterance or text can and often does participate in several genres (in Reid 1987: 97–98; condensed version Chapter 3, this volume). If we forget that, we are in danger of reductionism – and may commit errors when using or teaching genres.

6 The 'tyranny of genre' is normally taken to signify how generic structures constrain individual creativity. It should be taken also in a broader sense. As Miller suggests, 'what we learn when we learn a genre is not just a pattern of forms or even a method of achieving our own ends. We learn, more importantly, what ends we may have... As a recurrent, significant action, a genre embodies an aspect of cultural rationality' (1984: 165). To learn a generic form without becoming aware of tacit strategies, purposes, functions and values is not so much to master the genre as to become subject to it (cf. Luke 1994). To help someone learn generic forms without helping them also to that critical awareness and mastery may subject them to the genre more than empower them.

While considering the 'tyranny of genre' in this sense, it is worth remembering that one tacit social function of classical tragedy, according to both Aristotle and Burke, was politically conservative; by portraying the catastrophes that befell assertive individuals and thus 'dancing the attitude' that one should accept one's 'fate', however undeserved, these plays purged the audience's impulse to resist injustice, to question the existing social hierarchy. In tragic drama, Burke writes, 'important social relations involving superiority and inferiority could be translated into a set of 'mythic' equivalents... Whatever the social origins of such motives...converted into the fullness of tragedy they have become *cosmologized*' (1966: 126–7). What would be the ethical implications of teaching someone to write, or even to attend and enjoy, such plays without making them aware of the genre's political function?

References

ARISTOTLE (1954) *The Rhetoric and the Poetics*, (trans. R. Roberts and I. Bywater) New York: Random House.

BARTHES, R. (1972) *Mythologies*, (trans. A. Lavers) New York: Hill and Wang.

BARTHES, R. (1977) *Image-Music-Text*, (trans. S. Heath). Glasgow: Collins.

BURKE, K. ([1931] 1968) *Counter-Statement*, (reprint) Berkeley, CA: University of California Press.

BURKE, K. ([1941] 1957) *The Philosophy of Literary Form*, (revised abridged edn) New York: Vintage.

BURKE, K. (1947) 'Kinds of Criticism', *Poetry*, **68**, August, pp. 272–82.

BURKE, K. (1955) 'Linguistic Approach to Problems in Education', in HENRY, N. B. (ed.) *Modern Philosophies of Education*, Chicago, IL: National Society for the Study of Education, 54, Pt. 1, 259–303. (Distributed by University of Chicago Press.)

BURKE, K. (1966) *Language as Symbolic Action*, Berkeley, CA: University of California Press.

BURKE, K. (1968) 'Dramatism (Interaction)', *International Encyclopedia of the Social Sciences*, (ed. D. L. Sills) New York: Cromwell Collier and Macmillan, Vol. 7, pp. 445–52.

CHRISTIE, F. (1985) *Language Education*, Victoria, Australia: Deakin University Press.

COE, R. M. (1974) 'Rhetoric 2001', *Freshman English News*, **3**, pp. 1–13.

COE, R. M. (1975) 'Beyond Absurdity: Albee's Awareness of Audience in *Tiny Alice*, *Modern Drama*, **18**, pp. 232–7.

COE, R. M. (1992) 'Classical and Rogerian Persuasion: An Archeological/Ecological Explication', in TEICH, N. (ed.) *Rogerian Rhetoric*, Norwood, NJ: Albex, pp. 83–108.

COE, R. M. (1993) 'Beyond Diction: Using Burke to Empower Words – and Wordlings', *Rhetoric Review*, **11**, pp. 368–77.

COE, R. M. (1994) 'Metaphor', in *Encyclopedia of Rhetoric*, New York: Garland (forthcoming).

D'ANGELO, F. (1975) *A Conceptual Theory of Rhetoric*, Cambridgge, MA: Winthrop.

DERRIDA, J. (1974) 'White Mythology: Metaphor in the Text of Philosophy', (trans. F. C. T. Moore) *New Literary History*, **6**, pp. 5–74.

DEVITT, A. (1993) 'Generalizing about Genre', *College Composition and Communication*, **44**, pp. 573–86.

EAGLETON, T. (1983) *Literary Theory: An Introduction*, Oxford: Blackwell.

EDE, L. and LUNSFORD, A. (1984) 'Audience Addressed/Audience Invoked: The Role of Audience in Composition Theory and Pedagogy', *College Composition and Communication*, **35**, pp. 155–71.

FOUCAULT, M. (1972) *The Archaeology of Knowledge and the Discourse on Language*, (trans. A. M. Sheridan Smith) New York: Pantheon.

FREADMAN, A. (1987) 'Anyone for Tennis?' in REID, I. (ed.) *The Place of Genre in Learning*, Geelong, Australia: Deakin University, pp. 91–124.

FREEDMAN, A. (1993) 'Show and Tell? The Role of Explicit Teaching in the Learning of New Genres', *Research in the Teaching of English*, **27**, pp. 222–51.

HALLIDAY, M. A. K. and HASAN, R. (1985) *Language, Context and Text: A Social-Semiotic Perspective*, Geelong, Australia: Deakin University Press.

KINNEAVY, J. (1979) 'The Relation of the Whole to the Part in Interpretation Theory and in the Composing Process', in MCQUADE, D. (ed.) *Linguistics, Stylistics, and the Teaching of Composition*, Akron, OH: L & S, pp. 1–23.

KOJÈVE, A. (1969) *Introduction to the Reading of Hegel*, (trans. J. H. Nichols, Jr) New York: Basic.

LAKOFF, G. and JOHNSON, M. (1980) *Metaphors We Live By*, Chicago, IL: University of Chicago Press.

LEFEVRE, K. (1986) *Invention as a Social Act*, Carbondale, IL: Southern Illinois University Press.

LUKE, A. (1994) 'Genres of Power? Literacy Education and the Production of Capital, in HASAN, R. and WILLIAMS, G. (eds) *Literacy in Society*, London: Longman.

MALINOWSKI, B. (1923) 'The Problem of Meaning in Primitive Languages'. Supplement 1 in *The Meaning of Meaning*, (eds C. K. Ogden and I. A. Richards) London: Kegan Paul, pp. 296–336.

MILLER, C. (1984) 'Genre as Social Action', *Quarterly Journal of Speech*, **70**, pp. 151–67.

OHMANN, R. (1976) *English in America*, New York: Oxford University Press.

PERELMAN, C. (1982) *The Realm of Rhetoric*, (trans. W. Kluback) Notre Dame, IN: University of Notre Dame Press.

REID, I. (ed.) (1987) *The Place of Genre in Learning: Current Debates*, Victoria, Australia: Deakin University Centre for Studies in Literary Education, Typereader Publication 1.

RICHARDS, I. A. (1936) *The Philosophy of Rhetoric*, New York: Oxford University Press.

RICOEUR, P. (1973) 'Creativity in Language: Word, Polysemy, Metaphor', *Philosophy Today*, **17**, pp. 97–111.

RUECKERT, W. H. (1963) *Kenneth Burke and the Drama of Human Relations*, Minneapolis, MN: University of Minnesota Press.

WINTEROWD, W. R. (ed.) (1975) *Contemporary Rhetoric*, New York: Harcourt.

Chapter 12

'Do As I Say': The Relationship between Teaching and Learning New Genres*

Aviva Freedman

In the last 15 years, two distinct approaches to genre have developed in the English-speaking world: one largely in North America, and represented by chapters in this collection; and the second, largely in Australia and referred to as the 'Sydney School', because its leading proponents were students of M. A. K. Halliday at the University of Sydney.

Despite increased mobility among scholars and advances in communication technology, these two scholarly traditions have managed to develop largely independently and in isolation from each other. It is true, of course, that currents from the same intellectual *Zeitgeist* gave impetus to both approaches, especially the recent reorientation of interest from the psychological and the cognitive to the social and cultural as ways of understanding linguistic performance. Nonetheless, while both are socially oriented, the two approaches to genre have taken different courses – perhaps because of differences in the political environment of the different countries, and of concomitant responses by the educational system within those countries, but also because of the different scholarly traditions within which each approach has been framed.

The Sydney School genre movement is rooted in Hallidayan systemic linguistics and continues to foreground such linguistic analyses. More relevant to the argument of this chapter, its leading scholars have focused not just on the textual and the socio-cultural, but also and especially on the political dimensions of genre, and on a politically motivated project of genre education. The claim is that some genres are privileged in society and that their mastery confers power. For this reason, educators are enjoined to intervene directly with students who are economically and culturally disadvantaged, in order to help them master such genres and consequently gain access to the corridors of power. (For a description of the history and development of this movement, see Cope *et al.* 1993.)

*A somewhat different version of this chapter appeared as 'Show and Tell? The Role of Explicit Teaching in the Learning of New Genres', *Research in the Teaching of English*, **27**(3) (1993), pp. 222–51.

To achieve these ends – that is, the empowerment of the disadvantaged – the Sydney School genre educationists came out with a carefully developed and sequenced educational program. They began by identifying those genres that confer power (mainly school genres associated with the sciences and social sciences); they then explicated the features of these genres using the Hallidayan socially-based system of textual analysis. On that basis, they devised programs in which teachers were expected to explicate the features of these genres to their pupils, beginning in the earliest years of schooling. Thus Rothery first 'worked with teachers introducing the generic structure of genres and...analysing foregrounded aspects of their grammar – for example, the grammar of nominal groups in reports' (Cope *et al.* 1993: 298). Then teachers were shown how to explicate these features to students. For example, in order to teach their Grade 2 pupils to write narratives, Rothery instructed teachers to begin by 'modelling a genre *explicitly* by naming its stages; e.g., identifying the stages Orientation, Complication and Resolution in *Little Red Riding Hood*' (Martin *et al.* 1987: 69). As a result of such explication, students were expected to acquire these genres and consequently to be empowered – first in school and then in the workplace and social world beyond.

It is this educational aspect of the Sydney School approach to genre studies that I intend to address directly in this chapter, not just as a distant bystander surveying education in Australia, but also as an interested party who is deeply concerned lest precisely such teaching become attractive in North American jurisdictions, where educators are desperately seeking to respond to the ongoing onslaught about student 'illiteracy' from the media and the business community. The explicitness, the sequentiality, and especially the necessary authoritarianism implicit in the new genre pedagogy may be very appealing to educators who are daily being accused of lack of discipline, clear goals and explicit frameworks. Particularly seductive is the associated liberationist rationale: who would deny empowerment to the disadvantaged?

In a powerful critique of the Sydney School's assumptions, Luke (1994) has pointed to the political limitations of this enterprise. To summarize briefly, he first points out that, despite its ideological claims, the Sydney School approach is geared to 'allow for enhanced individual agency in mainstream institutions', rather than significant social change: 'emphasis on the direct transmission of text-types...leads to uncritical reproduction of the discipline' and the inequitable society. He also questions the naive assumption implicit in the program developed by these educationists: i.e. the assumption that the scientific genres that they privilege by teaching are ideologically neutral.

In addition, Luke objects to the Sydney School's conceptualization of genre as too simplistic – ignoring as it does the realities of contestation and the fact that genres are themselves sites for struggle. Finally, he points to the naivety of the theorizing about the relationship between genre and power. Their argument, he says, assumes a 'hypodermic' effect: power can be injected through some simple mechanism. By drawing on more sophisticated theories of power developed in the works of Foucault and especially Bourdieu, Luke shows that 'power is utterly sociologically contingent ... There are no guarantees of power: there are no genres of power.'

This chapter is intended to supplement Luke's argument. Rather than their political premises, I will interrogate the educational assumptions of the Sydney School movement: that explicit teaching of genre can in fact lead to its acquisition. In probing this issue, I will be raising questions not just about the programs promulgated by the Sydney School but also about assumptions underlying some conventional and widespread North American teaching, such as teaching the features of business writing in the secondary school classroom or in first-year engineering, or discussing discipline-specific genres in first-year composition.

Furthermore, the questions posed here are raised not just in response to Sydney School genre studies but also out of a sense that North American genre studies may also be moving teachers, less programmatically, towards greater explication of genre features. As we learn more about the nature of school and workplace genres, the urge to explicate this knowledge to our students, as a way of enhancing their learning, may be irresistible. As teachers, indeed as human beings, we all feel the same strong impulse to tell what we know, to share, especially with our students, what we have just discovered. But before we do so, we will need to ask ourselves what grounds we have for believing that such explication will in fact enhance their learning. What kind of research evidence is available to ground such a hypothesis? And how does such a hypothesis about learning mesh with our wider understanding of how we learn to write or with what we know about language learning in general?

The Question

In light of the educational program developed within the Sydney School, and in light of the current lively state of genre studies in North America which could easily lead to (and may already have led to) an explicit rule-based focus on genre in writing classrooms in the United States and Canada, I would like to address the following pedagogic question, with a view both to opening a communal professional discussion and to encouraging more specific, focused research: What role, if any, *can* or *should* the explicit teaching of genre features play in learning to write new genres? To be more precise, the question can be subdivided as follows:

- Is explicit teaching necessary?
- Is explicit teaching possible?
- If so, can it be useful?
- If so, when, at what stage in the evolution of a writer? and at what stage in the evolution of the writing? and by whom, i.e. what knowledge is necessary for the would-be intervener?

And as a counterpart throughout, we need to remember the implicit negative questions:

- Can explicit teaching be harmful?
- If so, when, and by whom?

By explicit teaching of genre, the following is intended: *explicit discussions, specifying the (formal) features of the genres and/or articulating underlying rules.* Because of current reconceptions of genre as social action, such teaching also may involve explication of the social, cultural and/or political features of the context which elicit the textual regularities. Typically, such teaching is also decontextualized, so that for example, would-be engineers are taught about workplace writing in the actual context of a university classroom or first-year students are taught about sociology papers in the context of a composition classroom. In both cases, teaching is in relation to assignments set and to a culture created by composition teachers.[1]

Contextualizing the Question

As preceding chapters in this volume have revealed, the notion of genre has in recent years been reconceived so that the recurring textual regularities which characterize genres are themselves seen as secondary to, and a consequence of, the action that is being performed through the texts in response to recurring socio-cultural contexts (Devitt 1993). Seminal theorists in this reconceptualization are Miller (1984, revised version Chapter 2, this volume), Bakhtin (1986), and Swales (1990).

Central to all these notions is the recognition that genres are social actions or rhetorical responses to recurring situations or contexts. Context, of course, is more and other than physical (or disciplinary) setting; the social motive that animates genre is experienced in response to recurrent socially constructed situations, which include a range of possible social, cultural political, ideological and discursive dimensions.

Such redefinitions themselves begin to pose the very questions that we are addressing in this chapter. If textual features are secondary to, and consequences of, the rhetorical action, is there any value to explicating these textual features by themselves, and out of context, as a way of teaching genre? In fact, if genres are responses to contexts, can they be learned at all out of context? In 'Reading and Writing as Social Action', Barnes and Barnes offer their clear answer: 'Learning to communicate is not only content-specific, but also context-specific' (1990: 60). They go on to say:

> Our ability to participate with others, to take on appropriate roles in writing to them, and to foresee what they need to know is a social competence that we learn for specific groups of people, and not in general... [It] depends on our awareness of the tacit meanings available in a group, and our ability to respond to the demands of a specific audience and situation. That is, [it] depends upon a participant's *experience of a social milieu*. (1990: 60; emphasis mine)

All this suggests a further question: can the complex web of largely tacitly understood social, cultural and rhetorical features to which genres respond ever be explicated fully, or in such a way that can be useful to learners?

While these redefinitions of genre form part of the backdrop for the argument that follows, additional support will be drawn from writing research and theory as well as research into and theory about first and second-language acquisition. In referring to this literature, I do not intend to blur the differences among the different linguistic processes. Clearly writing is different, in important ways, from conversing; adult language learning is not the same as acquisition in childhood; learning a second language is not identical to acquiring written discourse. However, there is enough that is analogous among these different language learning processes for comparisons to be considered. Certainly with respect to acquisition, the research evidence continues to point to fundamental overlap, and it is noteworthy that even a scholar like Myron Tuman, who focuses on identifying the differences between literacy and oral language, recognizes that 'the ontogeny of language and the ontogeny of literacy are...part of one and the same process' (1987: 99).

Two Hypotheses

As we will see, even when supplemented with evidence from first and second language acquisition, the research evidence concerning genre acquisition is limited; while some of the subquestions can be answered unequivocally on the basis of this evidence, others are open to more than one interpretation. For this reason, I intend to take advantage of an earlier example in linguistics (as well as a postmodern option) to offer the reader a choice between two models or hypotheses concerning the potential role of explicit teaching in genre acquisition.

The Strong Hypothesis will state that explicit teaching is unnecessary, for the most part, not even possible, and where possible, not useful (except during editing, for a limited number of transparent and highly specific features). Further, whenever explicit teaching does take place, there is risk of overlearning or misapplication.

The second hypothesis is the Restricted or limited version of the Strong Hypothesis. It is similar in stating that explicit teaching is neither necessary nor for the most part possible or useful, and it acknowledges as well the potential for harm in such teaching. However, the Restricted Hypothesis allows that, under certain conditions and for some learners, explicit teaching *may* enhance learning.

Both hypotheses can account for the research evidence that is currently available, and so this chapter is in part an argument and in part a plea for more focused research and related theorizing. And it is not just to researchers and theorists that this plea is addressed. Both models are also offered to practising teachers as hypotheses to be tested in the crucibles of their own experience and classrooms – to be supplemented, in other words, by what North (1987) calls 'lore' or what Phelps (1988) calls 'phronesis' or practical wisdom.

The Strong Hypothesis

Explicit Teaching is Not Necessary in the Acquisition of Genres

In the mid-1980s, my research assistants and I undertook a large-scale research project examining, among other things, the control of narrative structure in the scripts of some 7,500 schoolchildren in grades 5, 8 and 12 (see Freedman 1987a). The study revealed that even elementary schoolchildren showed considerable mastery and sophisticated manipulation of a structure that could be parsed by researchers using a highly developed story grammar (based on the model elaborated by Stein and Glenn 1979), a grammar that was unavailable either to teachers or students in explicit form. These children seemed to have no need for the explicit naming of the stages of narrative presented in the Sydney School model cited earlier. (Even with the most chauvinist intentions, I cannot point to cultural factors that might account for such a differernce.)

A plausible interpretation for this performance is that the young writers had inferred the appropriate schema for stories on the basis of their own reading or from hearing stories told or read aloud. This schema was internalized, without evidence of any prior explicit teaching and was brought to bear as tacit, shaping knowledge in the course of their writing in the context of the elicited task.

Still more interesting is a second piece of research we conducted in which we observed a group of undergraduate students as they produced writing that could be characterized as a distinctive genre or subgenre – through an analysis of its textual features and the social action performed (see Freedman 1987b, 1990, in press). Three related findings of that study are of note. First, the students consulted no models. Second, students were given no explicit instruction about the nature of this new genre. Third, the students themselves made no attempt to formulate the rules underlying the genre as they struggled with their writing tasks.

These facets of our findings, the distinctiveness of the genre and the absence of explicit instruction or conscious learning, provided one kind of answer to the question concerning the role of explicit teaching. *Clearly, explicit teaching is not necessary for the acquisition of even very sophisticated school genres.*

Further, while other studies investigating genre acquisition have not addressed this question directly, it is apparent in the accounts of the specialized genres acquired in distinct knowledge and discourse communities that (except with reference to gross features such as format) explicit teaching of the features of genre is not even attempted, and that the learning that takes place is tacit (see, for example, Herrington 1985 and McCarthy 1987).

All this is consistent with research undertaken into child language acquisition. While the role of caretakers and elder children in modelling appropriate language use and in providing facilitative contexts is essential, children learn the most sophisticated and complex rules of their native language with no explicit instruction.

The same can be said of second language acquisition for adult as well as child language-learners. Stephen Krashen (1981a, 1992) has long argued that nearly all second language learning entails what he calls 'acquisition': the subconscious inferring of the rules of language use on the basis of comprehensible examples of the target language during the process of authentic language tasks. There is considerable research evidence supporting Krashen's hypothesis. Such evidence includes 'studies showing that when acquirers obtain more comprehensible output, they acquire more of the target language. This is the case both outside of school (exposure and length of residence studies) and inside of school (method of comparison studies)' (1992: 400). (For a review of the relevant studies, see Krashen 1991 or Ellis 1990.)

Further corroboration comes from another source: recent work investigating everyday or practical cognition (see, for example, Lave and Wenger 1991). According to models developed within this literature, all learning is necessarily situated within communities of practice in which learners are enabled to perform by an intricately orchestrated process of coparticipation with old-time members. As Hanks explains in his introduction to Lave and Wenger, explication is not part of the learning process:

> The master's effectiveness at producing learning is not dependent on her ability to inculcate the student with her own conceptual representations. Rather, it depends on her ability to manage effectively a division of participation that provides for growth on the part of the student. (1991: 21)

The thrust in this literature is towards a model of learning as *performance in context*. Hanks explains that skilful performance 'involves a prereflective grasp of complex situations, which might be reported as a propositional description, but is not one itself' (1991: 20). In other words, although the relevant knowledge may be summarizable in propositional descriptions such as those put forward by Sydney School scholars or North American students of genre, such verbal explications are not themselves useful as modes of instruction. 'Quite simply, if learning is about increased access to performance, then the way to maximize learning is to perform, not to talk about it' (Hanks 1991: 22).

All this points to a new formulation of the question about explicit teaching. We have seen from these studies that explicit teaching may not be necessary. The relevant question now is different: Is explicit teaching even possible?

Explicit Teaching and Conscious Learning Are Not Possible Except for a Limited Number of Features

Krashen makes the following point in his monograph on *Writing*: 'The rules that describe written language. . .are simply too complex and too numerous to be explicitly taught and consciously learned' (1984: 27). There are three separate points to be considered here.

First, the rules for our language have not yet been described adequately even by the most sophisticated linguists. Those who discuss first language acquisition like to point to the tremendous complexity and sophistication of the laws of syntax, morphology, phonology – such that even Noam Chomsky cannot, at least yet, adequately formulate a set of rules to account entirely for the grammar of our language.

This is *a fortiori* true for the rules underlying written genres, where research and theory are still comparatively in their infancy and sometimes fraught with conceptual problems. (See, for example, Dixon's discussions, 1987, 1944, of the conceptual problems associated with the Australian work.) Even more daunting for any definitive explication of specific genres, however, is the fact of the fluid and dynamic nature of most genres. As Miller (1984: 163; revised version Chapter 2, this volume) writes, 'genres change, evolve, and decay'; certainly in the current everyday world of practical affairs where technological, material and political features of the rhetorical contexts are always changing, concomitant fluidity in the nature of the genres produced as rhetorical responses to these contexts is inevitable. In the end, we may never be able to specify or articulate with assurance the rules for such genres, except possibly historically and in retrospect.

Second, the rules that are known are simply too complex and too numerous to be explicitly taught in the context of writing or language instruction (as opposed to courses devoted to linguistics or discourse theory). Even a brief introduction to linguistics is enough to persuade one that the rules of syntax and phonology are extra-ordinarily complex and sophisticated. Research into academic and professional genres is just beginning to uncover the similarly complex set of processes and practices, as well as the fluid and dynamic interplay among them, that are all at play in the creation of such genres. We are beginning to learn how writers in the workplace, and in academia, respond in their writing to a wide variety of discoursal cues – social, cultural, conceptual, linguistic. In 'The Ecology of Writing', Cooper (1989) uses the metaphor of a web to capture the intricate, richly interwoven complexity of the processes at play. The complexity of such specific contexts, and of the subtle interplay among processes within these contexts, has been laid out in a number of highly sophisticated monograph-length studies by Bazerman (1988), Myers (1990), Swales (1990) and Yates (1989).

The third point to be taken from Krashen's statement has to do with what is possible for the learner, not the teacher. His argument is that the number of rules that can be applied in language production by the learner is very limited. As suggested earlier, Krashen's theories are based on a model of learning in which there are two distinct processes: 'learning' (which involves the conscious learning of rules such that they can be formulated explicitly by the learner), and 'acquisition' (which entails the unconscious inference of rules on the basis of exposure to the target language). Critical to this model is the notion that conscious learning can never become acquisition; the two are separate processes resulting in different kinds of knowledge, each stored separately, with no interface between the two possible.

Conscious learning can be called on in language production – but only for use by what Krashen calls the 'Monitor', or editing function. Only a small percentage of the rules of the language can be so used; these are restricted to the most general and obvious features of format and organization as well as very specific editing rules.

The fact that writers have more time than speakers to monitor means that they can, if they choose, apply this set of transparent rules more conscientiously. However, the far more subtle and complex rules at play cannot be so applied. Think, for example, of the delicate and nuanced set of conventions governing what constitutes appropriate *novelty* in student writing, as described by Kaufer and Geisler (1989). These rules, they argue, can only be acquired through 'insider status', which allows for the development of

> 'an insider's rhetoric' – a set of *tacit beliefs* that *accrue* to one who actively tries (and mostly fails) in the role of knowledge maker... [The relevant] conventions are learned *only* in the effort to be new and in the feedback one receives for one's effort. (1989: 306; emphasis mine)

Explicit Teaching Can Be Harmful

While Krashen concedes that language learners can call on a limited number of consciously learned rules as they edit, he is also quick to point to the danger that precisely such rules can be misapplied by overanxious and insecure writers. There are many examples in the second-language research literature (see Lightbown 1985; Weinert 1987; Ellis 1990), and Perl's (1979) study of basic writers documents evidence of just such overuse or misuse of conscious learning in the writing process.

A different kind of danger occurs when those who attempt to explicate the rules for a specific genre are not themselves members of the relevant community. A research study undertaken in British Columbia by Harper (1991) provides an instance that dramatizes the nature of my concern. Harper looks at the effects of an intervention by a group of university writing specialists within a professional discourse community. For our discussion, the relevant feature of this study is that even trained writing specialists, working in the context of authentic discourse and with very motivated learners, were not able to teach appropriately because they had not themselves understood the complex rhetorical role of some features of the discourse. For example, they had not understood the degree to which the specialized terminology ('jargon' to the layperson) was intimately related to the shared belief system as well as the intertextual nature of the genre. Similarly, they had not understood that the passives which they had tried to proscribe served not only to give objective status and hence authority to the findings but also to soften the oppositional discourse in order to preserve harmony within the community. As one writer explained later, 'We are not writing in a vacuum'. Indeed. But the resonance and the complicated interweaving network of relationships, purposes, audiences and agendas in the context were not easily understood by or made available even to sophisticated writing specialists working closely with members of the community.

Finally, I would like to cite my own experience conducting research into development in story writing, which provided a striking instance of how much more we know tacitly than we can say and of the consequent dangers for explicit teaching of the features of even familiar forms. Analysis using a model of story grammar developed in the 1970s revealed structural failure in a subset of stories, although these same stories seemed intuitively, to me and my researchers, to be more, rather than less, sophisticated. Fortunately, while we were analysing the data, a more complex model of story structure (Peterson and McCabe 1983) was reported in the literature. This model accounted for and recognized the sophistication of the stories that had seemed flawed according to the earlier analyses. My point is this: The first model was powerful and accounted for a great deal of data; a teacher could easily have been seduced by its clarity and the range of its explanatory power. Had there been direct explicit teaching based on that model (fortunately there was none), the students' writing might have been inhibited.

In linguistic matters, typically we know more than we can say. The danger in explicit teaching is that we may thereby prevent our students from enacting what they know tacitly. Acquisition itself is achieved through the intuition of rules at levels below the conscious.

What This Means for Teaching

None of this is meant to suggest that there is no role for the teacher. First, even the Strong Hypothesis leaves some room for explicit teaching. As suggested above, Krashen points to certain gross features that may be profitably taught explicitly for use in monitoring: overall features of format or organization, for example, and a limited set of rules regarding usage and punctuation. In addition to such transparent features of form, Krashen also suggests that composing strategies can be discussed explicitly: heuristic or invention strategies as well as revising techniques such as cutting and pasting, or their word-processing counterparts. Flower's (1989a) rhetorical problem-solving and Coe's (1990) metaheuristics are sophisticated versions of such strategies, including as they do techniques for analysing audience and context.

Beyond such explicit teaching though, teachers have a central role to play in setting up facilitative environments. This can take several forms. First, the Krashen model and research into reading–writing relationships suggest that a necessary prerequisite for the development of writing abilities is considerable reading experience. In fact, the relative lack of such exposure with respect to expository writing in general (and the writing of argument in particular) may explain, at least in part, students' relative lack of success in producing expository and argumentative genres (see, for example, discussions in Engelhard *et al.* 1992; Freedman and Pringle 1984; Stotsky 1983). And the tendency in some whole-language classes to focus only on fiction, accompanied by the tendency in some process classes to elicit only personal and narrative writing, does nothing to counter the paucity of exposure to the kind of reading that might prepare students for upper-level school demands as well as for workplace writing.

Indeed, it may be precisely these factors – limited kinds of whole-language and process teaching accompanied by students' relative failure to master school and workplace genres – that are fueling the genre movement in Australia. There are better solutions, however, to this problem. Teachers can, with some imagination and resourcefulness, stage-manage exposure to a wide range of expository genres. Then they can follow up by eliciting expository genres within appropriate contexts drawing on the approaches to be described below.

Before discussing such contexts and such approaches, there are two more points to note with respect to exposure. First, there is probably a threshold level of exposure: after that point, more reading is not going to make for better writing (Krashen 1981b). The difference between a Tolstoy and you or me is the not amount of fiction we have read. Further, the threshold level will vary with the individual and will depend on a host of variables relating to reading strategies, socio-cultural environment, developmental or experiential level, and general literacy background.

Beyond this, we must remember that exposure to written discourse is a *necessary but not a sufficient condition*. Reading alone is not enough, just as exposure to comprehensible input in a second language is not enough by itself to ensure acquisition. There are other prerequisites. Krashen points to the role of affect. For second language learning, anxiety is a key factor: the less the anxiety, the greater the learning. Motivation is also clearly important. And further research may uncover variations by personality type or learning style.

Perhaps most significant is the role of 'intention' – that is, having something to say, which itself implies exigence and context. In addition to exposure, then, what is necessary is an occasion and a need to mean: some kind of rhetorical exigency which will elicit performance. Current theoretical reconceptualizations of genre as recurring response to a rhetorical context highlight precisely these dimensions of social motive, rhetorical responsiveness and context.

School assignments can and do act as exigencies in this sense. It has become a cliché to speak of school activities as decontextualized. While that cliché has some validity with respect to the data dealt with in the classroom, it is meaningless in discussing contexts of composing. School writing has a real context – not the imaginary situation specified in some assignments (from 'you are an irate customer writing to the President of Air Canada' to elaborated 'cases'), but the classroom itself, and all that it entails.

In the law study, I was impressed by the richness and thickness of the texture of the context woven by the instructors, and by the degree to which the writing elicited was a respose to this context. This enabling context was established through the lectures, through the readings assigned, through the questions posed in the seminars to the students, and through the talk and social interaction in general in the lecture hall and seminar room. The assignment evolved naturally out of the disciplinary conversation, and in responding to it, the students were able to draw on the appropriate cues so that on the one hand, they all produced the same distinctive academic subgenre (writing for Law) and on the other hand, through this writing they enacted the ways of thinking and the ways of identifying, delimiting, construing and approaching phenomena characteristic of this discipline. (This kind of shaping is characteristic of many, if not most, content-area or disciplinary classrooms, and it is in this way, rather than through attempts at explicit formulation of rules, that formal instruction elicits the learning of new genres.)

This brings to mind a related notion, emerging from second language research: that is, the notion of 'pushed output' as developed by Swain (1985) in her research into immersion learning. The 'pushed output' hypothesis is conceived as an addition to Krashen's acquisition hypothesis. In addition to comprehensible input, students need to be 'pushed' to produce; they need opportunities for meaningful use of their linguistic resources, with their output being shaped by the assignments set and by feedback offered in response to these assignments.

This points to a different kind of facilitative role for teachers. In addition to staging the context for the writing, teachers can facilitate their students' learning far more directly – and still without explication. I have in mind the kind of guidance described by researchers into everyday or practical cognition as well as those studying child language acquisition. In the former field, the term used is 'guided participation' (Rogoff 1990), and in the latter, 'scaffolding'. (The latter term has been popularized by Bruner 1978 and Cazden 1979.) Both terms suggest collaborative performance by the expert and the novice, a kind of cooperative interaction over the work-in-progress, with the teacher probing and responding tactfully where necessary, and giving over more and more responsibility to the learner as the learning progresses.

This discussion immediately evokes both the approaches recommended by Don Murray, Donald Graves and the National Writing Project as well as the more traditional kinds of interactions between attuned editor and professional writer or between supervisor and graduate student in the creation of a dissertation. Many other kinds of teaching, however, fit the broad parameters suggested above: for example, Hillocks's (1986) 'environmental mode', in which the teacher carefully plans activities, selects materials, and especially structures tasks;[2] or his 'individual mode', which includes the individualized tutorials, offered in college and university writing centres, where tutors intervene and guide as students compose papers for disciplines across the curriculum.

In summary, the strict limits set on explicit teaching by the Strong Hypothesis still allow for many kinds of teaching, involving radically different goals and philosophies, and including both writing for personal development as well as writing in response to disciplinary and workplace demands. Whatever their curricular goal, teachers may draw on a range of strategies to ensure that students have sufficient exposure to relevant or related discourse, that they experience the rhetorical exigences as insiders within the relevant contexts, and that they are both 'pushed', and 'guided' in their attempts to respond appropriately to these exigencies.

The Restricted Hypothesis

On the other hand, there are reasons to qualify the Strong Hypothesis which states that explicit teaching is unnecessary, for the most part not even possible, and where possible not useful (except during editing, for a limited number of transparent features). The research evidence from genre studies is, in the end, scanty and suggestive, rather than conclusive. In the studies cited, it is true that students received no explicit guidance, and we can reasonably conclude that explicit guidance is not necessary. However, we cannot exclude the possibility that explicit guidance of some kind might have enhanced or accelerated the learning. The relevant research has yet to be done. Furthermore, while it is true that the formulation of the Strong Hypothesis is buttressed by theory (based on extensive research) from first and second language acquisition, it is also true that research and theory from the field of second language acquisition at least can also support a more qualified version of the hypothesis. It is this more qualified version that I would like to develop at this point, recognizing that it may provide a better fit with some teachers' personal experience or practical wisdom. I call this version the Restricted Hypothesis. Common to both hypotheses are the notions that explicit teaching and conscious learning are not necessary, and that, in any comprehensive sense, neither is possible. The Restricted Hypothesis, however, does allow for certain limited conditions under which explicit teaching may enhance learning – at least for certain learners. It is to these conditions that I will now turn.

The model I will present here is drawn from the field of second language acquisition, specifically from Rod Ellis's (1990) recent work. I draw on this model not because I believe that the processes of second language acquisition and the acquisition of written discourse are identical, but because there are enough important similarities to warrant considering the potential relevance or potential application of such a model (grounded as it is in considerable research evidence) to composition. Both processes involve the acquisition of complex and elaborate linguistic rules. Both may also involve the acquisition or application of general cognitive strategies or skills that allow the learner to use her or his linguistic knowledge eventually with some automaticity and fluency in increasingly more complex tasks. Further, Ellis's primary focus is to understand 'instructed', as opposed to natural language learning, something that is of particular relevance to composition theorists and teachers.

To contextualize this model within its own discipline, we need to refer again to the model proposed by Krashen to describe second language acquisition. Krashen's (1981a) hypothesis has provided a focus for developments in research and theory in that field since the 1970s. In the early and mid-1980s, Krashen's hypothesis was publicly questioned in the context of new research as well as meta-analyses of earlier findings (see, for example, Long 1983 and Ellis 1986). More recently, however, these later studies and meta-analyses have themselves been shown to be flawed or limited, and current thinking, which is best summarized in the Ellis model, involves a qualified version of the Krashen hypothesis – qualified in ways that have particular relevance for us.

Figure 12.1 presents a visual version of Ellis's (1990) model. I should point out that this model has been developed on the basis of a comprehensive integration of the rich research literature on second language acquisition. The account that follows

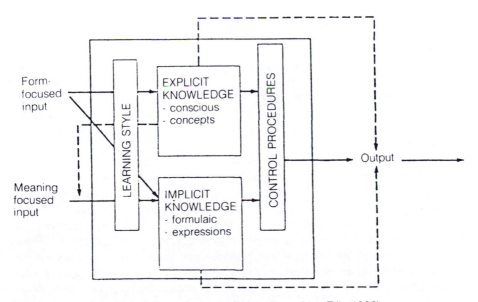

Figure 12.1   A model of instructed acquisition (based on Ellis 1990)

focuses only on the model itself; readers interested in the details of the corroborating research are referred to Ellis (1990). In observing the figure, note the following. Ellis distinguishes two kinds of instruction: form-focused instruction and meaning-focused instruction. Form-focused instruction involves explicit characterization of the features of discourse, or specific articulation of the linguistic (or other) rules underlying the discourse whose acquisition is targeted. Ellis hypothesizes that learners acquire two distinct kinds of knowledge: explicit knowledge (which allows the learner to specify features and rules) and implicit knowledge. Explicit knowledge is conscious and declarative; implicit knowledge is unconscious and procedural (i.e. the learner can enact the rules). Like Krashen, Ellis takes a non-interface position; these two kinds of knowledge do not interact. Ellis adduces a number of research studies to support this position (1990: 185–6), and we can all point to supporting phenomena: there are students who can recite rules without being able to enact them; and there are those who regularly enact complex and sophisticated rules without being able to articulate them.[3] Meaning-focused instruction, reading and writing for meaning, leads to implicit knowledge. Form-focused instruction leads to explicit knowledge. As opposed to Krashen, Ellis argues that form-focused instruction can lead to implicit knowledge in certain restricted cases. The most common such case involves the memorization of formulas; in composition these would include transitional phrases (however, on the other hand, etc.). Ellis's general conclusion is that, 'In practical terms, only instruction directed at formulaic phrases is likely to prove profitable. The principal source of implicit knowledge is meaning-focused instruction' (1990: 192).

All this is not very different from Krashen's hypothesis and is quite consistent with the Strong Hypothesis concerning explicit instruction. However, Ellis points to two other circumstances in which explicit teaching *can* lead to implicit knowledge, and this is where things get interesting for composition instruction.

In the first instance, Ellis argues that *some* structures can be explicitly taught and learned if the following conditions are met: the student is at the appropriate stage of development and has an appropriate learning style; the student is engaged in an authentic task that calls on the use of this structure. (This brings to mind Vygotsky's 1962 discussion of the conditions for concept-formation.) In other words, when interacting with students over work-in-progress either individually or in mini-lessons, certain kinds of explicit instruction may be useful to students who are ready and who have the appropriate learning style.

Even more suggestive is the following. Ellis hypothesizes that conscious knowledge may also be able to 'facilitate acquisition' in certain situations. That is, explicit teaching may be able to 'raise the consciousness' of some learners so that they will later notice and hence acquire features in meaning-focused input. For this process to occur, it is essential that the teaching and the opportunity for noticing be temporally in very close proximity. In other words, if certain features of a genre are pointed out explicitly to some learners during a period in which they are involved in reading other instances of that genre (say, other students' successful accomplishments of that genre), the learners may notice and acquire the rules governing those features.

To summarize, aside from the memorization of formulaic phrases, the two possibilities that Ellis specifies are these. First, if learners are developmentally ready and involved in authentic tasks, explicit teaching *may* result in acquisition in very specific instances. Second, as learners are immersed in meaningful, authentic reading and writing tasks, explicit teaching, which focuses on linguistic features of the discourse that is being read for meaning and/or being attempted in writing, *may* raise the consciousness of some learners in such a way that they will be sensitized to, and notice the occurrence of such features at a subsidiary attentional level, thereby acquiring that rule as part of their implicit knowledge so that it can be activated in future output.

What This Means for Teaching

These conditions offer very restricted qualifications to the Strong version of the theory. The teaching must always be done either in the context of, or in very close proximity to, authentic tasks involving the relevant discourse. Teaching first-year engineering students the discourse that will be required of them four years later as engineers (or even six months later, in their summer work) is somewhat too long a lag. On the other hand, teaching in the workplace, or a writing centre, or during an internship provides an ideal locale for this immediate kind of intervention because students are involved in authentic tasks and authentic contexts when the teaching takes place. Of course, the success of even such contextualized teaching depends upon the accuracy of the teacher's explicit knowledge and the congeniality of the student's learning style.

How does this differ from the scenario presented for the Strong Hypothesis? Not a great deal. The major difference is this: explicit discussions of the formal features of genre (always assuming that the instructor's description is accurate) may prove useful for those students whose learning styles are appropriate, but only when such discussions are presented while students are engaged in authentic reading and writing tasks, involving the targeted genre. For example, for a class of students who are all involved in writing sociology papers, there may be some merit in discussing some of the features of that genre, especially when that discussion precedes the reading of relevant models (good student papers, in this genre, for example) and attempts at writing in this genre. In one scenario, the explicit teaching itself becomes immediately internalized; in the other, the explicit teaching raises the learners' consciousness so that when they read or write, they will 'notice' the relevant features at an unconscious level and internalize at that point the rules that have been discussed.

Seminars for writers in the workplace may also fall into this category. If the presenters have accurate knowledge of the discourse under consideration (for example, legal briefs), and if the participants have been involved in reading and writing such briefs themselves, then explication of some features may raise the participants' consciousness so that not only will they be able to recognize during the seminars that the statements are accurate, but they may[4] also be able to incorporate this understanding in their subsequent composing.

The restrictions are severe though; proximity in time to exposure to authentic models is crucial. Teaching business writing to high school or even college students, years before their likely exposure to the relevant contexts, constitutes far too long a gap. In addition, the instructor must be sure that her or his descriptions of the genre are accurate. (In the Harper 1991 study described above, the writing specialists misunderstood the complex rhetorical dynamics at play in the genre they were attempting to teach. Similarly, early descriptions of story structure were too simplistic.) Finally, for some students at least, there are dangers in explicit teaching; they may overgeneralize the rules, as Perl's (1979) study showed, and distort their composing processes.

To respond to the questions posed at the outset, the Restricted Hypothesis argues tht explicit teaching is unnecessary, but is at least possible by those teachers who are in possession of accurate formulations of the genre elicited. Such explication may be useful, but only for students with the appropriate learning style, and at the appropriate level of development, and only during the process of composing, broadly conceived. At the same time, explicit teaching may be dangerous, if the instructor is an outsider or alternatively is an insider with inaccurate representations of the genre, or for those students who are likely to overgeneralize or place focal, rather than subsidiary, attention, to use Polanyi's terms, on formal features rather than on meaning.

Conclusion

Let me add one further qualification: none of this is intended to denegrate the value of critical literacy or reflective awareness. My point, however, is this: such critical consciousness becomes possible only *through* the performance: full genre knowledge (in all its subtlety and complexity) only becomes available *as a result of having written*. First comes the achievement or performance, with the tacit knowledge implied, and then, through that, the meta-awareness which can flower into conscious reflexive knowledge.

There is no question that such consciousness is empowering, potentially freeing the writer from the assumptions, interpretations and ideologies that have been tacitly at play. Such consciousness allows for the possibility of dissent and of informed choice. And this kind of liberation has increasingly become a goal of pedagogy for education, not just for composition. Coe, for example, has defined the task of the humanities as 'the raising or expansion of [students'] consciousness such that they can better comprehend, order, evaluate, and control their experience' (1974: 1).

My concern is not to argue against the possibility or the value of such reflexive consciousness, nor against the potential value of explication in extending such consciousness. My concern rather is to insist that however powerful such consciousness may be in allowing learners to reflect on, discrimate, and choose from among genres (hence from among ideologies and interpretations of reality), such consciousness is not itself a means of enabling learners to acquire such genres.[5]

To conclude, my presentation of the two hypotheses is intended to point to the necessity for further study, by researchers, theorists, teachers, and especially those who can test these hypotheses in the classroom and 'from within the matrix of practical experience' (Phelps 1988, 213). Let me end by acknowledging another set of generic realities. In her discussion of genre from a semiotic perspective, Anne Freadman (1987; condensed version Chapter 3, this volume) relies heavily on the analogy with a tennis match. According to the generic conventions of academic writing then, I will conclude by making explicit to my readers what they already know: The ball is now in your court.

Acknowledgement

I would like to thank Rick Coe, Richard Darville and Amy Devitt for their careful reading and provocative responses to an earlier version of this text.

Notes

1 My argument, in this chapter, focuses on the explicit teaching of genre – rather than on the broader issue of explicit teaching in general. The research reported here relates to genre acquisition and the hypotheses presented are placed primarily within the frame of genre theory. However, my guess is that, once we exempt explicit teaching of composing strategies, such as brainstorming, revising, etc. (as I do in this piece), most explicit teaching in the writing class is, in fact, genre-based, deriving from recurring features of form and context, and focusing on textual regularities and/or underlying rules tying form and substance to context.

2 As suggested in the text, Hillocks's (1986) meta-analyses provides some substantiation for the claim made in this chapter, given the relative success of the other modes of instruction in comparison to the presentational. I would argue, however, that the case may be even stronger than Hillocks's evidence suggests. His presentational teaching involves not only the explication of rules and a focus on form but also discussion and explication of the features of model texts. Exposure to models, however, can lead to 'acquisition', in Krashen's terms, even when the teacher's focus is on explicating rules. Simply by reading the models, students may be inferring the relevant rules for themselves, at a level below the conscious. In other words, their mode of learning may be quite different from what the mode of teaching implies. Because of this source of possible confusion in the data, I have chosen not to foreground this further piece of evidence.

3 Under the rubric of environmental teaching, one might include Bereiter and Scardamalia's (1987) 'procedural facilitations', sentence-combining, and the kind of exercises designed by Flower (1989b) to encourage greater conscious processing.

4 Ellis acknowledges that the research base for his non-interface position is not unshakeable. 'It is very difficult to tell what kind of knowledge a learner is using in any single performance. We cannot distinguish very easily editing by "feel" (which involves implicit knowledge) from editing with the "monitor" (which involves explicit knowledge)' (1990: 186). In the end, the non-interface position is his best guess on the basis of the research evidence available.

5 I emphasize the *may*, because this hypothesis must be tested. The ability to recognize, and even take pleasure in the discovery of, some discourse principle does not necessarily entail the ability to perform appropriately later. Bereiter and Scardamalia (1987) describe an experiment where students became able to articulate the features of argumentative form. The students were delighted and felt empowered; follow-up study, however, showed no carryover into their writing. Of course, adults may perform differently. There may be differences, relating to degree of readiness (relating to degree of exposure to the relevant context) and/or to the nature of the feature being taught. All this is researchable.

References

BAKHTIN, M. M. (1986) 'The Problem of Speech Genres', in *Speech Genres and Other Late Essays*, (ed. C. Emerson and M. Holquist, trans. V. W. McGee) Austin, TX: University of Texas Press.

BARNES, D. and BARNES, D. (1989) 'Reading and Writing as Social Action', in BEACH, R. and HYNDS, S. (eds) *Developing Discourse Practices in Adolescence and Adulthood*, Norwood, NJ: Ablex, pp. 34–64.

BAZERMAN, C. (1988) *Shaping Written Knowledge: The Genre and Activity of the Experimental Article in Science*, Madison, WI: Univrsity of Wisconsin Press.

BEREITER, C. and SCARDAMALIA, M. (1987) *The Psychology of Written Composition*, Hillsdale, NJ: Erlbaum.

BRUNER, J. (1978) 'The Role of dialogue in Language Acquisition, in SINCLAIR, A., JARVELLA, R. J. and LEVELT, W. J. M. (eds) *The Child's Conception of Language*, New York: Springer-Verlag, pp. 241–55.

CAZDEN, C. (1979) 'Peekaboo as an Instructional Model: Discourse Development at Home and at School', *Papers and Reports of Child Language Development*, **17**, pp. 1–29.

COE, R. (1974) 'Rhetoric 2001', *Freshman English News*, **3**, pp. 1–12.

COE, R. (1990) *Process, Form, and Substance*, 2nd edn, Englewood Cliffs, NJ: Prentice Hall.

COOPER, M. (1989) 'The Ecology of Writing', in COOPER, M. M. and HOLZMAN, M. (eds) *Writing as Social Action*, Portsmouth, NH: Boynton/Cook Heinemann, pp. 1–13.

COPE, W., KALANTZIS, M., KRESS, G. and MARTIN, J.; compiled by MURPHY, L. (1993) 'Bibliographic Essay: Developing the Theory and Practice of Genre-Based Literacy', in COPE, W. and KALANTZIS, M. (eds) *The Literacies of Power and the Powers of Literacy*, London: Falmer Press, pp. 295–315.

DEVITT, A. J. (1993) 'Generalizing about Genre: New Conceptions of an Old Concept', *College Composition and Communication*, **44**, pp. 357–86.

DIXON, J. (1987) 'The Question of Genre', in REID, I. (ed.) *The Place of Genre in Learning*, Geelong, Australia: Deakin University, pp. 9–21.

DIXON, J. (1994) 'Writing in Response to Each Other', in FREEDMAN, A. and MEDWAY, P. (eds) *Teaching and Learning Genre*, Portsmouth, NH: Boynton/Cook Heinemann.

DOHENY-FARINA, S. (1992) *Rhetoric, Innovation, Technology*, Cambridge, MA: MIT Press.

ELLIS, R. (1986) *Understanding Second Language Acquisition*, Oxford: Oxford University Press.

ELLIS, R. (1990) *Instructed Second Language Acquisition: Learning in the Classroom*, Oxford: Blackwell.

ENGELHARD, G. JR, GORDON, B. and GABRIELSON, S. (1992) 'The Influences of Mode of

Discourse, Experiential Demand, and Gender on the Quality of Writing', *Research in the Teaching of English*, **26**, 315–36.

FLOWER, L. (1989a), 'Rhetorical Problem Solving: Cognition and Professional Writing', in KOGEN, M. (ed.) *Writing in the Business Professions*, Urbana, IL: National Council of Teachers of English, pp. 3–36.

FLOWER, L. (1989b) 'Taking Thought: The Role of Conscious Processing in the Making of Meaning', in MAIMON, E. B., NODINE, B. F. and O'CONNOR, F. W. (eds) *Thinking, Reasoning and Writing*, New York: Longman, pp. 185–212.

FREADMAN, A. (1987) 'Anyone For Tennis?' in REID, I. (ed.) *The Place of Genre in Learning*, Geelong, Australia: Deakin University, pp. 91–124.

FREEDMAN, A. (1987a) 'Development in Story Writing', *Applied Psycholinguistics*, **8**, pp. 153–69.

FREEDMAN, A. (1987b) 'Learning to Write Again', *Carleton Papers in Applied Language Studies*, **4**, pp. 95–116.

FREEDMAN, A. (1990) 'Reconceiving Genre', *Texte*, **8/9**, pp. 279–92.

FREEDMAN, A. (1995) 'Genres of Argument and Argument as Genre', in BERRILL, D. (ed.) *Perspectives on Written Argument*, Norfolk, NJ: Hampton Press.

FREEDMAN, A. and PRINGLE, I. (1984) 'Why Students Can't Write Arguments', *English in Education*, **18**, pp. 73–84.

HANKS, T. (1991) 'Foreword' to LAVE, J. and WENGER, E. *Situated Learning: Legitimate Peripheral Participation*, Cambridge: Cambridge University Press, pp. 13–24.

HARPER, J. (1991) 'Shaping Discourse, Shaping Culture: The "Finding" Genre at the Workers' Compensation Board', unpublished Master's thesis, Simon Fraser University, Vancouver, BC.

HERRINGTON, A. (1985) 'Writing in Academic Settings: A Study of the Contexts for Writing in Two College Chemical Engineering Courses', *Research in the Teaching of English*, **19**, pp. 331–61.

HILLOCKS, G., JR. (1986) *Research on Written Composition*, Urbana, IL: National Conference on Research in English and ERIC Clearinghouse on Reading and Communication Skills.

KAUFER, D. and GEISLER, C. (1989) 'Novelty in Academic Writing', *Written Communication*, **6**, pp. 286–311.

KRASHEN, S. D. (1981a) *Second Language Acquisition and Second Language Learning*, Oxford: Pergamon Press.

KRASHEN, S. D. (1981b) 'The Role of Input (Reading) and Instruction in Developing Writing Ability', paper presented at Carleton University, Ottawa, Ontario, October.

KRASHEN, S. D. (1984) *Writing: Research, Theory, and Applications*, Oxford: Pergamon Press.

KRASHEN, S. D. (1991) 'The Input Hypothesis: An Update', paper presented at the Georgetown University Round Table on Languages and Linguistics, Washington, DC, March.

KRASHEN, S. D. (1992) 'Another Educator Comments', *TESOL Quarterly*, **26**, pp. 409–11.

LAVE, J. and WENGER, E. (1991) *Situated Learning: Legitimate Peripheral Participation*, Cambridge: Cambridge University Press.

LIGHTBOWN, P. (1985) 'Exploring Relationships between Developmental and Instructional Sequences in L2 Acquisition', in SELIGER, H. and LONG, M. (eds) *Classroom Oriented Research in Second Language Acquisition*, Rowley, MA: Newbury House, pp. 217–43.

LONG, M. (1983) 'Does Second Language Instruction Make a Difference? A Review of the Research', *TESOL Quarterly*, **17**, pp. 359–82.

LUKE, A. (1994) 'Genres of Power? Literacy Education and the Production of Capital', in HASAN, R. and WILLIAMS, G. (eds) *Literacy in Society*, London: Longman.

MCCARTHY, L. M. (1987) 'A Stranger in Strange Lands: A College Student Writing across the Curriculum', *Research in the Teaching of English*, **21**, pp. 233–65.

MARTIN, J. R., CHRISTIE, F. and ROTHERY, J. (1987) 'Social Processes in Education: A Reply to Sawyer and Watson (and Others)', in REID, I. (ed.) *The Place of Genre in Learning*, Geelong, Australia: Deakin University, pp. 58–82.

MILLER, C. (1984) 'Genre as Social Action', *Quarterly Journal of Speech*, **70**, pp. 151–67.

MYERS, G. (1990) *Writing Biology*, Madison, WI: University of Wisconsin Press.

NORTH, S. M. (1987) *The Making of Knowledge in Composition*, Upper Montclair, NJ: Boynton/Cook.

PERL, S. (1979) 'The Composing Processes of Unskilled College Writers', *Research in the Teaching of English*, **13**, pp. 317–36.

PETERSON, C. and MCCABE, A. (1983) *Developmental Psycholinguistics*, New York: Plenum Press.

PHELPS, L. W. (1988) *Composition as a Human Science*, New York: Oxford University Press.

POLANYI, M. (1964) *Personal Knowlege*, New York: Harper and Row.

ROGOFF,.B. (1990) *Apprenticeship in Thinking*, New York: Oxford University Press.

STEIN, N. L. and GLENN, C. L. (1979) 'An Analysis of Story Comprehension in Elementary School Children', in FREEDLE, R. (ed.) *New Directions in Discourse Processing*, Vol. 2, Norwood, NJ: Ablex, pp. 53–120.

STOTSKY, S. (1983) 'Research on Reading/Writing Relationships: A Synthesis and Suggested Directions', in JENSEN, J. (ed.) *Composing and Comprehending*, Urbana, IL: National Conference on Research in English and ERIC Clearinghouse on Reading and Communication Skills, pp. 7–22.

SWAIN, M. (1985) 'Communicative Competence: Some Roles of Comprehensible Input and Comprehensible Output in its Development', in GASS, S. and MADDEN, C. (eds) *Input in Second Language Development*, Rowley, MA: Newbury House, pp. 234–53.

SWALES, J. (1990) *Genre Analysis*, Cambridge: Cambridge University Press.

TUMAN, M. C. (1987) *A Preface to Literacy*, Tuscaloosa, AL: University of Alabama.

VYGOTSKY, L. (1962) *Thought and Language*, (trans. E. Hanfmann and G. Vakar) Cambridge, MA: MIT Press.

WEINERT, R. (1987) 'Processes in Second Language Development', in ELLIS, R. (ed.) *Second Language Acquisition in Context*, Englewood Cliffs, NJ: Prentice-Hall, pp. 83–99.

YATES, J. (1989) *Control through Communication*, Baltimore, MD: Johns Hopkins University Press.

Chapter 13

Traffic in Genres, In Classrooms and Out

Russell A. Hunt

Fifteen years ago now I conducted an experiment with a 2-year-old.[1] At the request of a colleague in psychology who wanted to see whether it was possible to replicate a study of elicited imitation published five years earlier (Slobin and Welsh, 1973), I spent a couple of hours playing a game called 'say what I say'. The subject – my daughter – seemed to find the game great fun, and eventually we wound up with quite a lot of audio tape, which demonstrated beyond any reasonable doubt that although Kate could repeat pretty long utterances – 17 to 20-word sentences, for example – virtually verbatim, she could not repeat even close to verbatim any sentence with a relative clause in it.

> *Experimenter*: Can you say, 'The kitty in the water is sad'?
> *Kate*: [patiently explaining] I already did.
> *Experimenter*: Ohh...I guess you already did. That's right. [pause] What's the puppy doing?
> *Kate*: Well, he's reaching those orange.
> *Experimenter*: He's reaching those orange. And what happens to the oranges?
> *Kate*: They fell down there.
> *Experimenter*: And is the puppy happy?
> *Kate*: Yes.
> *Experimenter*: [incredulity] He's happy!?!
> *Kate*: But he's sad there.
> *Experimenter*: Can you say, 'The puppy who spilled the oranges is sad'?
> *Kate*: I already did.
> *Experimenter*: No, you didn't.
> *Kate*: The puppy, mmm, mmm, the puppy is, mmm, is fall that and, uh, the, uh, the oranges is fell down and and the basket there spilled all the oranges...[pause 5.5 seconds]
> *Experimenter*: [under his breath] I'll be darned.

Whether Kate's struggle was really, as I thought at the time, against the recalcitrant limits of her own grammatical competence, or whether it was something quite different, we can only guess. The workings of people's minds are difficult of access, even to their owners – much less to those who must construct long inferential chains based on tiny fragments of behaviour like Kate's stumbling over expressing the relationships between the spilling, the oranges, the puppy and sadness.

One thing that seemed most difficult to account for in trying to describe the limits of Kate's competence was her ability, on her own, to generate and handle precisely the same kinds of complex relationships she was unable (or perhaps unwilling) to replicate when offered them by her father.

Kate: You ate my ice cream. You was all sad. I can't find my own ice cream what is sad...

Experimenter: What kind of ice cream was it?

Kate: It was green.

Experimenter: It was green?!

Kate: Yeah.

Experimenter: Yuck. Can you say, 'It was terrible ice cream'?

Kate: It was terrible ice cream. And I can't eat it, uh, it's green.

Experimenter: Can you say, 'I can't eat the ice cream that was green'?

Kate: I can't eat the ice cream at, it was green. It...was green. The guy says, green, it's green...

Experimenter: Can you say, 'Some white ice cream and some green ice cream was here'?

Kate: The white ice cream and and, uh, green ice cream is here. – There's no ice cream here.

Experimenter: There's no ice cream here now, is there? Can you say 'There was ice cream here yesterday'?

Kate: There was ice cream here yesterday.

Experimenter: Can you say, 'The ice cream that was here yesterday is gone'?

Kate: It's gone. The ice cream was here all yesterday was gone.

Experimenter: Those are hard sentences, aren't they?

Kate: But you ate my ice cream, it was gone.

I found this exercise engaging and resonant in a way that the Slobin and Welsh presentation of essentially the same kinds of exploration had not been. In part this was a result of the fact that I actually felt in a real situation the resistance to the relative clause – I know *I* hadn't been cooking the data; *I* hadn't been subconsciously trying to keep Kate from imitating relative clauses because of my own covert hypothesis about principles of language development.

Another reason for the resonance of this first encounter with what seemed to be the psychological actuality of a grammatical structure was that about that same time I was becoming aware of sentence combining as a strategy for teaching writing. Within a couple of years I was going to be engaged in working through an experimental composition class based on Daiker *et al.* (1982), and discovered what seemed to me a detailed parallel to what I thought of as Kate's 'relative-clause blindness'; virtually none of my first-year students seemed to have as part of their written language repertoire the grammatical construction known as the nominative absolute. Although they seemed to *understand* the construction ('*Flags flying*, the boat sailed out of the harbor'), they often seemed utterly incapable of *producing* such a structure, even when given the 'kernel sentence' components of such a sentence, and a model to work from.

One thing about the nominative absolute that I found particularly interesting was the reflection that it is a very highly literate grammatical device. Not only does one almost never hear such a construction in speaking, it seems very unlikely that it could ever have come to exist without the advent of written language, which allows the kind of flexibility of processing and suspension of closure needed to understand – and, perhaps even more, to create – such a structure.

At the time, it seemed perfectly obvious to me what was happening in both cases. I was exploring the treacherous, shifting and fertile ground right along the edge of someone's knowledge, getting as close as I ever had to the process of learning itself. My explanation of Kate's – and my first-year students' – language situation would have been something like this: the learner is in a position where the specific grammatical construction (relative clause for Kate, nominative absolute for my students) can be interpreted with the strong support of its immediate context, but the structure isn't clearly enough situated in the learner's mind to be generalized to a new context and used. What seemed a clear analogy was my memory of the way a word might have been part of my reading (or even listening) vocabulary long before I found myself in sure enough control of its meaning to use it in one of my own sentences.

The neat parallel between the three instances – the learning of a specific word, of a specific oral grammatical structure, and of a particularly literate grammatical structure – reinforced my growing conviction that language learning was not a process that changed much through the years. That is, although the specific aspects of language that were being learned might change out of recognition, the mental machinery at work seemed to be essentially the same from the cradle to the grave.

More recently, I've begun to wonder how it was that Kate did, sometime in the next few years, learn how to create a relative clause – more specifically, perhaps, how she learned to create relative clauses that served her intention to say something. One thing of which I'm certain is that that afternoon's game was as close as anyone ever got to teaching her what a relative clause is (at least before high school, by which time they'd been a part of her oral and written repertoire for at least a decade).

What I learned from that study – and from the work of even closer observers of early language development like Michael Halliday (1981), Harste *et al.* (1984), Judith Newman (1984), Kenneth Kaye (1982) and many others – was that language development was a 'normal process'. That is, it's something people do, not something that's done to them, but, on the olther hand, it isn't a developmental pattern like the growth of a flower. It happens, it was clear, because people need it to happen. Both the children who were developing and the adults who were participating with them in that development needed it to happen. It seemed to me, much of what I was learning illuminated the processes of learning I was watching as my undergraduate students struggled with the unfamiliar language of academic discourse – both as they learned to read texts as though they mattered, and as they learned to write as though someone cared about what they had to say.

I was left with a hole in my understanding, however. Just as when I'd been a teenager trying to learn how a radio worked, I had both ends but not the middle. On the one hand, I'd known how to solder a connection, what a capacitor looked like and how to read the markings on a resistor; and on the other I'd known about moving electrons, electrical potential, and Ohm's law. But they weren't connected for me, and in fact even though I spent a year in electrical engineering as an undergraduate they never really did connect for me. Now, a decade later, I was terrified that my understanding of how language development looked in Kenneth Kaye's neonates and Jerry Harste's preschoolers was never going to connect to what I knew, as a scholar of literature and an investigator of literary reading, about linguistics and the structure of language, the nature of metaphor and the music of irony.

It was my rediscovery of Mikhail Bakhtin, while on sabbatical leave in Australia and Germany in 1988–89, that enabled me to begin making the connection I'd been afraid might never be made.

The Bakhtin I discovered, by the way, was not the one I had been familiar with – the one who is primarily known as a theorist of literature and the author of (or at least the major figure in the group which authored) the studies of the novel and Dostoevsky. What I found was the one who is a theorist of the ways in which language and languaging are social. He is the author of *Marxism and the Philosophy of Language* (1973) and (especially) of the essays collected in *Speech Genres and Other Late Essays* (1986). This Bakhtin told me that it is the utterance, not the phoneme, the word, the sentence or the text, that is the basic unit of analysis for understanding language (oral or written). He defined the utterance for me as any instance of language in use, bounded by a change of speakers – one utterance ends, another is a response to it, and still another is a response in turn. He showed me that the utterance is always created and formed and shaped as a response to a previous utterance or utterances, and that it is always created and formed and shaped in anticipation of a responding utterance. Language, he said, is an unending dialogic web of cross-connected utterances and responses, each piece of writing or speaking, each utterance, depending on its occasion and context for its very existence, for its comprehensibility. 'As an utterance', he says, '(or part of an utterance) no one sentence, even if it has only one word, can ever be repeated: it is always a new utterance (even if it is a quotation)' (Bakhtin 1986: 108).

Bakhtin's views began to give me a tool for understanding how someone might learn a behaviour like the relative clause or the nominative absolute – or the academic paper. I began to see that Kate's inability to construct a relative clause at the age of two and a half, and her effortless and unself-conscious mastery of it at the age of five, didn't have to do with the biological maturing of an organism, but with socialization. Her relations with her family required that she learn relative clauses, not because we wanted her to, but because as she entered more and more deeply into social relationships there were ideas that could only be expressed with relative clauses. There's a difference between 'Kit is in the kitchen and has a cookie' and

'Kit, who is in the kitchen, has a cookie' – and it has to do with the social agreement that one part of that second sentence is focal (the cookie) and the other part is subsidiary. But just as my undergraduate students couldn't learn to construct a nominative absolute outside of a situation in which an interlocutor actually needed to have the distinction made, so Kate needed to *intend* to say the thing the relative clause conveys. 'Intending' involved creating an utterance, as part of a dialogic chain.

Work (most important, that of Freedman 1993, condensed version Chapter 12, this volume) on the implicit learning of genres – along with the radical insight made available to us by Polanyi (1958) about the distinctions between tacit and focal awareness, and the productive distinction Krashen (1981) forged between what he calls 'acquisition' and 'learning' (I'm not crazy about the words, but I find the distinction extremely useful) has begun to illuminate this process. It has made it possible for me to begin to see what the mechanics of Kate's learning were – and what the mechanics of my students' learning are as they internalize the habits of discourse that allow them to participate in communities in which they want to participate. (Such communities, by the way, almost never have any use for the nominative absolute.)

Such a view of language has powerful implications for the concept of genre and for our ideas about how genres are learned (or, as Krashen would say, 'acquired'). These are suggested most directly in Bakhtin's essay 'The Problem of Speech Genres' (1986: 60–102) – perhaps especially in the very title, in the concept that the *kinds* of language, like the other elements of language that we have traditionally thought in terms of, should be brought down out of the realm of ideas ('language'; Saussure's *langue*) and put back into the realm of practice ('speech'; Saussaure's *parole*) in order to be understood. It is almost equally important that, as with his other reversals of our traditional ways of understanding language, Bakhtin begins with speech rather than writing, with the obviously contingent and context-bound rather than the apparently clear and stable, and makes spoken, conversational language the norm in terms of which other kinds of language can be understood (it is almost as an aside that he notes that 'everything we have said here also pertains to written and read speech, with the appropriate adjustments and additions' (1986: 69).

I'm thinking here, however, primarily as a practitioner, rather than a theoretician. For the past 10 years at least my work as a teacher has been most centrally an attempt to break down the conceptual barriers separating speech from writing and listening from reading, and to bring to bear on written language the insights about learning and use that we are offered by researchers on spoken language – particularly the branch of the socio-linguistics of language that studies the rules under which speakers exchange utterances, the patterns that arise out of those exchanges, and thus the ways in which speech genres arise in conversation. Bakhtin's parenthetical invocation of written language into his discussion of speech I take as an invitation to think about my teaching of written language, and the situations that support that teaching in my classrooms – and, as well, about my and Vipond's research on the reading of literature (Vipond and Hunt 1984, 1988; Hunt and Vipond 1985, 1986, 1992; Vipond *et al.* 1990) – as though the analogies between written and oral language were powerful and illuminating (for a quite different, but I think equally compelling argument that this is the case, see Brandt's *Literacy as Involvement*, 1990).

Accepting Bakhtin's invitation has forced me to abandon the idea that genres were external, fixed forms, which (like language itself, in that view) we learn by importing models and examples from outside, more or less consciously. That view suggested that we learn a new genre (the sonnet, for instance, or the term paper or the personal letter), by encountering a number of instances of the form, being told (or discovering) what its 'rules' are, internalizing that abstract definition, and using it as an algorithm to generate new examples: fourteen lines, iambic pentameter, grouped into an octave and a sestet, rhymed in an elaborate pattern; or state a thesis, acknowledge objections through a literature review, marshal evidence and arguments, conclude. Knowing that sort of thing, I once comfortably assumed, enabled me to understand Shakespeare's or Donne's sonnets, or read a research paper, and gave me the basic tools to write my own.

Bakhtin's proviso that what he says about speech applies as well to writing makes it at least defensible to argue that literacy learning, like oral language learning, is in large measure the 'social invention' (in LeFevre's phrase, 1987) of speech genres. It also seems reasonable to think that, as in the development of oral language, authentic engagement in dialogue is the most powerful promoter of such learning. (By 'authentic dialogue', here and elsewhere, I mean exchanges of language in which each party's intention is to infer the other party's intentions, as manifested in language, and respond to them; I mean to exclude situations in which the language is used as an example of language, or otherwise directly attended to in ways which ignore, or 'bracket out', speakers' pragmatic intentions.)

Such a notion is consistent with what we can see in educational situations. Looking at typical classroom and institutional contexts for writing, it seems clear that there is in more situations in schools and universities virtually no opportunity for written language to serve as the medium for direct and authentic dialogue. I have dealt with this idea at more length elsewhere (Hunt 1993).

There is an apparent inconsistency between that view of what happens in school and the statement that all language is dialogic. If *all* language is dialogic, how can 'school language' be different? Consider, as I recently did, an essay on the topic 'current efforts to create life by artificial means are/are not beneficial to human society'. This essay was written on assignment by a student with no particular interest in the subject and with the sole aim of demonstrating the ability to invent or find, and marshal, arguments (the student, incidentally, is the same one who had such trouble with the relative clause at the age of two). It was read by a teacher with no particular interest in the subject, and with the avowed intention of assessing the mechanical fluency of the student's language and deciding whether she had successfully fulfilled the formal and stated requirements of the genre 'persuasive essay'. That teacher had no intention to 'respond', in the Bakhtinian sense of an instrumental response (nor, indeed, is there any practical possibility that she *could* respond in that way).

The transaction constituted by that writing and that reading may, in some sense, be a dialogue, but, if so, it is a very peculiar and asymmetrical sort of dialogue. It is neither direct nor authentic. The discourse was neither created by the student nor understood by the teacher as an itterance; rather, it was bracketed, set aside, considered, evaluated. If it is a dialogue, it is one conducted *around* the actual text, one which brackets the text out as a sort of hypothetical instance. Anne Freadman, describing a similar phenomenon in French classes, has observed that in such classes any instance of language inevitably becomes 'an example of French' (1988: 6).

It is not, I believe, by exchanging examples that we invent our genres; it is by engaging in dialogue, whether in writing or in speech. As a practitioner, as I have said, my intention is to render permeable the barriers between spoken and written discourse. My central means of achieving this is to create situations in which written language can serve as a medium for authentic dialogue – that is, can be created and understood as utterance.

In recent years I have adopted a method of teaching called 'collaborative investigation', which is being developed at my university. I will not describe it in detail here (for elaboration, see Parkhill 1988; Reither 1988, 1990; Hunt 1989, 1991, 1993; Reither and Vipond 1989; Hunt and Reither, in press), but I need to say that it employs a set of fundamental and related strategies that have the consequence of creating situations in which students use written language in dialogic ways and are put in the position of having to invent new genres of language for these new situations.

The central strategy is called 'inkshedding' (the word is originally, apparently, from Carlyle, and is analogous to 'bloodshed' rather than to 'woodshed' or 'watershed'). I owe the word to my colleague Jim Reither, who came up with it in the early stages of the development of the concept. Briefly, it entails informal or impromptu writing which is immediately read, used and responded to by others, and then often discarded. A typical inkshedding situation might occur as a response to a conference paper – the audience might immediately write for a few minutes, then read a half-dozen other participants' writing, and then move to oral discussion based on the reading. The writing might then be thrown away. Or the participants might, as they were reading, have marked sections worth consideration by the whole group; those sections might then be transcribed, photocopied, and distributed to that group. There are many variants of this process, but all share at least one charactgeristic: they afford using written language in dialogic ways. What is immediately relevant is that over the near decade in which this strategy has been in use at St Thomas University and at various conferences (including the annual Inkshed conference, now in its eleventh year), I have observed colleagues and students jointly inventing, and reinventing, a new written genre, the 'inkshed', with a unique set of common characteristics and expectations. These characteristics have never, to my knowledge, been explicitly described, but include elements such as these: dispensing with formal openings and closings, general address (writing to the whole group), assumptions of a common frame of reference, informality of structure and diction, acceptance of abbreviations.

This strategy has been extended to include a wide range of forms of collaboration in writing, through the medium of writing. Collaborative writing is often considered to be restricted to joint authorship, but as the work of LeFevre (1987), Reither and Vipond (1989) and Paré (1992), among others, has shown, collaboration extends across the text to include its readers in collaborative (and dialogic) relations. 'Writing', in Reither and Vipond's phrase, '*is* collaboration', just as, in Bakhtin's language *is* dialogue.

In these particular cases, the collaborative dialogue occurs as part of the process of collaborative investigation. Let me make this process concrete by describing one example, as it occurred in an actual course. I do something like this in all my courses; it so happens that this one was an undergraduate seminar in Restoration and eighteenth century literature, enrolling 13 students, which makes it rather atypical, but I work toward essentially similar writing and learning situations in whatever I teach.

The course began with my handing everyone a long written introduction to the course and giving everyone time to read it silently. I also handed out, as I do at the beginning of most sessions, a document headed 'In Class Today'. In September 1992, that document said, in part:

> As you'll discover, one of my central beliefs as a teacher is that reading and writing are powerful tools, and ones we don't use as often as we might. One of the ways in which that belief is acted out in my teaching is that I write a lot, ask you to read it, and expect you to write a lot and expect others (including me, sometimes) to read it. But I don't expect that the writing is going to be used in the way most educational writing is used – that is, as a basis for evaluating the writer (can she (*sic*) write? does she know what she's supposed to know?). I expect it's going to be used the way you'll use most of these handouts – to see what I have to say, and respond to it in some meaningful way (by doing what it asks, or arguing that what it asks doesn't make sense, for example).

That handout also asked everyone to write about the eighteenth century for ten or fifteen minutes. What the document said was this:

> the second part of the class will involve everyone writing about the literature of the eighteenth century, reading each other's writing, and generating responses and questions. This is a way of ascertaining the sorts of things we all know, and need to know, about the period, about its literature, and about literary study, and generating some issues and concerns that we're going to be addressing over the first few weeks.

During that class session, by reading each others' writing and responding in the margins, reading the responses and discussing them orally, the class generated a set of questions about the eighteenth century. At the end of class, we had divided them into questions that no one expected could be answered, questions that could only be answered after a good deal of study and learning, and questions that might be answered by a group of two or three students who spent some time in the library over the next week. I divided the class into groups, the groups picked a question of the third kind (they included questions on comedy in the period, on changes between this period and the seventeenth century, on what an ode was and on who were important playwrights at the time), and we were off. Next week, each group had completed a draft of a report and keyed it into the computer network through which we share most of our work. (This network was based in a small basement lab with

five PCs networked together and connected to the slightly larger university lab.)
Printed copies were distributed and in class we inkshedded about those, exchanged
and read them, and generated further questions for each of the groups, who went
back to the library to elaborate or revise their reports.

In the meantime, we began a running conversation on the electronic bulletin board
set up on the computer network. Everyone was required to log on and read the board
– and contribute something – at least once a week. The contributions varied from
Merry Christmas messages and complaints about the heat in the computer lab to
an extended, multi-voiced discussion of whether Moll Flanders should be regarded
as primarily the author of her own fate or a victim of society. Everyone was also
required to touch base with me regularly through the (more private) electronic mail
system. Letters there varied from 'nothing to report this week' to long exchanges
about the reasons why some people find it harder to participate in oral discussions
than in written ones (that one, in fact, later expanded into a bulletin board discussion).

Between that fall and the succeeding March, according to a rough count, the
13 students in the course generated over 40,000 words on the bulletin board and
over 30,000 words in electronic notes to me. How much they may have generated
in notes to each other I have no way of knowing, but it is considerable. Even without
that, the total works out to a bit over 5000 words per student.

Beyond that, of course, there was a great deal of in-class hand-written inkshedding,
question generating, commenting on other people's reports, questioning them, and
so forth, which I have no way of counting or tracking.

Perhaps most important there was all the electronic writing done in the more
formal context of written reports to the rest of the class, and comments on those
reports by their readers. Although the mechanics of this varied as the course (and
our familiarity with the computer network) developed, the last cycle of reports, all
of which had to do with some facet of the class's reading of various texts of Pope
and Johnson, were handled this way. Questions and issues were discussed (in part
through in - and out-of-class inksheddings) and then proposed individually, in files
in a common directory on the network. Each person in the class was invitged to
read the questions posed by all the others and add comments and suggestions to the
individual files. As the comments accumulated, the authors read them; in some cases
these led to modifications of the questions, and in some the authors were offered
strategies for finding answers; in most there was a good deal of comment suggesting
that others were interested in the questions. Over the next week or so, as the authors
began finding answers to their questions, they began putting drafts into the same
file, immediately following the sets of questions and comments. As the drafts
lengthened, others read them and added comments on, and questions and suggestions
about, the drafts in the same files, following the drafts. As authors checked back
on the responses to their work, they regularly edited and changed the drafts in response
to their audience's questions. Comments on the bulletin board suggested that this
was, from most of the students' point of view, the most successful way of managing
this collaborative form of writing we had yet tried.

It is difficult in a few pages to give any flavour of the discussion in these files,
and I didn't move fast enough to save the original drafts, so as I read through the

files it isn't clear how the comments on first drafts affected subsequent modifications, but let me pull a few examples out of one such file. This file began with the following question from Darice (all the names but mine have been changed):

> My question has to do with Pope's repulsiveness both physically and personality wise as I feel his ability to write satiric literature may be connected (simply because I'm sure since he is described as looking like a toad that he knew that people found him repulsive and therefore promoted this repulsiveness in his personality, which ultimately led to an ingenious ability to compose satiric literature as a way to overcome the public's view of him). I may be way off, but I feel that this may be the case as Russ explained in class that Pope used to get very irate if someone had said his parents had been poor and also that not many people who knew Pope liked him. If I'm unable to get any information upon this connection between his physical and personality repulsive character which may have influenced his poetic ability, then I thought I might just pursue the reasons beind his physical deformity.
>
> Any suggestions? What do you think: a dead path or possibility? I realize this is not a question orientated specifically to historical background, but more a background on Pope (Russ is this o.k.)?

Some of the comments on this question included the following:

> Darice: This sounds interesting. It's nice to get another side of things – a background, or at least some kind of sense of this sort of thing.'
> – Gwen

> There are arguments about some of these issues (different diographers have different views). One way to focus it would be to present some views of it, specifically ascribed to the authors; it's certainly a question worth asking.
> – Russ

> Darice,
> I didn't pick up on the fact that Pope wasn't a 'very handsome' fella, or as you say 'repulsive'! I think you might have to look at Biographies etc. to see what his background was like and family life which might have influenced his personality, but (not to discourage) I think it would be difficult to determine that someone's physical appearance affected their personality.
> – Greta

> Darice,
> I just read something that described when Pope developed his disease and the pain it caused him. The book relates that as a young man Pope was first stricken with the disease and was convinced he was dying. He even went so far as to write letters of goodbye to his friends. Perhaps the constant expectance of death influenced his nasty attitudes and helped sharpen his satirical tongue.
> – Tamara

I just read something else about him too: a description of him at fourteen: 'He is small and pale, fragile, and already not quite straight in the back...but he has a frighteningly sensitive face, large wondering eyes, and an enchanting voice which will earn him the name of "the little nightingale" '.

I don't know if this is relevant to what you are doing, but I thought it might be nice to hear a pleasant description of the poor guy.

– Tamara

Pope was often described in quite attractive terms by his friends, often quite similar to what you found, Tamara. (Who is that, by the way?)

– Russ

I took the quote from Bonamy Dobree's book Alexander Pope, published in 1952.

– Tamara

In response to those questions, Darice produced an 850-word report on Pope's early life, drawn primarily from George Sherburn's and John Russo's books. Her report included passages like this (just to give you a sense of the tone):

Since they were Catholics at a time when England's religion was Protestant, the Popes were forced by antipapist legislation to move often, which prompted Mr Pope to retire from his successful linen business. There is little known of Pope as a child, except that he experienced several traumatic experiences. Although Pope was not physically deformed as a child, his half sister, Mrs Rackett informed Pope's biographer, Mr Spence that when he was between the age of three and five 'a wild cow that was driven by the place where he was filling a little cart with stones struck at him with her horns, tore off his hat which was tied under the chin, wounded him in the throat, beat him down, and trampled over him' (Russo, p. 27). Further Pope studied under four priests, one of which was said to have whipped and ill-used him for writing a satire (isn't that ironic!).

Most of the comments on the report were appreciative; a few raised further questions.

Darice,
I enjoyed this report very much; it was an interesting way to look at Pope and his work. However, I think you may have overlooked something of relative importance: what can explain his friends' kind attitudes towards him? Surely, he must have had some attractive qualities. For instance, his voice was quite enchanting – could that have affected his ability to create such rhythmic, lyrical verses? Perhaps not, but I do think his positive attributes should also be explored.

– Tamara

Darice, I have been fascinated with the physical descriptions of Pope since reading about him. This report is very helpful in giving me a more vivid picture. Have you read Johnson's 'From the Lives of Poets', the section on Pope? I read it for this week and I must say, it is a very informative piece. Not only does it talk about his works, but about his personal life too. It said that he 'never took tea without a strategem' – his mind was always on the go. It also said he thought quite highly of himself. My question is, did his brilliantly sharp mind and maybe, his somewhat conceited air have something to do with his physical deformities – was his mind compensating for something else? Something to think about and you should read it if you have not already – it's really interesting.

– Barb

Darice, Isn't the nature of a wild cow to attack, regardless of one's physical appearance! Or should I have interpreted it as a joke?

  – But what about his friends, I'm sure they didn't reject their sickly friend? Also it's sad that a man who so sparks our enjoyment and laughter, didn't himself. It is interesting that you see to suggest without his illness, he wouldn't have produced such satire.

– Greta

Some of the comments, like the one about the cow, were responded to in the version I now have (the first one is lost in the electrons, unfortunately, but suggested inadvertently that the cow trampled Pope because he was deformed).

That there is change occurring, and that it involves learning new genres, seems to me incontrovertible. Near the end of term, in preparing for a conference presentation, I asked my students, if they had a chance, to look back over the writing they did for the course in the first few weeks, and at what they'd done more recently, and reflect on what differences they saw (with examples, if possible). Here's one example, chosen by Barb as typical of her writing in September:

> Ultimately, the relationship between comedy and its audience cannot be measured because society is not homogenous in nature; there can be no absolute because there is no universal standard.

About that sentence, Barb said:

> I found my initial report to be very formal. I think we were trying to impress you, the professor, rather than our classmates because that is what we are used to doing. I think when we write essays we tend to try to aspire to academic heights and we try to sound as academic as possible. When we write for the benefit of our classmates, we know that they are at the same academic level, so we don't have to sound so professional. The writing in class is more friendly; more personal and less formal.
>
> I think, too, I am more relaxed in my writing because there isn't the pressure of a paper that is worth 40% of the mark. With this type of class, I am able to relax and this changes my writing style, I believe.

Here's the sentence she chose from her more recent writing.

> From what I've read about the often diseased food at the time, I don't think
> I would have wanted to have eaten back then.

I do not want to contend that that second sentence necessarily represents 'better' writing than the first. I am not arguing that it has a more authentic voice, that it's more concrete and personal and therefore more effective, or that the student has found a superior register in which she should now attempt to produce her papers for her other literature courses. I believe the first, more formal and abstract, kind of writing is as necessary and as useful as the second, and, further, that the only criteria that could possibly be used to judge which is 'better' writing are functions of the site in which the composing occurs. What I would argue, and what I think the student is arguing, is that the second kind of writing is 'better' in a situation where what she is doing is writing to engage and inform the other students in the class. Now, the first piece was written, as well, in just such a situation – but it is clear, I think, that she hadn't yet begun to make the sorts of adjustments to the situation that are apparent when you contrast the two. Most important in this context, I want to suggest that what she was doing there was inventing a genre. (Whether the first sentence is a 'good' instance of its genre, or the second of its, is another, separate question. Which sentence is evidence of language learning is yet another.)

I should reiterate that both the genres she has written here – and, as well, the genre represented by the note to me explaining her writing – are examples of what Bakhtin calls 'relatively stable and normative forms of the utterance' (1986: 81). They are not new, but she has invented them in response to a dialogic demand, in a context which provided rich support for such invention.

I think, as well, there is similar invention going on in other situations in this class. One place I find it most obvious is in the postings to the electronic bulletin board. It is widely noted among participants in email networks and bulletin boards that new forms of discourse are being invented to respond to the new social situation posed by informal written language which is almost as quickly interactive as face-to-face conversation, but which lacks the resources of voice tone, body language, shared environment, and so forth. New or newly elaborate devices have to be invented for such problems as referring to specific parts of someone else's utterance, for signalling irony, humour, anger, etc., for indicating or enacting addressivity (who one is responding to and to whom the posting is particularly addressed), for indicating closure on a topic or exchange. The genre (or genres) that are evolving in these situations are an extremely powerful example of the way in which parallel devices will develop quite separately from each other in response to the same social situation.

Here are the first three postings to the first strand I set up on the bulletin board (to start things off, I invited contributors to reflect on what had been going on during the first three or four weeks of the course).

From: DARICE PARKS
Date: 10/09/91 10:46
Topic: Reflections

In reflecting on what I've learned about the 18thc, I find that through research and class discussions that I'm able to see the 18thc as a time which is connected with our present time. Before this class, the 18thc didn't have much meaning to my life, it was just a period in history that I was learning about in order to complete the necessary requirements for my honors degree. I guess that I reached this realization in last class when Russ suggested that the 18thc could be seen as the blueprint for today's society, as it marked the beginnings of things that are typical in our present society, such as $$$, companies, jobs, etc. It is this connection with present time that the 18thc becomes meaningful to me.

From: TAMARA SCOTT
Date: 10/09/91 12:29
Topic: Reflections

Today when I was walking to school I started thinking about some of the things I've learned about the eighteenth century so far. I was amazed at the amount of things I came up with. I have a much broader understanding of what life was like and how people lived. I still think of frilly shirts and white wigs when I think of the eighteenth century, but if I had to write another blurb on what I know about the eighteenth century I'd be able to say A LOT more. You know, the range in this class is amazing – I'm picking up bits of information that perhaps I wouldn't put in a traditional English essay, but nonetheless are useful to me as a person, rather than as a student.

From: KATHY FELLOWS
Date: 10/10/91 11:48
Topic: Reflections

Over this past week, I have found myself learning more and more about the 18th century. By preparing and researching the reports I have learned a great deal, especially in my own group on 18th century Children's Literature. By doing this report I learned a vast amount of information on the subject. I also find that by picking a topic that is interesting to me, and then by going and researching it, that I learn a lot more than if someone picked the topic for me (perhaps because it is a topic that I myself am interested in). Overall, this past week I must say that I have learned a lot more about children's literature and about the 18th century in general, and I look forward to researching this week's report.

When I first read those, they seemed unremarkable to me. I noticed the formal and abstract language, of course: in the third, for instance, we find phrases like 'learned a great deal', 'a vast amount of information', 'I myself', 'I must say', 'I look forward to'. Whoever it is whose words Kathy's speech is overflowing with was without question an academic. But it did not become clear to me how much change was occurring until I went back and compared those early postings with, for example, some of the late January argument about Moll Flanders to which I've already referred. It began this way:

From: KARL GAMBELL
Date: o1/15/92 14:20
Topic: Moll: actor or acted

The responses to my report on casuistry brought up what I thought might be an interesting question to discuss on the bulletin board (if for no other reason than to get some additional input for my revision). The question was originally brought up by Barb during a smokebreak, and consists simply of 'Did you like the character of Moll?' Answers to this question, I would think, would have to address the question of Moll's actions versus Moll's circumstances. Would you agree that Moll does not act so much as she is acted upon? If you agree with the latter, then we like Moll. If you disagree, then you don't. Obviously, I liked Moll and thought she was a manufactured deviant (for any Soc. people out there), she was forced by her society to be a thief and a whore and the blame is not hers. I'd be very interested to know what other people think about this for responses to this question determine reaction to the novel...Ay wot?

From: JANE MACFARLANE
Date: 01/16/92 15:15
Topic: Moll: actor or acted

Karl, that is an interesting question about Moll's character. I must agree that Moll is more acted upon by society than anything else. When you consider Maria's report on employment for women, you realize that there wasn't much else that Moll could do for a living. As well, I kind of admire her thieving abilities – if you're forced to be a thief for a living, you might as well be a good one!

Besides the growing concreteness and specificity, what I am struck with here is the new consciousness of this medium as a device for forging and maintaining social relationships as well as carrying on an intellectual discussion. The casual and efficient references to the positions of others ('The question was originally brought up by Barb'), to other documents in the class ('When you consider Maria's report on employment for women'), the in-jokes ('for any Soc. people out there'), all suggest a context and relation between writer and readers very different from what is implied in those early messages. And by three or four weeks and a couple of dozen messages later we find this sort of interaction:

From: GRETA STEINBRETT
Date: 01/21/92 11:10
Topic: Moll: actor or acted

I wish I re-read Moll so I could get in on some of this juicy discussion, but here it goes anyway. Like many others in the class, I was appalled by Moll's abandoning of her children, but I was wondering if people reading this in the C18 would have felt the same way we do? I doubt it, but it would be difficult to determine. I liked what Maria said about Moll being conscious of her actions, but then why do we like her? I mean, in the passage Karl cited she admits her life was one of 'whoredom, adultry, incest, lying, theft; and in a word everything but murder and treason'. Of course we probably like her simply because she is so colorful, and maybe even because she admits what she is. Hell, I don't know – but we don't think she's inherently evil or anything, do we? Maria also suggested that maybe Defoe was trying to make us sympathize with Moll by portraying her as a mother figure, but if he did it sure didn't work. If I sympathize with her it's because of her childhood and circumstances, not because she's a mother . . .

From: KARL GAMBELL
Date: 01/21/92 12:03
Topic: Moll: actor or acted

In response to the question of what was Defoe's judgement of Moll, I'd tend to agree with Starr in saying that Defoe 'seeks a verdict of guilty, but also a suspended sentence, and even, in some cases, a full pardon'. I think that Moll is one of those cases where a pardon is in order due to the circumstances. Moll's casuistry didn't convince me of this, Defoe's rhetoric did. Again I pose the question of how can one be judged by moral standards in a society that placed emphasis on personal gain (or greed), individual beauty (vanity), and social stature (class)? If we are a product of our society (which I believe) then Moll was simply pursuing those ends that her society cherished as good things. How can we find fault with that?

From: TAMARA SCOTT
Date: 01/22/92 14:12
Topic: Moll: actor or acted

O.K. Karl, Moll IS a product of society and yes, she is acting in ways dictated by that society. BUT, I still don't believe one can be justified simply in that way. Moll is not simply pursuing her own goals, she is affecting other people's lives too. I'm sure all those people she stole from would appreciate having their stuff back so they could pursue their goals! Perhaps that is the point where I must stop accepting Moll's behaviour and begin to hold her responsible. What further makes me judge Moll as an actor as well as acted upon is the attitudes she expresses. She says is sorry for the banker, yet her sentiment is overshadowed by her actions – she still takes advantage of him. She acknowledges that she is doing wrong, she knows she is deceiving people, she realizes that her actions bring pain to others, and still she continues to do these things. What justification does she offer – her actions benefit herself and that's her main concern. This selfishness can also be related to Carrie's comment about how lacking in emotional baggage she is.

From: KARL GAMBELL
Date: 01/23/92 14:26
Topic: Moll: actor or acted

Well, I guess we've pretty much beat this to pieces, ay? Not to say that it wasn't fun, but I guess I'm not going to be able to convince you that Moll was more acted than actor, and you convince me of the opposite. BUT, the questions of morality, (what's 'right', what's 'wrong'), which you raise and which are perfectly legitimate objections, could be equally applied to say Jesse James, Billy the Kid, Blackbeard, Bluebeard, Bartles and James, and a whole bunch of other villains who we don't necessarily agree with, but nonetheless are fascinated by . . .

I could go on quoting from these discussions (remember, I have 40,000 words worth of them), but it seems to me more important to reflect on what they may mean from the point of view of an educational practitioner, and raise a couple of questions about what they mean from a more theoretical point of view.

There is an increasing consensus (at least among the educational writers and practitioners I have the most respect for) that the best sort of teaching is the kind that engages people in what Smith (1983; see also Dixon and Stratta 1984) calls 'an enterprise' and then observes closely to see what they can do, what they actually do, what – as Vygotsky (1962, 1986) insisted – they can almost do, and can do with a little help from their friends; and then finds ways to promote learning that's specific to where each learner is and to where she or he needs to be. I think, in general, that's what's going on in classes conducted like the one I have described. I think, as well, that a large part of what I see the students in courses like this one learning can be described as new genres.

It is not yet clear to me however, that in learning or inventing these new genres they are learning something that goes beyond the simple matter of knowing yet another isolated new genre (the bulletin board posting, the email letter, the question–response–question sequence involved in developing a research report, the various research reports, etc.). These might be interesting forms, and it might even be useful to know them at some point, but they are as subject to being rendered irrelevant or obsolete by circumstance as the 'persuasive essay' or the essay exam question or the sonnet. I am not raising here the issue of the learning about the ostensible subject matter of the course – in my case, the literature of the English Restoration and eighteenth century – but rather wondering whether it is possible to find out whether learning these new written genres in this new context has consequences for their learning of further genres in the world beyond my classroom, in learning the kinds of genres – the kinds of literacies – they'll be confronted with in some unimaginable future.

None of us had anywhere in our minds the notion that Kate might need the relative clause some day while she was busy learning it. Had we tried to put together a list of the grammatical forms she was going to need, we'd have failed miserably – and not only because none of those talking with her were grammarians. What we *did* do was provide the situation in which she could not only learn what she needed, but continue to be a language learner – one who would continue to be able to acquire the conventions and forms needed to take a role in the new groups she became part of. It seems reasonable to me that we should be trying to do no less for our students.

Note

1 For a different theoretic contextualization for some of the classroom data discussed in this article, see Hunt (1994).

References

BAKHTIN, M. M. (1973) *Marxism and the Philosophy of Language* ('By V. N. Volosinov') (trans. L. Matejka and I. R. Titunik) New York: Harvard University Press.

BAKHTIN, M. M. (1986) *Speech Genres and Other Late Essays* (ed. C. Emerson and M. Holquist, trans. V. W. McGee) Austin, TX: University of Texas Press.

BRANDT, D. (1990) *Literacy as Involvement: The Acts of Writers, Readers, and Texts,* Carbondale, IL: Southern Illinois University Press.

CHOMSKY, N. (1957) *Syntactic Structures* The Hague: Mouton.

DAIKER, D. A., KEREK, A. and MORENBERG, M. (eds) (1982) *The Writer's Options: Combining to Composing,* 2nd edn, New York: Harper and Row.

DEWEY, J. (1938) *Experience and Education,* The Kappa Delta Pi Lecture Series, New York: Macmillan.

DEWEY, J. and BENTLEY, A. F. (1949) *Knowing and the Known,* Boston, MA: Beacon Press.

DIXON, J. and STRATTA, L. (1984) 'Student Enterprises with Personal and Social Value', Series B: Writing 14 to 18, Discussion Booklet 3, ERIC Document No. ED268522.

FREADMAN, A. (1988) ' "Genre" and the Reading Class', *Typereader: The Journal of the Centre for Studies in Literary Education,* 1, November, pp. 1–7.

FREEDMAN, A. (1991) 'Genre as Social Action: Implications for Pedagogy', paper presented at the Conference on College Composition and Communication, Cincinnati, OH, March.

FREEDMAN, A. (1993) 'Show and Tell? The Role of Explicit Teaching in the Learning of New Genres', *Research in the Teaching of English,* 27, pp. 222–51.

HALLIDAY, M. A. K. (1978) *Language as Social Semiotic: The Social Interpretation of Language and Meaning,* Baltimore, MD: University Park Press.

HALLIDAY, M. A. K. (1981) *Learning How to Mean: Explorations in the Development of Language,* London: Edward Arnold.

HARSTE, J. C., BURKE, C. L. and WOODWARD, V. A. (1984) *Language Stories and Literacy Lessons,* Portsmouth, NH: Heinemann Educational.

HUNT, R. A. (1989) 'A Horse Named Hans, a Boy Named Shawn: The Herr von Osten Theory of Response to Writing', in ANSON, C. M. (ed.) *Writing and Response: Theory, Practice, and Research*, Champaign-Urbana, IL: National Council of Teachers of English, pp. 80–100.

HUNT, R. A. (1991) 'Modes of Reading, and Modes of Reading Swift', in CLIFFORD, J. (ed.) *The Experience of Reading: Louise Rosenblatt and Reader*-Response Theory, Portsmouth, NH: Heinemann-Boynton/Cook, pp. 105–26.

HUNT, R. A. (1993) 'Texts, Textoids and Utterances: Writing and Reading for Meaning, In and Out of Classrooms', in STRAW, S. B. and BOGDAN, D. (eds) *Constructive Reading: Teaching Beyond Communication*, Portsmouth, NH: Heinemann-Boynton/Cook, pp. 113–29.

HUNT, R. A. (1994) 'Speech Genres, Writing Genres, School Genres, Computer Genres', in FREEDMAN, A. and MEDWAY, P. (eds) *Teaching and Learning Genres*, Portsmouth, NH: Boynton/Cook Heinemann.

HUNT, R. A. and REITHER, J. A. (1994) 'A Workshop: Knowledge in the Making in Writing, Englilsh, and Other Content Courses', in STEVEN, L. and SCHRYER, C. (eds) *Contextual Literacy*, Winnipeg: Inkshed Publishing Initiative.

HUNT, R. A. and VIPOND, D. (1985) Crash-Testing a Transactional Model of Literary Reading, *Reader*, **14**, pp. 23–39.

HUNT, R. A. and VIPOND, D. (1986) 'Evaluations in Literary Reading', *Texte*, **6**, pp. 53–71.

HUNT, R. A. and VIPOND, D. (1992) 'First, Catch the Rabbit: The Methodological Imperative and the Dramatization of Dialogic Reading', in BEACH, R., GREEN, R. J., KAMIL, M. and SHANAHAN, T. (eds) *Multidisciplinary Perspectives on Literacy Research*, Urbana, IL: National Conference on Research in English.

KAYE, K. (1982) *The Mental and Social Lives of Babies: How Parents Create Persons*, Chicago, IL: University of Chicago Press.

KRASHEN, S. D. (1981) *Second Language Acquisition and Second Language Learning*, New York: Pergamon Press.

LeFEVRE, K. B. (1987) *Invention as a Social Act*, Carbondale, IL: Southern Illinois University Press.

NEWMAN, J. (1984) *The Craft of Children's Writing*, Portsmouth, NH: Heinemann Educational.

PARÉ, A. (1992) 'Ushering "Audience" Out: From Oration to Conversation', *Textual Studies in Canada*, **1**, pp. 45–64.

PARKHILL, T. (1988) 'Inkshedding in Religious Studies: Underwriting Collaboration', *Inkshed*, **7**(4), pp. 1–4.

PEIRCE, C. S. ([1940] 1955) *Philosophical Writings of Peirce* (ed. J. Buchler) New York: Dover.

PEIRCE, C. S. (1958) *Values in a Universe of Chance: Selected Writings of Charles S. Peirce* (ed. P. P. Wiener) Stanford, CA: Stanford University Press.

POLANYI, M. (1958) *Personal Knowledge: Towards a Post-Critical Philosophy*, Chicago, IL: University of Chicago Press.

REITHER, J. A. (1988) 'Writing and Knowing: Toward Redefining the Writing Process', in TATE, G. and CORBETT, E. P. J. (eds) *The Writing Teacher's Sourcebook*, 2nd edn, New York: Oxford University Press, pp. 140–8.

REITHER, J. A. (1990) 'The Writing *Student* as Researcher: Learning From Our Students', in DAIKER, D. A. and MORENBERG, M. *The Writing Teacher as Researcher: Essays in the Theory and Practice of Class-Based Research*, Portsmouth, NH: Boynton/Cook Heinemann, pp. 247–55.

REITHER, J. A. and VIPOND, D. (1989) 'Writing as Collaboration', *College English*, **51**, December, pp. 855–67.

SAUSSURE, F. DE (1960) *Course in General Linguistics* (trans. W. Baskin, compiled by C. Bally and A. Sechehaye, with A. Riedlinger) London: R. Owen.

SLOBIN, D. I. and WELSH, C. A. (1973) 'Elicited Imitation as a Research Tool in Developmental Psycholinguistics', in FERGUSON, C. A. and SLOBIN, D. I. (eds) *Studies of Child Language Development*, New York: Holt, Rinehart and Winston, pp. 607–19.

SMITH, F. (1983) *Essays Into Literacy*, London: Heinemann.

VIPOND, D. and HUNT, R. A. (1984) 'Point-Driven Understanding: Pragmatic and Cognitive Dimensions of Literary Reading', *Poetics*, **13**, June, pp. 261–77.

VIPOND, D. and HUNT, R. A. (1988) 'Literary Processing and Response as Transaction: Evidence for the Contribution of Readers, Texts, and Situations', in MEUTSCH, D. and VIEHOFF, R. *Comprehension of Litgerary Discourse: Results and Problems of Interdisciplinary Approaches*, Berlin: De Gruyter, pp. 155–74.

VIPOND, D., HUNT, R. A., JEWETT, J. and REITHER, J. A. (1990) 'Making Sense of Reading', in BEACH, R. and HYNDS, S. (eds) *Developing Discourse Practices in Adolescence and Adulthood, Advances in Discourse Processes*, 34, Norwood, NJ: Ablex, pp. 110–35.

VYGOTSKY, L. S. (1962) *Thought and Language* (ed. and trans. E. Hanfmann and G. Vakar) Cambridge, MA: MIT Press.

VYGOTSKY, L. S. (1986) *Thought and Language* (translation newly edited and revised by A. Kozulin) Cambridge, MA: MIT Press.

Notes on Contributors

Charles Bazerman is Professor, English Department, University of California, Santa Barbara. His books include *Constructing Experience, Shaping Written Knowledge: The Genre and Activity of the Experimental Article in Science*, and *The Informed Writer*. He also coedited *Textual Dynamics of the Professions*. His research interests include the psycho-social dynamics of writing, the rhetoric of science and technology, and rhetorical theory. Currently he is working on a study of the rhetorical and representational work that made Edison's incandescent light a social reality, entitled *The Languages of Edison's Light*.

Richard M. Coe, Professor of English at Simon Fraser University Burnaby, BC, has taught in Canada, China and the United States. His *Toward a Grammar of Passages* (Southern Illinois University Press, 1988) introduced an instrument for studying generic structures. In 1990, Prentice-Hall published a thoroughly revised edition of his innovative textbook under the new title, *Process, Form and Substance: A Rhetoric for Advanced Writers*. He is presently writing *How to Read Kenneth Burke* and planning *The Rhetoric and Ecology of Genre*.

Anne Freadman teaches semiotics, literary theory and French in the Department of Romance Languages in the University of Queensland, Australia. She has published widely on genre, including, with Amanda Macdonald, *What is this Thing called 'Genre'?* and is currently working on a book-length study, *Charles Peirce and the Sign Hypothesis*. Her next project will be on the intersections of genre and gender.

Aviva Freedman is Professor of Linguistics and Applied Language Studies at Carleton University, Ottawa. She has written, coedited and coauthored several books and many articles on rhetorical theory and writing research. A continuing research interest relates to what had been called development in writing abilities and what can, in the light of current reconceptions, be defined as expansion of generic repertoires. She has recently coedited (with Peter Medway) a second volume on genre, *Learning and Teaching Genre*, which focuses more directly on educational practice, and is participating in a large-scale longitudinal project comparing university and workplace genres.

Janet Giltrow teaches in the English Department at Simon Fraser University, Burnaby, British Columbia. She has published articles applying linguistic-pragmatic measures of style to literary and non-literary texts, as well as articles on cultural definitions of literacy, and composition instruction and its context. She has also published a textbook, *Academic Writing*.

Russell A. Hunt teaches literature at St Thomas University in Fredericton, New Brunswick. Since the early 1980s he has been attempting to teach in ways which make student writing and reading instrumental and meaningful, and which invite students to take responsibility for initiating and assessing their own learning in social contexts. He studied eighteenth-century literature and critical theory at Northwestern University, and has written on the socio-linguistic processes of literary reading, teaching and other matters in various journals and edited collections. He is currently Learning and Teaching Development Officer at St Thomas, and says he is working on a book on literacy learning through literacy use.

Peter Medway taught English and humanities for 15 years in British secondary schools, worked on the London University Writing across the Curriculum Project, and at Leeds University on technical and vocational education and on English teaching in secondary schools. He moved in 1991 to the Department of Linguistics and Applied Language Studies in Carleton University, Ottawa, where he is engaged in research on language in architectural education and practice. He has recently coedited a second collection on written genres, *Learning and Teaching Genre*, with Aviva Freedman.

Carolyn R. Miller is Professor of English at North Carolina State University, Raleigh. Her primary research interests are rhetorical theory and rhetorical analysis, specifically as applied to scientific and technical discourse. She has served on the editorial boards of the *Journal of Business and Technical Communication*, *College Composition and Communication* and *Written Communication*, and on the executive committees of several professional organizations. She is president-elect of the Rhetoric Society of America.

Anthony Paré is Director of the Centre for the Study and Teaching of Writing and Assistant Professor in the Faculty of Education, McGill University, Montreal, Quebec, Canada. His teaching and research interests include genre, language across the curriculum and non-academic writing, especially social work writing.

Catherine F. Schryer is an Assistant Professor of English in the Rhetoric and Professional Writing program at the University of Waterloo, Waterloo, Ontario, Canada. She has published on the topic of genre in *Written Communication* and on the topic of literary history in *Textual Studies in Canada*. Her research interests include literacy, qualitative research methods and professional writing.

Graham Smart is the Coordinator of Writing Training at the Bank of Canada in Ottawa and has taught as a sessional lecturer in Carleton University's Department of Linguistics and Applied Language Studies and the University of Ottawa's Faculty of Education and as an independent study tutor at l'Université de Québec à Hull.

He has researched workplace documents, composing processes and reading practices from a socio-textual perspective and has reported on this research in journal articles and book chapters as well as at scholarly conferences.

A. D. Van Nostrand has written two books that bear on genre development from different perspectives. *The Denatured Novel* addresses the economics of publishing and its effects on genre characteristics. *Everyman His Own Poet* is a literary study of romantic cosmologies. Having coauthored two textbooks on writing, he has since focused his interests in rhetoric and genre study on systems of knowledge production. He is an emeritus professor of both Brown University, Providence, RI and Georgia Institute of Technology, Atlanta, GA.

Eugenia N. Zimmerman has been a member of the French Department at Carleton University, Ottawa, since 1968. Originally specialized in twentieth-century French literature, particularly the work of Jean-Paul Sartre, she now does most of her research in terms of Aristotelian and Perelmanian rhetoric. She has recently completed a book-length manuscript entitled 'Coercion/Demonstration/Persuasion: On the Margins of Rhetoric', which she sees as a synthesis of her past and present intellectual preoccupations.

Index